FIVE ELIZABETH

W. Bradley 19/10/75

# FIVE ELIZABETHAN TRAGEDIES

EDITED
WITH AN INTRODUCTION BY
A. K. McILWRAITH

OXFORD UNIVERSITY PRESS

LONDON OXFORD NEW YORK

1971

*Oxford University Press*

LONDON OXFORD NEW YORK

GLASGOW TORONTO MELBOURNE WELLINGTON

CAPE TOWN SALISBURY IBADAN NAIROBI DAR ES SALAAM LUSAKA ADDIS ABABA

BOMBAY CALCUTTA MADRAS KARACHI LAHORE DACCA

KUALA LUMPUR SINGAPORE HONG KONG TOKYO

ISBN 0 19 281119 3

First published in The World's Classics, 1938

First issued as an Oxford University Press paperback
by Oxford University Press, London, 1971

*Printed lithographically in Great Britain by
The Camelot Press Ltd, London and Southampton*

# CONTENTS

# INTRODUCTION

THIS volume is designed as a complement to the selections of Pre-Shakespearean and Elizabethan Comedies published as part of a series of anthologies of the English drama. Marlowe and Shakespeare need more room than an anthology can spare, and are reserved for special treatment. When they are set aside, and the term 'Elizabethan' is used in its strict sense to denote the reign of Queen Elizabeth (1558–1603) without its conventional extension to the outbreak of the Civil War forty years later, the selection almost makes itself. *Gorboduc*, *The Spanish Tragedy*, and *A Woman Killed with Kindness* must be here, and earlier domestic tragedy is best represented by *Arden of Feversham*. If Chapman wrote *Bussy D'Ambois* in 1600 it should have made the fifth; but it is usually dated 1604, and even if it should prove to have been written earlier it belongs in spirit to a new age, and an example of the Elizabethan Seneca has been preferred. The influence of Seneca on Elizabethan tragedy has been often proclaimed and never disputed, but it is believed that Jasper Heywood's translation of *Thyestes*, made at the very beginning of Elizabeth's reign, is now first reprinted in modern spelling.

Seneca probably meant his plays to be read aloud or recited by a single speaker, not to be acted or spoken by a company of players. Physical action on a large scale was therefore out of the question, even if it had not been discountenanced by the example of his Greek models; and even the conflict of wills and passions and fates set forth in rapid dialogue, which characterizes classical tragedy, Greek and French alike, was no more effective than long speeches of narration or reflection in which physical or mental action and suffering were described and reported. Most of his plays, moreover, are concerned with Greek myths and legends which were well known to his hearers, so that he would have bored them if he had spent much time on the actual course of events.

In the fifteen centuries that divided him from Renaissance Europe this characteristic of Seneca's art had been lost to memory, and however his plays were treated in his own day they were acted on the stages of Italy, France, and England. They were being acted at Rome before 1500, and as early as 1551 *Troas* was acted in Latin at Trinity College, Cambridge. The plays, with new Latin imitations of them, soon grew into favour for amateur entertainments in the Inns of Court and the Universities, during the time when the comedies of Plautus and Terence and English plays modelled on them were becoming popular for performance by the boys of some schools and of the choirs of the royal chapels.

The earliest translations into English are three which Jasper Heywood, Fellow of All Souls College, Oxford, made between 1558 and 1561, of which *Thyestes* is the second. (*Troas* was the first and *Hercules Furens* the third.) Twenty years later all of Seneca's plays had been rendered into English by various hands, and in 1581 Thomas Newton edited an 'omnibus volume' of these translations under the title of *Seneca his Tenne Tragedies*, from which the Argument to *Thyestes* is here reprinted.

Heywood perhaps derived a feeling for the stage from his father, John Heywood, the writer of interludes,[1] and his versions are not intolerably unfaithful to the sometimes imperfect Latin texts available to him. He did not try to imitate Seneca's variety of metres, but was generally content with rhymed quatrains in lines of ten syllables for the choruses and rhymed couplets of fourteen syllables for the dialogue. (Since the

[1] See *Five Pre-Shakespearean Comedies*, ed. F. S. Boas (Oxford Paperbacks 219).

'fourteener' was too long for the width of the page, the original printer had to arrange it as two lines of eight and six syllables, and for the same reason it has unfortunately been necessary to follow his example in this reprint.) This measure later fell into disfavour and was condemned for its monotony, but it answers Heywood's purpose well, and he sometimes achieves with it an effect of dreadful grandeur which is well in keeping with Seneca's theme:

A loathsome spring stands under shade, and slothful course doth take
With water black, even such as is of irksome Stygian lake
The ugly wave, whereby are wont to swear the Gods on high.
Here all the night the grisly ghosts and Gods of death to cry
The fame reports. With clinking chains resounds the wood each where.
The sprites cry out, and everything that dreadful is to hear
May there be seen. Of ugly shapes, from old sepúlchres sent,
A fearful flock doth wander there; and in that place frequent
Worse things than ever yet were known. Yea, all the wood full oft
With flame is wont to flash, and all the higher trees aloft
Without a fire do burn; and oft the wood, beside all this,
With triple barking roars at once. Full oft the palace is
Affright with shapes, nor light of day may once the terror quell.
Eternal night doth hold the place, and darkness there of Hell
In midday reigns.

The rumbling accumulation of horror upon horror is by no means ineffective. Heywood's most tiresome fault is his fondness for inversion, a vice in which he has few rivals. That passage has some examples, but he is often worse, even in the address of 'The Translator

to the Book', where there can be no defence that he
was influenced by the word-order of a Latin original:

> If deed so rash of mine he do reprove,
> That I thee dare attempt to send him to.

Here the natural order of words in the second line is:

> 1   2   4      5     6   7   3   9   8
> That I dare attempt to send thee to him.

With practice most of these dislocated sentences can
be reset at sight, but there are many of them. More
characteristic of Heywood are such passages of almost
straightforward eloquence as this from the Chorus to
the Second Act, which might not have seemed wholly
out of place in Gray's *Elegy*:

> Not riches make a king, or high renown;
>   Not garnish'd weed with purple Tyrian dye;
> Not lofty looks, or head enclos'd with crown;
>   Not glitt'ring beams with gold, and turrets high.
> A king he is, that fear hath laid aside,
>   And all affects that in the breast are bred;
> Whom impotent ambition doth not guide,
>   Nor fickle favour hath of people led.

*Thyestes* was perhaps the most popular of the
tragedies of Seneca, and we can see echoes of it in
several of the plays which follow. *Gorboduc* insists
again on the evils of a divided realm; a ghost and a
spirit of Revenge form the framework to set off the
action of *The Spanish Tragedy*—and there is a ghost in
*Hamlet*; the murky journey of Arden and Franklin in
the Fourth Act of *Arden of Feversham* has the mood of
horror which broods over the homecoming of Thyestes
in Act III. And other resemblances may suggest
themselves.

The step from translation to imitation was soon
taken. *Gorboduc*, the first English tragedy, was written
by Thomas Norton and Thomas Sackville to be acted
in the Inner Temple during the Christmas festivities

of 1561–2, and was acted again before the Queen
early in the New Year. The young lawyers imitated
their Senecan model in many ways. They chose from
British legend a story perhaps as familiar to their
audience as the Grecian myths were in ancient Rome;
they reduced action to the vanishing-point, and
adopted the classical Messenger to narrate events;
they divided their play into five acts with choruses
between, as they found Seneca's plays in the printed
editions. In other ways they were more original. For
one thing, they neglected, to the regret of Sir Philip
Sidney, the Unities of Time and Place; and if their
story is of the usual sort it is at least one which had
not been put to dramatic use before; they also introduced each act with a dumb show symbolizing the
lesson it was to teach and employed the Chorus at the
end to recall and expound the dumb show, a scheme
for which no precedent is known; and finally they
abandoned the rhymed decasyllables and fourteeners
of Heywood and the other translators in favour of
blank verse, which had not been used for plays before,
and which was to remain for three centuries the usual
medium of English tragedy. We need not neglect
Matthew Arnold's warning against letting the his-
torical interest of Norton and Sackville as innovators
blind us to any artistic faults we may find in *Gorboduc*,
but we have become accustomed, since he wrote, to
seeing the stage used as a pulpit for moral, social, and
political harangues, and we may be more ready than
a Victorian critic to forgive the authors for their
lecturing of Queen Elizabeth on the vital problem of
providing a single indisputable heir to the throne,
and for driving the lesson home with the gloomy
picture which they draw of the doom of a land wherein the succession is divided or uncertain.

Both these plays were written for the sophisticated
circles of the Universities and the Inns of Court, which
were then more a general centre of post-graduate

study and recreation than they are to-day, but Thomas Kyd, the son of a scrivener, wrote *The Spanish Tragedy* in the 1580's for the stage of the public theatres which had been springing up in London since 1576. He showed a singular genius in combining popular with academic tradition, and both of these with a knowledge of the limitations and the possibilities of the theatre of his day. His only real rival at this date was Marlowe, and at first Marlowe was a better poet than dramatist.

Men who had watched strolling players in inn yards liked blood and rant to thrill them and rough horse-play to make them laugh, and if one play pleased them in both ways so much the better. A typical example of this crude medley is Thomas Preston's *Lamentable Tragedy of Cambyses*, written at any rate before 1570, a mad jumble of (*a*) ranting scenes based (ultimately) on Herodotus, (*b*) knock-about farce of the King's servants Ruff, Huff, and Snuff and the medieval 'Vice' Ambidexter, and (*c*) allegorical characters of the *Everyman* type like Cruelty, Murder, &c. Preston's metres are meant to be those used by Jasper Heywood, but his verse is rough and clumsy in comparison. Kyd learned from the inn-yard tradition that the presentation of violence and bloodshed can move an audience more than the narration of it, and the dramatic irony of Pedringano's trial (Act III, Scene vi) has this in common with the 'mixed' plays, that it is nearer to laughter than the dramatic irony of Greek tragedy usually is. Yet it is very far from being irrelevant or incongruous, and our reactions to it involve no abrupt change of mood.

From Seneca Kyd learned to keep his play to a single theme, and to relax tension without changing the tone. Clearly he also borrowed, in *The Spanish Tragedy*, the idea of a dead man's ghost and the spirit of Revenge, though by giving to these two (who appear only at the beginning of *Thyestes*) the part played by Seneca's Chorus he conveys an eerie feeling of the insignificance of his human actors against their timeless background of the dead. Another thing he has learned, not from Seneca but from the English Senecans, is the trick of blank verse. About the same time Marlowe did it better, but Kyd's verse far more than that of *Gorboduc* has power to lead us through

> the gates of horn,
> Where dreams have passage in the silent night.

It is a commonplace that the stage of the Elizabethan public theatre, unlike the modern 'picture' stage, had little scenery or properties, and left the actors usually surrounded on three sides by the audience. Some conventions would therefore seem perfectly natural on it which would look grossly artificial on the stage we know. In Act II, Scene ii, Kyd has two conversations going on at once, one between Horatio and Bellimperia—no doubt at the front of the projecting stage—and another between Pedringano's protégés as he leads them on to the back of the stage and conducts them up to the balcony whence they overlook and overhear the lovers. Such 'eavesdropping scenes' were common in the Elizabethan drama, and were perhaps easier to act on their stage than they are on ours.

Kyd has been generally praised for his technical skill in making the best use of the available resources. He has also been accused of using his skill for merely melodramatic ends; and that charge seems unjust. In the play as he wrote it, as it was first printed, and as it is here reprinted, there is a perfectly credible study of Hieronimo's[1] character and of the strain which drove him mad. He is suspicious from the first

---

[1] *Hieronimo* and *Jeronimo* are different forms of the same name, and there is little to choose between them except that the former is Kyd's spelling. In verse it may be pronounced as four syllables or as five to suit the metre.

(Act I, Scene ii) that the Court is jealous of his son; from the night scene (II. v) where he finds that son's murdered body hanging in his bower he is a man driven out of his reason gradually and by natural steps: by the difficulties first of learning for certain who the murderers were and second of contriving a revenge which should for certain fall on all who were guilty. He must 'be not credulous' of the 'bloody writ' which accuses Lorenzo (III. ii), for it may be a trap laid for him by the Court which he suspects; the tardy delivery of Pedringano's letter (III. vii) answers the first question, but it leaves him the second: how to ensure the completeness of his just revenge. Only under this strain, increased by his wife's breakdown (III. viii), do his thoughts begin to wander (III. xi). Thereafter his distraught mind pursues its aim until the revenge is accomplished through the device of the 'play within the play' (IV. iv), and it is not till then that his silence and secrecy become an irrational obsession, when there is no more need for his (oft-quoted) caution,

Hieronimo, beware! go by, go by!

The story Kyd told was reasonable, not false to life or melodramatic; but the play was popular, the audience liked to see Hieronimo mad, and so the theatrical agent Philip Henslowe in 1601 and 1602 advanced to Ben Jonson a large sum on account of certain additions, and a revised version duly appeared in 1602, with extra scenes of Hieronimo's madness, the first of them inserted as early as II. v. We cannot tell whether or not the additions we have were written by Jonson, but they can hardly have been Kyd's, and they were certainly not part of the play as he first wrote it. Poetically Lamb may have been right in calling them 'the very salt of the old play', but they make nonsense of the plot and of Hieronimo's character, and dramatically there is more truth in the opinion attributed to a silly spectator in Jonson's

*Cynthia's Revels* (1600), that 'the old *Hieronimo*, (as it was first acted), was the only best, and judiciously penn'd play of Europe'. These additions have usually been printed in the text or as footnotes beneath it, but they are here tucked away in a remote appendix so that the play may be first read as it was first written. It will be easier for a reader who wants them to look them up than it would have been for a reader who did *not* want them to neglect them.

It is Kyd's grasp of human character and his portrayal of it that make good his claim to greatness, and it is on them, together with some punning allusions which have been found in contemporary pamphlets, that his further claim rests to be the author of a lost play which may have been rewritten by Shakespeare as *Hamlet*. The weakness of puns as evidence is that the best may be incidental and signify nothing. There are similarities between *The Spanish Tragedy* and *Hamlet*, but they tell in both directions: in both plays the theme is revenge; in both the revenge is delayed; in both there is a 'play within the play'. Yet in each resemblance there is a difference: the revenger is different, the motive for delay is apparently different, and the purpose of the included play is different. The question has been posed and is still debated, but there is no sure answer yet.

Shakespeare and Kyd are further linked by the anonymous tragedy of *Arden of Feversham*. It was ascribed to Shakespeare (without much plausibility) by an eighteenth-century scholar, and it is now attributed to Kyd by several critics on grounds of style and vocabulary. Despite its obvious dissimilarities it bears some sort of resemblance to *The Spanish Tragedy*. It combines a bloody tale of physical violence with a delicate psychological study, and the savage irony of the scene of Pedringano's trial answers the same purpose as the breath-taking mishaps which repeatedly thwart the would-be murderers, when at

the crucial moment Black Will is stunned by a closing
shutter (II. ii) or Shakebag falls into a ditch in the
fog (IV. iii).

It is possible to conceive that a single author might
have written both plays; but, unlike its fellow, *Arden
of Feversham* has a native middle-class English setting,
and deals with an actual crime some forty years old
recorded in Holinshed's *Chronicle*. It is thus one of
the earliest English 'domestic tragedies', in which
the chief characters are common people in familiar
life and not kings and princes unreal and remote in
time (as in *Gorboduc*) or in place and nation (as
in *The Spanish Tragedy*). The successive murderous
attempts and failures of the hired cut-throats are
repeated too often, and begin to grow wearisome or
ludicrous to our taste, but it was just these things that
gave the old murder the notoriety which kept it
alive, and the dramatist could hardly have left them
out without disappointing his audience, to whom, in
a curious epilogue, he offered

> this naked tragedy,
> Wherein no filed points are foisted in
> To make it gracious to the ear or eye,

explaining what happened afterwards to all the minor
characters except that

> The painter fled, and how he died we know not.

What he added from his own imagination is his picture
of Alice and Mosbie and their alternations between
desire and distrust, as their passion is soured and
warped by their insistent awareness that they are
doing wrong. There is nothing mechanically sym-
metrical here, nothing crude in the different reactions
of the man and the woman. There is a sickening
reality, as there is too about the final messy killing and
the tell-tale blood in the snow, which is far from the
heroics of melodrama.

The fall of Alice and Mosbie is not brought about by a moulding of external events by Fate in conformity with moral law, nor by other people following such a law, but by their own consciousness of their own sin, which makes them distrust each other and so wrecks their plans. Moral law is here a fact, of which good men and bad are equally aware, and it operates in no mysterious way, but quite simply. each has given proof of falseness, so neither can trust the other.

The advantages of the Elizabethan platform stage, with its general paucity of scenery, are exploited in *Arden of Feversham* in what has been called 'continuous staging', where the actors remain on the stage and the dialogue continues while the imaginary setting is supposed to change. The first act is surely meant to wander in and out of Arden's house and about the neighbourhood without any precise definition of place, and the first three scenes of Act III, and the second. third, and fourth scenes of Act IV, are not to be interrupted while a curtain is lowered and the scene is changed. In Act IV, Scene iv, we are to see not the spot at which Franklin and Arden meet Alice and Mosbie, but the progress of the two parties toward their meeting. And there are two scenes at least in *A Woman Killed with Kindness* where Heywood has adopted the same device (IV. v and v. iv).

Heywood[1] also chose a contemporary setting, but his story was an imaginary one, and it left him free to plan his play as he liked. He avoids the repetition of too similar effects, but the tale he tells has to be eked out not only with comic relief among Frankford's servants, which is logically related to the main plot and helps to build up the everyday setting, but also

[1] Thomas Heywood (*d.* 1641) was born in Lincolnshire to a father newly come from Cheshire, and there is no reason to connect him with Jasper Heywood the translator, or with John Heywood the writer of interludes.

with the almost unconnected story of Mountford and his sister Susan, in the same key as that of Frankford, his wife, and Wendoll. *The Spanish Tragedy* and *Arden of Feversham* were ahead of their time in dramatic art; *A Woman Killed with Kindness* was behind its time. Yet it marks a moral advance, for there is in it a new gentleness of spirit, the kindness which is all Frankford's revenge on his false wife and the contriteness of Mountford for a murder in hot blood. It is typical of Heywood's greater charity that the servants here are faithful, whilst those in *Arden of Feversham* are false and selfish. It is not easy to attach a precise meaning to Lamb's description of Heywood as 'a sort of *prose* Shakespeare', but perhaps he had recognized a generous warmth of heart for which a comparison with Shakespeare appeared to him to be a merited praise, if not a very apt one.

Without Marlowe and Shakespeare this survey is incomplete, but they are the founders of a new age, and Heywood, though he lived till the Civil War, is a survival of the old; whilst Kyd, like Marlowe, died young before the turn of the century. It is their faith in the justice of moral law that seems to distinguish the tragic dramatists of the end of Elizabeth's reign.[1] Earlier, the authors of *Gorboduc* saw the inevitability of Fate, and the events of their play are the logical outcome of Gorboduc's action; but his decision was not taken in the knowledge that it was wicked, and its fatal consequences are the expression of a law which escapes man's moral sense. Later than our period, writers like Chapman saw the value of moral judgements but were no longer unquestioningly sure which moral judgements were correct. From Chapman to Ford there are tragedies of men and women who act as they think right, and claim our admiration for

---

[1] On the change of spirit here discussed see the penetrating study of U. M. Ellis-Fermor, *The Jacobean Drama*, 1936.

doing so, but suffer because other people think differently about right and wrong. It is chiefly in these ten years between the old world and the new that we find such clear-cut tragedies of people who know what it is right for them to do and who yet act otherwise. Alice and Mosbie are swept by lust beyond their reason, and Mistress Frankford knows at the moment when she yields to Wendoll's wooing that

My soul is wand'ring and hath lost her way.

\* \* \* \* \* \*

In reprinting these texts the spelling and punctuation have been modernized but the forms and inflexions of words have not, so that *furder* appears for *further*, *moe* for *more*, *sithens* for *since*, and so on, and verbs with plural subjects may appear to be singular in form. In the matter of elision the governing idea has been to use a modern spelling which may represent the old, so that *walk'd* might stand for *walkt*, *walkd*, or *walkde*, and *walked* for a spelling that included a second vowel. Probably the spelling of the original was often left to the printer and does not always tell us how the author meant the word to be pronounced, but the pronunciation indicated is frequently required by the metre, and it seems better to preserve what hints there are than to bury them in a drab uniformity.

In the original editions only *Thyestes* and *Gorboduc* are divided into acts and scenes; *The Spanish Tragedy* has the acts marked, but not the scenes; and the other two are not divided at all. The divisions marked in the originals are of course preserved, and for convenience of reference those introduced by modern editors are also kept when they do not distort or obscure the author's meaning. Localizations of a scene in 'A Room in the House' or 'The Open Country', sometimes with a train of followers in 'Another Part of the

Same', are false to the technique of the Elizabethan stage and have no place in an Elizabethan play.

The text of each play is taken from the standard modern edition (though it does not necessarily follow it in every detail), and most of the notes are taken either from the standard editions or from the *Oxford English Dictionary*. Indebtedness to an edition is implied by its citation at the head of the play.

The notes do not attempt to deal learnedly with textual corruptions or major difficulties of interpretation; they are meant to help readers who are not quite at home in Elizabethan English.

In *The Spanish Tragedy*, Hieronimo's play 'in sundry languages, was thought good to be set down in English, more largely, for the easier understanding to every public reader'. Such dictates of humanity failed to deter Kyd from making his characters interlard their speeches, sometimes at length, with passages in Latin and other languages. Some of these have been recognized as quotations or adaptations from one or more Latin writers; others have not been identified, and may be original. They are not always easy to translate, but a loose rendering is attempted in the notes.

1938                                         A. K. McI.

# THYESTES

BY

## LUCIUS ANNAEUS SENECA

TRANSLATED BY

## JASPER HEYWOOD

# LUCIUS ANNAEUS SENECA (†A.D. 65)
# JASPER HEYWOOD (1535–98)

## *Thyestes*

### Translated and printed in 1560.

[Heywood's translations of *Troas*, *Thyestes*, and *Hercules Furens* were edited by H. de Vocht, in *Materialien zur Kunde des älteren englischen Dramas*, vol. xli, 1913 (with introduction and notes in English). *Seneca his Tenne Tragedies, Translated into English*, collected by Thomas Newton, were printed in 1581, and were reprinted with an introduction by T. S. Eliot, 2 vols., in the Tudor Translations, Second Series, 1927.]

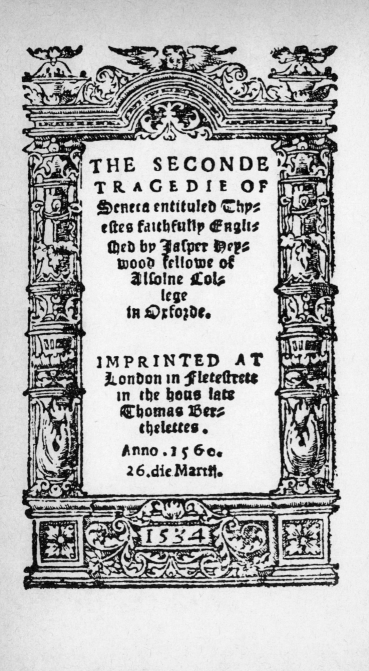

# THE SECONDE TRAGEDIE OF

Seneca entituled Thy-
estes faithfully Englis-
hed by Jasper Hey-
wood fellowe of
Alsolne Col-
lege
in Oxforde.

## IMPRINTED AT

London in Fletestrete
in the hous late
Thomas Ber-
thelettes.

Anno . 1 5 6 0 .
26. die Martij.

1534

# To the Right Honourable Sir *John Mason*, Knight, one of the Queen's Majesty's Privy Council, his daily orator Jasper Heywood wisheth health with increase of honour and virtue.

As bounden breast doth bear the poorest wight
   That duty doth in trifling token send,
As he that doth with plenteous present quite,
   Of prouder price, and glitt'ring gold, his friend.
Whoso repay'th with money's mighty mass
   The good that he at other's hands hath found,
Remembrance of the benefit doth pass,
   He thinks himself to him no longer bound.
The poor, whose power may not with price repay
   The great good gifts that he receiv'd before,     10
With thankful thought yet gudgeon gift doth sway
   Above the peise of pearl and gold, great store.
If puissant prince at poor man's hand once took
   A radish root, and was therewith content,
Your Honour, then, I pray, this little book
   To take in worth, that I to you present;
Which, though itself a volume be but small,
   Yet greater gift it gives than ween ye might:
Though it a barren book be, throughout all
   Full fruitless, yet not faithless sign in sight     20

heading: Sir John Mason] *Lived 1503–66, Chancellor of Oxford, 1552–6.*     3 quite] requite, repay     11 gudgeon] worthless     12 peise] weight     13 If puissant prince &c.] *Alluding to a story told in* Tales, *and quicke answeres, a jest-book of 1535.* (*De Vocht.*)     15 in worth] in good part

It shows of him that for your Honour prays
  (As deeds of yours of him deserved have)
That God above prolong your happy days
  And make the skies your seat soon after grave.


## The Translator
## to the book.

Thou, little book, my messenger must be,
  That must from me to wight of honour go;
Behave thee humbly, bend to him thy knee,
  And thee to him in lowly manner show.
But do thou not thyself to him present
  When with affairs thou shalt him troubled see;
Thou shalt perhaps, so, worthily be shent,
  And with reproof he thus will say to thee:
'So proudly thus presume how darest thou
  At such a time so rashly to appear?                10
With things of weight thou seest me burden'd now,
  I may not yet to trifles give mine ear.'
Spy well thy time; when thou him seest alone,
  An idle hour for thee shall be most meet;
Then step thou forth in sight of him anon
  And, as behoves, his Honour humbly greet.
But now take heed what I to thee shall tell,
  And all by rote this lesson take with thee;
In everything thyself to order well
  In sight of him, give ear and learn of me.        20
First, what or whence thou art if he would wit,
  Then see that thou thy title to him show;
Tell him thy name is in thy forehead writ,
  By which he shall both thee and me well know.
Then, when he hath once look'd upon thy name,
  If yet he shall neglect to read the rest,
Or if he chide, and say thou art to blame,
  With trifles such to have him so oppress'd:

7 shent] put to shame

Beseech him yet thereof to pardon thee,
    Since thou art but thy master's messenger;      30
Excuse thyself, and lay the fault in me,
    At whose commandment thus thou com'st in there.
If my presumption then accuse he do,
    If deed so rash of mine he do reprove,
That I thee dare attempt to send him to,
    Beware thou speak nothing for my behove,
Nor do thou not excuse my fault in ought,
    But rather yet confess to him the same,
And say there may a fault in me be thought,
    Which to excuse, it doubleth but the blame.      40
Yet with my boldness him beseech to bear,
    And pardon give to this my enterprise;
A worthy thing in wight of honour were
    A present poor to take in thankful wise.
For tell him, though thou slender volume be,
    Ungreeing gift for state of honour guest,
Yet dost thou sign of duty bring with thee,
    And pledge thou art of truly bounden breast.
And thou for him art come for to confess,
    His beadman bound to be for his desart      50
And how to him he grants he ow'th no less,
    Nor gives no more, but note of thankful heart.
In all the rest that he to thee shall say
    Thy wit shall serve an answer well to make.
Thou hast thine errand, get thee hence away.
    The Gods thee speed, to them I thee betake.

## The Argument of this Tragedy.

Megaera, one of the Hellish Furies, raising up
Tantalus from Hell, incited him to set mortal hatred

36 behove] behoof, benefit      46 ungreeing] unfit
50 beadman] servant who prays for his lord    desart] desert
Argument] *Printed in the edition of 1581. The first edition has
instead an interesting verse preface of 684 lines which is not
directly concerned with the play.*

between his two nephews Thyestes and Atreus, being brothers, and reigning as kings over Mycenae by interchangeable turns, that is to-wit Thyestes to reign the one year, and Atreus the other. Now Atreus enraged with fury against his brother, partly for defiling and deflowering his wife Aerope by policy and partly for taking from him a Ram with a Golden Fleece, practised with his servant how to be revenged of his brother. This Atreus, therefore, dissembling a reconciliation ˙ and inviting Thyestes to Mycenae, secretly and unknown to him set before him at a banquet the flesh of his own children to eat. Afterward Atreus, having also given to his said brother the blood of his children in a goblet to drink, did lastly command the heads also to be brought in; at the doleful sight whereof Thyestes, greatly lamenting, knowing that he had eaten his own children, was wonderfully anguished. But Atreus, for that he had thus revenged himself, took therein great pleasure and delectation.

22

## The Speakers.

| | |
|---|---|
| Tantalus. | Megaera. |
| Atreus. | Servant. |
| Thyestes. | Phylisthenes. |
| Messenger. | Chorus. |

10 practised] plotted
Speakers 4 Phylisthenes] *Early editions of Seneca gave a part to Phylistenes in act III; later editions give it to Tantalus, and mention Plisthenes as an actor who appears without speaking. Heywood follows the early editions.*

# THYESTES OF
## Seneca

### The First Act.

#### Tantalus.  Megaera.

*Tan.*  What fury fell enforceth me
 to flee th'unhappy seat,
That gape and gasp with greedy jaw
 the fleeing food to eat?
What God to Tantalus the bowers
 where breathing bodies dwell
Doth show again?  Is ought found worse
 than burning thirst of Hell
In lakes alow?  Or yet worse plague
 than hunger is there one,    10
In vain that ever gapes for food?
 Shall Sisyphus his stone,
That slipper restless rolling peise,
 upon my back be borne?
Or shall my limbs with swifter swinge
 of whirling wheel be torn?
Or shall my pains be Tityus' pangs,
 th'encreasing liver still,
Whose growing guts the gnawing gripes
 and filthy fowls do fill,    20
That still by night repairs the paunch
 that was devour'd by day,
And wondrous womb unwasted li'th
 a new-prepared prey?

5 bowers] habitations  9 alow] below  13 slipper] slippery  peise] weight  15 swinge] sweep, impetus  19 gripes] vultures

What ill am I appointed for?
　O cruel judge of sprites,
Who-so thou be, that torments new
　among the souls delights
Still to dispose, add what thou canst
　to all my deadly woe,                                    30
That keeper, even, of dungeon dark
　would sore abhor to know,
Or Hell itself it quake to see;
　for dread whereof likewise
I tremble would: that plague seek out.
　Lo, now there doth arise
My brood, that shall in mischief far
　the grandsire's guilt outgo,
And guiltless make; that first shall dare
　unventur'd ills to do.                                   40
Whatever place remaineth yet
　of all this wicked land
I will fill up: and never once
　while Pelops' House doth stand
Shall Minos idle be.

*Meg.*                                        Go forth,
　thou detestable sprite,
And vex the Gods of wicked House
　with rage of Furies' might.
Let them contend with all offence,
　by turns and one by one                                  50
Let swords be drawn; and mean of ire
　procure there may be none,
Nor shame; let Fury blind enflame
　their minds and wrathful will;
Let yet the parents' rage endure,
　and longer-lasting ill
Through children's children spread; nor yet
　let any leisure be

---

26 sprites] spirits　　44 Pelops] *Son of Tantalus and*
*father of Atreus and Thyestes.*　　45 Minos] *Judge of the*
*shades of the dead in Hades.*　　51 mean] moderation

The former fault to hate, but still
    more mischief new to see,      60
Nor one in one; but, ere the guilt
    with vengeance be acquit,
Increase the crime; from brethren proud
    let rule of kingdom flit
To runagates; and swerving state
    of all unstable things,
Let it by doubtful doom be toss'd
    between th'uncertain kings.
Let mighty fall to misery,
    and miser climb to might;      70
Let chance turn th'empire up-so-down,
    both give and take the right.
The banished for guilt, when God
    restore their country shall,
Let them to mischief fall afresh,
    as hateful then to all
As to themselves; let ire think nought
    unlawful to be done.
Let brother dread the brother's wrath,
    and father fear the son,      80
And eke the son his parent's power.
    Let babes be murdered ill,
But worse begot. Her spouse betrapp'd
    in treason's train to kill
Let hateful wife await, and let
    them bear through seas their war;
Let bloodshed lie the lands about,
    and every field afar,
And over conquering captains great
    of countries far to see      90
Let lust triumph; in wicked house
    let whoredom counted be

---

65 swerving] tottering     70 miser] wretch     71 up-
so-down] upside down     91 triumph] *Pronounced* triúmph
*as a verb*.

The light'st offence; let trust that in
  the breasts of brethren breeds,
And truth, be gone; let not from sight
  of your so heinous deeds
The Heavens be hid, about the Pole
  when shine the stars on high
And flames with wonted beams of light
  do deck the painted sky.           100
Let darkest night be made, and let
  the day the heavens forsake.
Disturb the Gods of wicked House;
  hate, slaughter, murder make.
Fill up the house of Tantalus
  with mischiefs and debates.
Adorned be the pillars high
  with bay, and let the gates
Be garnish'd green; and worthy, there,
  for thy return to sight          110
Be kindled fire! Let mischief, done
  in Thracia once, there light
More manifold! Wherefore doth yet
  the uncle's hand delay?
Doth yet Thyestes not bewail
  his children's fatal day?
Shall he not find them where with heat
  of fires that under glow
The cauldron boils? Their limbs each one
  a-pieces let them go          120
Dispers'd! Let father's fires, with blood
  of children filed be!
Let dainties such be dress'd! It is
  no mischief new to thee
To banquet so. Behold, this day
  we have to thee releas'd,
And hunger-starved womb of thine
  we send to such a feast!

122 filed] defiled

With foulest food thy famine fill,
    let blood in wine be drown'd,        130
And drunk in sight of thee!  Lo now
    such dishes have I found
As thou wouldst shun.  Stay, whither dost
    thou headlong way now take?

*Tan.*  To pools and floods of Hell again,
    and still-declining Lake,
And flight of tree full-freight with fruit
    that from the lips doth flee,
To dungeon dark of hateful Hell
    let leeful be for me        140
To go!  Or, if too light be thought
    the pains that there I have,
Remove me from those Lakes again
    in midst of worser wave
Of Phlegethon to stand, in seas
    of fire beset to be.
Whoso beneath thy pointed pains,
    by Destiny's decree,
Dost still endure; whoso thou be
    that underliest alow        150
The hollow den, or ruin who
    that fears, and overthrow
Of falling hill, or cruel cries
    that sound in caves of Hell
Of greedy roaring lions' throats;
    or flock of Furies fell
Who quakes to know; or who the brands
    of fire, in direst pain
Half-burnt throws off: Hark to the voice
    of Tantalus, again        160
That hastes to Hell!  And, whom the truth
    hath taught, believe well me:
Love well your pains, they are but small.
    When shall my hap so be

136 still-declining] ever-receding (*from his parched mouth*)
140 leeful] lawful

To flee the light?

*Meg.*                         Disturb thou first
  this House with dire discord:
Debates and battles bring with thee,
  and of th'unhappy sword
Ill love to kings; the cruel breast
  strike through, and hateful heart,                170
With tumult mad.

*Tan.*                         To suffer pains
  it seemeth well my part,
Not woes to work.  I am sent forth
  like vapour dire to rise
That breaks the ground, or poison like
  the plague, in wondrous wise
That slaughter makes.  Shall I to such
  detested crimes apply
My nephews' hearts?  O parents great
  of gods above the sky,                          180
And mine (though sham'd I be to grant)
  although with greater pain
My tongue be vex'd, yet this to speak
  I may no whit refrain,
Nor hold my peace: I warn you this,
  lest sacred hand with blood
Of slaughter dire, or frenzy fell
  of frantic fury wood
The altars stain, I will resist,
  and guard such guilt away.                      190
With stripes why dost thou me affright?
  why threat'st thou me to fray
Those crawling snakes? or famine fix'd
  in empty womb, wherefore
Dost thou revive?  Now fries within,
  with thirst enkindled sore,

179 parents] *Heywood several times has a plural where the
Latin has the singular which the sense requires.*    188 wood]
mad       192 fray] frighten       194 womb] belly

My heart; and in the bowels burnt
the boiling flames do glow.

*Meg.*   I follow thee!  Through all this House
now rage and fury throw!      200
Let them be driven so, and so
let either thirst to see
Each other's blood!  Full well hath felt
the coming-in of thee
This House, and all with wicked touch
of thee begun to quake!
Enough it is.  Repair again
to dense and loathsome Lake
Of flood well-known.  The sadder soil
with heavy foot of thine      210
Aggrieved is.  Seest thou from springs
how waters do decline,
And inward sink? or how the banks
lie void by droughty heat?
And hotter blast of fiery wind
the fewer clouds doth beat?
The trees be spoil'd, and naked stand
to sight in wither'd woods;
The barren boughs whose fruits are fled;
the land between the floods,      220
With surge of seas on either side
that wonted to resound
And nearer fords to separate
sometime with lesser ground,
Now broader spread, it heareth how
aloof the waters rise.
Now Lerna turns against the stream;
Phoronides likewise,
His pores be stopp'd; with custom'd course
Alpheus drives not still      230
His holy waves; the trembling tops
of high Cithaeron hill,

227–30 Lerna . . . Phoronides . . . Alpheus] *Rivers of the Peloponnese.*

They stand not sure; from height adown
   they shake their silver snow,
And noble fields of Argos fear
   their former drought to know.
Yea, Titan doubts, himself, to roll
   the world his wonted way,
And drive by force to former course
   the backward-drawing day.       240

Chorus.

This Argos town, if any God be found,
   And Pisey bowers that famous yet remain,
Or kingdoms else, to love of Corinth's ground,
   The double havens, or sunder'd seas in twain—
If any love Taÿgetus his snows
   (By winter which when they on hills be cast
By Boreas' blasts, that from Sarmatia blows,
   With yearly breath, the summer melts as fast),
Where clear Alpheus runs, with flood so cold,
   By plays well-known, that there Olympics hight—
Let pleasant power of his from hence withhold   11
   Such turns of strife, that here they may not
     light!
Nor nephew worse than grandsire spring from us,
   Or direr deeds delight the younger age!
Let wicked stock of thirsty Tantalus
   At length leave off, and weary be of rage!
Enough is done, and nought prevail'd the just
   Or wrong; betray'd Myrtilus is, and drown'd,
That did betray his dame; and with like trust
   Borne as he bare, himself hath made renown'd   20

2 Pisey] Pisaean, belonging to Pisa (*an ancient colony of Elis*).     4 double havens . . . sunder'd seas] *Alluding to the position of Corinth on the Isthmus dividing the Aegean on the east from the Gulf of Corinth on the west.*
8 yearly] seasonal     10 plays] games; (*the Olympic Games are of legendary antiquity*).     18 Myrtilus] *A charioteer drowned in the Aegean by Pelops for treachery.*

With changed name the sea, and better known
  To mariners thereof no fable is.
On wicked sword the little infant thrown,
  As ran the child to take his father's kiss,
Unripe for th'altar's off'ring fell down dead;
  And with thy hand, o Tantalus! was rent,
With such a meat for Gods thy boards to spread.
  Eternal famine for such food is sent,
And thirst; nor for those dainty meats un-mild
  Might meeter pain appointed ever be.         30
With empty throat stands Tantalus beguil'd;
  Above thy wicked head there leans to thee
Than Phiney's fowls in flight a swifter prey;
  With burden'd boughs declin'd on every side,
And of his fruits all bent to bear the sway,
  The tree deludes the gapes of hunger wide.
Though he full greedy feed thereon would fain,
  So oft deceiv'd, neglects to touch them yet:
He turns his eyes, his jaws he doth refrain,
  And famine fix'd in closed gums doth shet.     40
But then each branch his plenteous riches all
  Lets lower down, and apples from on high
With lither leaves they flatter, like to fall,
  And famine stir: in vain that bids to try
His hands, which when he hath rought forth anon
  To be beguil'd, in higher air again
The harvest hangs, and fickle fruit is gone.
  Then thirst him grieves, no less than hunger's pain;
Wherewith when kindled is his boiling blood
  Like fire, the wretch the waves to him doth call,  50
That meet his mouth: which, straight, the fleeing flood
  Withdraws, and from the dried ford doth fall,
And him forsakes that follows them. He drinks
The dust so deep, of gulf that from him shrinks.

26 Tantalus] *He cut his son Pelops in pieces, boiled them,
and set them before the gods at a repast.*     33 Phiney's fowls]
*The Harpies who plagued the blind soothsayer Phineus.*
40 shet] shut     43 lither] yielding     45 rought] reached

## The Second Act.

### Atreus. Servant.

*Atr.* O dastard, cow'rd, o wretch! and (which
    the greatest yet of all
To tyrants check I count, that may
    in weighty things befall)
O unrevenged! After guilts
    so great, and brother's guile,
And truth trod down, dost thou provoke
    with vain complaints the while
Thy wrath? Already now to rage
    all Argos' town throughout      10
In armour ought of thine, and all
    the double seas about
Thy fleet to ride; now all the fields
    with fervent flames of thine
And towns to flash, it well beseem'd,
    and everywhere to shine
The bright, drawn sword. All under foot
    of horse, let every side,
Of Argos' land resound, and let
    the woods not serve to hide      20
Our foes, nor yet, in haughty top
    of hills and mountains high,
The builded towers. The people all,
    let them *To Battle!* cry,
And clear forsake Mycenas' town.
    Whoso his hateful head
Hides and defends, with slaughter dire
    let blood of him be shed.
This princely Pelops' palace proud
    and bowers of high renown      30
On me, so on my brother too,
    let them be beaten down!
Go to, do that which never shall
    no after-age allow,

12 double seas] *See note on Act I Chorus line 4.*  34 allow] approve

Nor none it whisht; some mischief great
  there must be ventur'd now,
Both fierce and bloody, such as would
  my brother rather long
To have been his. Thou never dost
  enough revenge the wrong         40
Except thou pass. And fiercer fact
  what may be done so dire
That his exceeds? doth ever he
  lay down his hateful ire?
Doth ever he the modest mean
  in time of wealth regard,
Or quiet in adversity?
  I know his nature: hard,
Untractable, that broke may be,
  but never will it bend.         50
For which, ere he prepare himself,
  or force to fight intend,
Set first on him! Lest while I rest
  he should on me arise.
He will destroy, or be destroy'd;
  in midst the mischief lies,
Prepar'd to him that takes it first.

*Serv.*     Doth fame of people nought,
Adverse, thee fear?

*Atr.*               The greatest good
  of kingdom may be thought       60
That still the people are constrain'd
  their Princes' deeds as well
To praise, as them to suffer all.

*Serv.*     Whom fear doth so compel
To praise, the same his foes to be
  doth fear enforce again;
But who indeed the glory seeks
  of favour true t'obtain,

He rather would with hearts of each
   be prais'd than tongues of all.         70

*Atr.*  The truer praise full oft hath happ'd
   to meaner men to fall:
The false, but unto mighty man.
   What nill they, let them will!

*Serv.*  Let first the King will honest things
   and none the same dare nill.

*Atr.*  Where leeful are to him that rules
   but honest things alone,
There reigns the King by others' leave.

*Serv.*     And where that shame is none,     80
Nor care of right, faith, piety,
   nor holiness none stay'th,
That kingdom swerves.

*Atr.*             Such holiness,
   such piety and faith,
Are private goods: let kings run on
   in that that likes their will.

*Serv.*  The brother's hurt a mischief count
   though he be ne'er so ill.

*Atr.*  It is but right to do to him
   that wrong to brother were.     90
What heinous hurt hath his offence
   let pass to prove? or where
Refrain'd the guilt? My spouse he stale
   away for lechery,
And reign by stealth; the ancient note
   and sign of empery
By fraud he got; my House by fraud
   to vex he never ceas'd.
In Pelops' House there foster'd is
   a noble, worthy beast,     100
The close-kept Ram: the goodly guide
   of rich and fairest flocks,

74, 76 nill] will not    77 leeful] lawful    83 swerves]
totters    92 prove] try    93 stale] stole

By whom throughout on every side
  depend a-down the locks
Of glitt'ring gold, with fleece of which
  the new kings wonted were
Of Tantal's stock their sceptres gilt
  and mace of might to bear.
Of this the owner reigneth he:
  with him of House so gret      110
The fortune fleeth; this sacred Ram
  aloof in safety shet
In secret mead is wont to graze,
  which stone on every side,
With rocky wall encloseth round,
  the fatal beast to hide.
This beast, advent'ring mischief great,
  adjoining yet for prey
My spoused mate, the traitor false
  hath hence convey'd away.      120
From hence the wrongs of mutual hate
  and mischief all up-sprong;
In exile wander'd he throughout
  my kingdoms all along;
No part of mine remaineth safe
  to me from trains of his.
My fere's deflower'd, and loyalty
  of empire broken is;
My House all vex'd, my blood in doubt,
  and nought that trust is in      130
But brother foe. What stay'st thou yet?
  At length, lo now, begin!
Take heart of Tantalus to thee,
  to Pelops cast thine eye:
To such examples well beseems
  I should my hands apply.

104 depend] hang      110 gret] great      112 shet]
shut      116 fatal] fateful      122 up-sprong] sprang up
126 trains] tricks      127 fere] wife

        Tell thou which way were best to bring
          that cruel head to death.

*Serv.*   Through-pierc'd with sword let him be slain,
          and yield his hateful breath.       140

*Atr.*   Thou speak'st of th'end; but I him would
          oppress with greater pain.
        Let tyrants vex with torment more!
          should ever in my reign
        Be gentle death?

*Serv.*               Doth piety
        in thee prevail no whit?

*Atr.*   Depart thou hence, all piety,
          if in this House as yet
        Thou ever wert! And now let all
          the flock of Furies dire,       150
        And full of strife Errinyes come,
          and double brands of fire
        Megaera shaking; for not yet
          enough with fury great
        And rage doth burn my boiling breast:
          it ought to be replete
        With monster more.

*Serv.*            What mischief new
        dost thou in rage provide?

*Atr.*   Not such a one as may the mean
          of wonted grief abide.       160
        No guilt will I forbear, nor none
          may be enough despite.

*Serv.*   What, sword?

*Atr.*            Too little, that!

*Serv.*                    What, fire?

*Atr.*   And that is yet too light!

*Serv.*   What weapon then shall sorrow such
        find fit to work thy will?

*Atr.*   Thyestes' self!

*Serv.*           Than ire itself
        yet that's a greater ill.

        151 Errinyes] Eumenides, Furies

*Atr.*   I grant; a tumbling tumult quakes
     within my bosoms, lo,        170
    And round it rolls; I moved am
     and wot not whereunto.
    But drawn I am: from bottom deep
     the roaring soul doth cry,
    The day so fair with thunder sounds,
     and House as all from high
    Were rent, from roof and rafters cracks;
     and Lares turn'd about
    Have wry'd their sight. So be't, so be't!
     Let mischief such be sought      180
    As ye, o Gods, would fear!

*Serv.*                What thing
     seek'st thou to bring to pass?

*Atr.*   I note what greater thing my mind—
     and more than wont it was,
    Above the reach that men are wont
     to reach—begins to swell,
    And stay'th with slothful hands. What thing
     it is, I cannot tell;
    But great it is. Be't so, my mind,
     now in this feat proceed!      190
    For Atreus and Thyestes both
     it were a worthy deed!
    Let each of us the crime commit!
     The Thracian House did see
    Such wicked tables once; I grant
     the mischief great to be,
    But done ere this. Some greater guilt,
     and mischief more, let ire
    Find out. The stomach of thy son,
     o father, thou inspire,      200
    And sister eke, like is the cause;
     assist me with your power,

---

178 Lares] household gods      179 wry'd] averted
183 note] know not

And drive my hand! let greedy pa-
rents all his babes devour,
And glad to rent his children be,
and on their limbs to feed!
Enough, and well it is devis'd;
this pleaseth me indeed!
In meantime, where is he? So long
and innocent, wherefore                                    210
Doth Atreus walk? Before mine eyes
already, more and more,
The shade of such a slaughter walks:
the want of children cast
In father's jaws! But why, my mind,
yet dread'st thou so, at last,
And faint'st, before thou enterprise?
It must be done, let be.
That which in all this mischief is
the greatest guilt to see,                                 220
Let him commit!

*Serv.*                          But what deceit
may we for him prepare,
Whereby betrapp'd he may be drawn
to fall into the snare?
He wots full well we are his foes.

*Atr.*        He could not taken be
Except himself would take, but now
my kingdoms hopeth he.
For hope of this, he would not fear
to meet the mighty Jove,                                   230
Though he him threaten'd to destroy
with lightning from above!
For hope of this, to pass the threats
of waves he will not fail,
Nor dread no whit by doubtful shelves
of Lybic seas to sail.

203–4 parents] *See note on* 1. i. 179.        205 rent] rend
217 enterprise] undertake        235 shelves] shoals

For hope of this (which thing he doth
   the worst of all believe)
He will his brother see.

Serv.                     Who shall
   of peace the promise give?                    240
Whom will he trust?

Atr.                    His evil hope
   will soon believe it well.
Yet to my sons the charge which they
   shall to their uncle tell
We will commit: that home he would
   from exile come again,
And miseries for Kingdom change,
   and over Argos reign
A King of half; and though, too hard
   of heart, our prayers all                    250
Himself despise, his children yet—
   nought woting what may fall,
With travels tir'd, and apt to be
   entic'd from misery—
Requests will move.  On th'one side his
   desire of empery,
On th'other side his poverty,
   and labour hard to see,
Will him subdue, and make to yield,
   although full stout he be.                    260

Serv.  His travails now the time hath made
   to seem to him but small.

Atr.   Not so, for day by day the grief
   of ill encreaseth all.
'Tis light to suffer miseries,
   but heavy them t'endure.

Serv.  Yet other messengers to send
   in such affairs, procure.

Atr.   The younger sort the worse precepts
   do eas'ly hearken to.                         270

Serv.  What thing against their Uncle now
   you them instruct to do,

  Perhaps with you to work the like
   they will not be a-dread.
  Such mischief wrought hath oft return'd
   upon the worker's head.

*Atr.* Though never man to them the ways
   of guile and guilt have taught,
  Yet kingdom will.  Fear'st thou they should
   be made by counsel naught?   280
  They are so born.  That which thou call'st
   a cruel enterprise,
  And direly deemest done to be,
   and wickedly likewise,
  Perhaps is wrought against me there.

*Serv.* And shall your sons of this
  Deceit be ware, that work you will?
   No secretness there is
  In their so green and tender years:
   they will your trains disclose.  290

*Atr.* A privy council close to keep
   is learn'd with many woes.

*Serv.* And will ye them, by whom ye would
   he should beguiled be,
  Themselves beguilde?

*Atr.*        Nay, let them both
   from fault and blame be free.
  For what shall need, in mischiefs such
   as I to work intend,
  To mingle them?  Let all my hate
   by me alone take end.   300
  Thou leav'st thy purpose ill, my mind:
   if thou thine own forbear,
  Thou sparest him.  Wherefore of this
   let Agamemnon here
  Be minister; and client eke
   of mine for such a deed,
  Let Menelaus present be:
   truth of th'uncertain seed

280 naught] bad   295 beguilde] beguile

By such a practice may be tried;
   if it refuse they shall,          310
Nor of debate will bearers be,
   if they him uncle call,
He is their father.  Let them go.
   But much the fearful face
Bewrays itself; even him that feigns
   the secret weighty case,
Doth oft betray; let them therefore
   not know how great a guile
They go about.  And thou these things
   in secret keep the while.          320

*Serv.*  I need not warned be, for these
   within my bosom deep
Both faith and fear, but chiefly faith,
   doth shet and closely keep.


### Chorus.

The noble House, at length, of high renown,
   The famous stock of ancient Inachus,
Appeas'd, and laid the threats of brethren down.
   But now what Fury stirs and drives you thus,
Each one to thirst the other's blood again,
   Or get by guilt the golden mace in hand?
Ye little wot, that so desire to reign,
   In what estate or place doth kingdom stand.
Not riches make a king, or high renown:
   Not garnish'd weed with purple Tyrian dye;          10
Not lofty looks, or head enclos'd with crown;
   Not glitt'ring beams with gold, and turrets high.
A king he is, that fear hath laid aside,
   And all affects that in the breast are bred;
Whom impotent ambition doth not guide,
   Nor fickle favour hath of people led.


  2 Inachus] *The most ancient hero of Argos.*
10 weed] robe          14 affects] passions          15 impotent]
headstrong

Nor all that West in metals' mines hath found,
    Or channel clear of golden Tagus shows,
Nor all the grain that threshed is on ground,
    That with the heat of Lybic harvest glows,      20
Nor whom the flash of lightning flame shall beat,
    Nor Eastern wind that smites upon the seas,
Nor swelling surge with rage of wind replete,
    Or greedy gulf of Adria displease;
Whom not the prick of soldier's sharpest spear,
    Or pointed pike in hand hath made to rue,
Nor whom the glimpse of sword might cause to fear,
    Or bright drawn blade of glitt'ring steel subdue.
Who in the seat of safety sets his feet
    Beholds all haps, how under him they lie,      30
And gladly runs his fatal day to meet,
    Nor ought complains or grudgeth for to die.
Though present were the princes everichone,
    The scattered Dakes to chase that wonted be,
That shining seas beset with precious stone,
    And Red Sea coasts do hold, like blood to see;
Or they which else the Caspian mountains high,
    From Sarmats strong with all their power withhold;
Or he that on the flood of Danuby
    In frost afoot to travel dare be bold,      40
Or Seres in whatever place they lie,
    Renown'd with Fleece that there of silk doth spring,
They never might the truth hereof deny:
    It is the mind that only makes a king.
There is no need of sturdy steeds in war,
    No need with arms, or arrows else, to fight,
That Parthus wonts with bow to fling from far,
    While from the field he falsely feigneth flight.
Nor yet to siege no need it is to bring
    Great guns in carts to overthrow the wall,      50
That from far off their batt'ring pellets sling.
    A king he is that feareth nought at all.

    33 everichone] every one      34 Dakes] Dacians
41 Seres] *A people of Eastern Asia.*

Each man himself this kingdom gives at hand.
    Let whoso list with mighty mace to reign
In tickle top of court delight to stand;
    Let me the sweet and quiet rest obtain:
So set in place obscure, and low degree,
    Of pleasant rest I shall the sweetness know.
My life, unknown to them that noble be,
    Shall in the step of secret silence go.                    60
Thus when my days at length are overpass'd,
    And time without all troubles tumult spent,
An aged man I shall depart at last,
    In mean estate to die full well content.
But grievous is to him the death, that, when
    So far abroad the bruit of him is blown
That known he is too much to other men,
    Departeth yet unto himself unknown.


## The Third Act.

### Thyestes.    Philisthenes.

*Thy.*  My country bowers so long wish'd for,
        and Argos' riches all,
    Chief good that unto banish'd men
        and misers may befall,
    The touch of soil where born I was,
        and Gods of native land,
    (If Gods they be), and sacred towers
        I see of Cyclops' hand,
    That represent than all man's work
        a greater majesty!                                     10
    Renowned stadies to my youth,
        where noble sometime I
    Have not so seld as once the palm
        in father's chariot won!

55 tickle] insecure    1 bowers] habitations    4 misers]
wretches        11 stadies] stadia, *where the Games were held.*
13 seld] seldom

All Argos now, to meet with me,
   and people, fast will run;
But Atreus too!  Yet rather lead
   in woods again thy flight,
And bushes thick, and hid among
   the brutish beasts from sight          20
Like life to theirs, where splendent pomp
   of court, and princely pride,
May not with flatt'ring, fulgent face
   allure thine eyes aside.
With whom the Kingdom given is
   behold, and well regard,
Beset but late with such mishaps
   as all men count full hard
I stout and joyful was, but now
   again thus into fear                    30
I am return'd; my mind misdoubts,
   and backward seeks to bear
My body hence, and forth I draw
   my pace against my will.

*Phyl.*  With slothful step—what meaneth this?—
   my father standeth still,
And turns his face, and holds himself,
   in doubt what thing to do.

*Thy.*  What thing, my mind, consider'st thou?
   or else so long whereto                 40
Dost thou so easy counsel wrest?
   Wilt thou to things unsure
Thy brother and the Kingdom trust?
   Fear'st thou those ills t'endure
Now overcome, and milder made?
   And travails dost thou flee
That well were plac'd?  It thee avails
   a miser now to be.
Turn hence thy pace, while leeful is,
   and keep thee from his hand.             50

47 thee avails] profits thee      48 miser] wretch

*Phyl.*  What cause thee drives, o father dear,
    thus from thy native land
    Now seen to shrink?  What makes thee thus,
    from things so good, at last
    Withdraw thyself?  Thy brother comes,
    whose ires be overpass'd,
    And half the Kingdom gives, and of
    the House dilacerate
    Restores the parts, and thee restores
    again to former state.                    60
*Thy.*  The cause of fear that I know not
    thou dost require to hear.
    I see nothing that makes me dread,
    and yet I greatly fear.
    I would go on, but yet my limbs
    with weary legs do slack.
    And other way than I would pass
    I am withholden back.
    So, oft, the ship that driven is
    with wind and eke with oar,          70
    The swelling surge, resisting both,
    beats back upon the shore.
*Phyl.*  Yet overcome whatever stays
    and thus doth let your mind,
    And see what are at your return
    prepar'd for you to find.
    You may, o father, reign!
*Thy.*                        I may,
    but then when die I mought.
*Phyl.*  Chief thing is power!
*Thy.*                        Nought worth at all
    if thou desire it nought.          80
*Phyl.*  You shall it to your children leave.
*Thy.*  The Kingdom takes not twain.
*Phyl.*  Who may be happy, rather would
    he miser yet remain?

74 let] hinder     78 mought] might     84 miser] wretch

*Thy.* Believe me well, with titles false
　　the great things us delight,
And heavy haps in vain are fear'd.
　　While high I stood in sight,
I never stinted then to quake,
　　and self-same sword to fear          90
That hanged by mine own side was.
　　Oh how great good it were
With none to strive, but, careless, food
　　to eat, and rest to know!
The greater guilts, they enter not
　　in cottage set a-low;
And safer food is fed upon
　　at narrow board alway,
While drunk in gold the poison is;
　　by proof well taught I say          100
That evil haps before the good
　　to love, it likes my will.
Of haughty house that stands aloft
　　in tickle top of hill
And sways aside, the city low
　　need never be afright:
Nor in the top of roof above
　　there shines no ivory bright,
Nor watchman none defends my sleeps
　　by night, or guards my rest.          110
With fleet I fish not, nor the seas
　　I have not backward press'd
Nor turn'd to flight with builded wall;
　　nor wicked belly I
With taxes of the people fed;
　　nor parcel none doth lie
Of ground of mine beyond the Getes
　　and Parthians far about;
Nor worshipped with frankincense
　　I am, nor (Jove shet out!)          120

96 alow] lower      104 tickle] insecure      117 Getes]
Getae        120 shet out] shut out, forbid

My altars decked are; nor none
 in top of house doth stand
In garden trees, nor kindled yet
 with help of each man's hand
The baths do smoke; nor yet are days
 in slothful slumbers led,
Nor nights pass'd forth in watch and wine
 without the rest of bed.
We nothing fear; the house is safe
 without the hidden knife,    130
And poor estate the sweetness feels
 of rest and quiet life.
Great kingdom is to be content
 without the same to live.

*Phyl.* Yet should it not refused be
 if God the kingdom give.
*Thy.* Not yet desir'd it ought to be.
*Phyl.* Your brother bids you reign.
*Thy.* Bids he? The more is to be fear'd!
 There lurketh there some train.   140
*Phyl.* From whence it fell, yet piety
 is wont to turn, at length;
And love unfeign'd repairs again
 his erst-omitted strength.
*Thy.* Doth Atreus then his brother love?
 Eke Ursa first, on high,
The seas shall wash, and swelling surge
 of seas of Sicily
Shall rest, and all assuaged be,
 and corn to ripeness grow   150
In bottom of Ionian seas,
 and darkest night shall show
And spread the light about the soil;
 the waters with the fire,
The life with death, the wind with seas,
 shall friendship first require,
And be at league.
  140 train] trick  156 require] seek

*Phyl.*                 Of what deceit
       are you so dreadful here?
*Thy.*   Of everichone; what end at length
       might I provide of fear?          160
       In all he can he hateth me.
*Phyl.*   To you what hurt can he?
*Thy.*   As for myself, I nothing dread;
       you little babes make me
       Afraid of him.
*Phyl.*              Dread ye to be
       beguil'd, when caught ye are?
       Too late it is to shun the train,
       in middle of the snare!
       But go we on; this, father, is
       to you my last request.         170
*Thy.*   I follow you, I lead you not.
*Phyl.*   God turn it to the best
       That well-devised is for good.
       Pass forth with cheerful pace.


## The Second Scene.

### Atreus.    Thyestes.

*Atr.*   Entrapp'd in train the beast is caught,
       and in the snare doth fall;
       Both him, and eke of hated stock
       with him, the offspring all
       About the father's side I see;
       and now in safety stands,
       And surest ground, my wrathful hate.
       Now comes into my hands
       At length Thyestes! Yea, he comes,
       and all at once, to me!         10
       I scant refrain myself, and scant
       may anger bridled be.

159 everichone] every one

So when the bloodhound seeks the beast
  by step, and, quick of scent,
Draws in the leam, and pace by pace
  to wind the way he went
With nose to soil doth hunt,
  while he the boar aloof hath found
Far off by scent, he yet refrains
  and wanders through the ground          20
With silent mouth; but when at hand
  he once perceives the prey,
With all the strength he hath he strives
  with voice, and calls away
His ling'ring master, and from him
  by force out breaketh he.
When ire doth hope the present blood,
  it may not hidden be.
Yet let it hidden be.  Behold,
  with ugly hair, to sight,          30
How irksomely deform'd with filth
  his foulest face is dight!
How loathsome lies his beard unkempt!
  But let us friendship fain.—
To see my brother me delights;
  give now to me again
Embracing long desired for!
  Whatever strife there was
Before this time between us twain,
  forget, and let it pass.          40
Fro this day forth, let brother's love,
  let blood, and law of kind,
Regarded be; let all debate
  be slak'd in either's mind.
*Thy.*  I could excuse myself, except
  thou wert as now thou art.
But, Atreus, now I grant, the fault
  was mine in every part,

15 leam] leash          31 irksomely] hideously
32 dight] dirtied          42 kind] nature, kindred

And I offended have in all.
   My cause the worse to be       50
Your this-day's kindness makes! Indeed
   a guilty wight is he
That would so good a brother hurt
   as you, in any whit.
But now with tears I must entreat,
   and first I me submit.
These hands, that at thy feet do lie,
   do thee beseech and pray
That ire and hate be laid aside,
   and from thy bosom may       70
Be scraped out, and clear forgot.
   For pledges, take thou these,
O brother dear, these guiltless babes.

*Atr.*    Thy hands yet from my knees
Remove, and rather me to take
   in arms, upon me fall!
And ye, o aids of elders' age,
   ye little infants all,
Me clip and coll about the neck!
   This foul attire forsake,       80
And spare mine eyes that pity it,
   and fresher vesture take,
Like mine to see. And you, with joy,
   the half of empery,
Dear brother, take! The greater praise
   shall come to me thereby,
Our fathers' seat to yield to you,
   and brother to relieve.
To have a Kingdom is but chance,
   but virtue, it to give.       90

*Thy.*  A just reward for such deserts,
   the Gods, o brother dear,
Repay to thee! But on my head
   a regal crown to wear

79 clip and coll] hug and embrace

My loathsome life denies; and far
    doth from the scepter flee
My hand unhappy.  In the midst
    let leeful be for me
Of men to lurk!

*Atr.*              This kingdom can
    with twain full well agree.          100

*Thy.*  Whatever is, o brother, yours,
    I count it mine to be.

*Atr.*  Who would Dame Fortune's gifts refuse
    if she him raise to reign?

*Thy.*  The gifts of her, each man it wots,
    how soon they pass again.

*Atr.*  Ye me deprive of glory great,
    except ye th'empire take.

*Thy.*  You have your praise in off'ring it,
    and I, it to forsake;          110
And full persuaded to refuse
    the Kingdom am I still.

*Atr.*  Except your part ye will sustain,
    mine own forsake I will.

*Thy.*  I take it then, and bear I will
    the name thereof alone;
The rights and arms, as well as mine
    they shall be yours each one.

*Atr.*  The regal crown, as you beseems,
    upon your head then take;       120
And I th'appointed sacrifice
    for gods, will now go make.


### Chorus.

Would any man it ween!  That cruel wight
    Atreus, of mind so impotent to see,
Was soon astonied with his brother's sight!
    No greater force than piety may be.

1 ween] believe        2 impotent] unrestrained
3 astonied] astounded

Where kindred is not, lasteth every threat;
  Whom true love holds, it holds eternally.
The wrath but late with causes kindled great
  All favour brake, and did *To battle!* cry,
When horsemen did resound on every side,
  The swords each where then glister'd more and
    more:                                        10
Which raging Mars with often stroke did guide
  The fresher blood to shed yet thirsting sore.
But Love the sword against their will doth swage,
  And them to peace persuades, with hand in hand.
So sudden rest amid so great a rage
  What God hath made? Throughout Mycenae's land
The harness clink'd, but late, of civil strife;
  And for their babes did fearful mothers quake;
Her armed spouse to leese, much fear'd the wife,
  When sword was made the scabbard to forsake, 20
That now by rest with rust was overgrown.
  Some to repair the walls that did decay,
And some to strength the towers half overthrown,
  And some the gates with gins of iron to stay,
Full busy were; and dreadful watch by night
  From turret high did overlook the town.
Worse is than war itself the fear of fight.
  Now are the threats of cruel sword laid down,
And now the rumour whists of battles sown,
  The noise of crooked trumpet silent lies,      30
And quiet peace returns to joyful town.
  So, when the waves of swelling surge arise,
While Corus' wind the Brutian seas doth smight,
  And Scylla sounds from hollow caves within,
And shipmen are with wafting waves affright,
  Charybdis casts that erst it had drunk in;
And Cyclops fierce his father yet doth dread,
  In Etna bank, that fervent is with heats,

13 swage] pacify     19 leese] lose     23 strength]
strengthen     24 gins] bars     29 whists] falls silent
35 wafting waves] seas that bear them

Lest quenched be with waves that overshed
  The fire, that from eternal furnace beats;      40
And poor Laertes thinks his kingdoms all
  May drowned be, and Ithaca doth quake.
If once the force of winds begin to fall,
  The sea li'th down more mild than standing lake;
The deep, where ships so wide full dreadful were
  To pass, with sails on either side outspread,
Now fall'n a-down, the lesser boat doth bear;
  And leisure is, to view the fishes dead
Even there where late, with tempest beat upon,
  The shaken Cyclads were with seas aghast.      50
No state endures. The pain and pleasure, one
  To other yields; and joys be soonest past.
One hour sets up the things that lowest be.
  He that the crown to Princes doth divide,
Whom people please with bending of the knee,
  And at whose beck their battles lay aside
The Medes, and Indians eke, to Phoebus nigh,
  And Dakes that Parthians do with horsemen threat—
Himself yet holds his scepters doubtfully,
  And men of might he fears, and chances great    60
(That each estate may turn), and doubtful hour.
  O ye, whom lord of land and waters wide,
Of life and death grants here to have the power,
  Lay ye your proud and lofty looks aside;
What your inferior fears of you amiss,
  That your superior threats to you again.
To greater King, each King a subject is.
  Whom dawn of day hath seen in pride to reign,
Him overthrown hath seen the evening late.
  Let none rejoice too much, that good hath got; 70
Let none despair of best, in worst estate.
  For Clotho mingles all, and suff'reth not
Fortune to stand, but Fates about doth drive.
  Such friendship find with Gods yet no man might

58 Dakes] Dacians

That he the morrow should be sure to live.
  The God our things all toss'd and turned quite
Rolls with a whirlwind.


## The Fourth Act.

### Messenger.  Chorus.

*Mess.* What whirlwind may me headlong drive,
      and up in air me fling,
    And wrap in darkest cloud, whereby
      it might so heinous thing
    Take from mine eyes? O wicked House
      that even of Pelops ought
    And Tantalus abhorred be!
*Chor.*    What new thing hast thou brought?
*Mess.* What land is this? Li'th Sparta here,
      and Argos, that hath bred       10
    So wicked brethren? And the ground
      of Corinth lying spread
    Between the seas? Or Ister else,
      where, wont to take their flight,
    Are people wild? Or that which wonts
      with snow to shine to bright,
    Hyrcana land? Or else do here
      the wand'ring Scythians dwell?
*Chor.* What monstrous mischief is this place
      then guilty of? That tell,       20
    And this declare to us at large,
      whatever be the ill.
*Mess.* If once my mind may stay itself,
      and quaking limbs, I will.
    But yet of such a cruel deed
      before mine eyes the fear
    And image walks! Ye raging storms
      now far from hence me bear,
    And to that place me drive, to which
      now driven is the day       30

      Thus drawn from hence!

*Chor.*                Our minds ye hold
      yet still in doubtful stay.
      Tell what it is ye so abhor;
      the author thereof show.
      I ask not who, but which of them:
      that quickly let us know.

*Mess.* In Pelops' turret high, a part
      there is of palace wide,
      That toward the south erected leans;
      of which the outer side           40
      With equal top to mountain stands,
      and on the city lies,
      And people, proud against their prince,
      if once the traitors rise,
      Hath underneath his batt'ring stroke.
      There shines the place in sight
      Where wont the people to frequent,
      whose golden beams so bright
      The noble spotted pillars gray,
      of marble, do support.              50
      Within this place well-known to men,
      where they so oft resort,
      To many other rooms about
      the noble Court doth go.
      The privy Palace underlieth
      in secret place alow,
      With ditch full deep, that doth enclose
      the wood of privety
      And hidden parts of kingdom old;
      where never grew no tree          60
      That cheerful boughs is wont to bear,
      with knife or lopped be,
      But tax, and cypress, and with tree
      of holm, full black to see,

---

32 stay] pause         39 leans] faces         63 tax]
yew-tree

Doth beck and bend the wood so dark;
  aloft above all these
The higher oak doth overlook,
  surmounting all the trees.
From hence with luck the reign to take
  accustom'd are the Kings,                    70
From hence in danger aid to ask,
  and doom in doubtful things.
To this affixed are the gifts:
  the sounding trumpets bright,
The chariots broke, and spoils of sea
  that now Myrtoön hight;
There hang the wheels once won by craft
  of falser axle-tree,
And every other conquest's note;
  there leeful is to see                       80
The Phrygian tire of Pelops' head,
  the spoil of en'mies here,
And, of barbarian triumph left,
  the painted gorgeous gear.
A loathsome spring stands under shade,
  and slothful course doth take
With water black, even such as is
  of irksome Stygian lake
The ugly wave, whereby are wont
  to swear the Gods on high.                   90
Here all the night the grisly ghosts
  and Gods of death to cry
The fame reports. With clinking chains
  resounds the wood each where.
The sprites cry out, and everything
  that dreadful is to hear
May there be seen. Of ugly shapes,
  from old sepulchres sent,

72 doom] sentence, judgement        76 hight] is called
80 leeful] lawful (*but the phrase hardly means more than* there
may be seen)        88 irksome] loathsome        95 sprites]
spirits

A fearful flock doth wander there;
   and in that place frequent                        100
Worse things than ever yet were known.
   Yea, all the wood full oft
With flame is wont to flash, and all
   the higher trees aloft
Without a fire do burn; and oft
   the wood, beside all this,
With triple barking roars at once.
   Full oft the palace is
Affright with shapes, nor light of day
   may once the terror quell.                        110
Eternal night doth hold the place,
   and darkness there of Hell
In midday reigns.  From hence, to them
   that pray, out of the ground
The certain answers given are,
   what time with dreadful sound
From secret place the fates be told,
   and dungeon roars within
While of the God breaks out the voice.
   Whereto when enter'd in                            120
Fierce Atreus was, that did with him
   his brother's children trail,
Deck'd are the altars: who, alas!
   may it enough bewail?
Behind the infants' backs anon
   he knit their noble hands,
And eke their heavy heads about
   he bound with purple bands.
There wanted there no frankincense,
   nor yet the holy wine,                             130
Nor knife to cut the sacrifice,
   besprink'd with leavens fine.
Kept is in all the order due,
   lest such a mischief gret

132 besprink'd] sprinkled        leavens] *The salted meal
of the sacrifice.*        134 gret] great

Should not be order'd well.
*Chor.*                              Who doth
　　　his hand on sword then set?
*Mess.* He is himself the priest, and he
　　　himself the deadly verse,
With prayer dire, from fervent mouth
　　　doth sing and oft rehearse.                    140
And he at th'altars stands, himself;
　　　he them assign'd to die
Doth handle and in order set
　　　and to the knife apply;
He lights the fires.  No rites were left
　　　of sacrifice undone.
The wood then quak'd, and all at once
　　　from trembling earth anon
The palace beck'd, in doubt which way
　　　the peise thereof would fall,                  150
And shaking as in waves it stood.
　　　From th'air and therewithal
A blazing star, that foulest train
　　　drew after him, doth go.
The wines that in the fire were cast,
　　　with changed liquor flow,
And turn to blood; and twice or thrice
　　　th'attire fell from his head.
The ivory bright in temples seem'd
　　　to weep and tears to shed.                     160
The sights amaz'd all other men,
　　　but steadfast yet alway
Of mind, unmoved Atreus stands,
　　　and even the Gods doth fray
That threaten him; and, all delay
　　　forsaken, by and by
To th'altars turns, and therewithal
　　　aside he looks awry.

149 beck'd] shook        150 peise] weight        166 by
and by] very soon

As hungry tiger wonts, that doth
  in Gange woods remain,      170
With doubtful pace to range and roam
  between the bullocks twain,
Of either prey full covetous,
  and yet uncertain where
She first may bite, and roaring throat
  now turns the t'one to tear
And then to th'other straight returns,
  and doubtful famine holds:
So Atreus dire between the babes
  doth stand, and them beholds     180
On whom he points to slake his ire.
  First slaughter where to make
He doubts, or whom he should, again,
  for second off'ring take.
Yet skills it nought; but yet he doubts,
  and such a cruelty
It him delights to order well.
*Chor.*   Whom take he first to die?
*Mess.* First place (lest in him think ye might
  no piety to remain)     190
To grandsire dedicated is;
  first Tantalus is slain.
*Chor.* With what a mind and countenance could
  the boy his death sustain?
*Mess.* All careless of himself he stood,
  nor once he would in vain
His prayers leese; but Atreus fierce
  the sword in him at last,
In deep and deadly wound doth hide
  to hilts, and gripping fast     200
His throat in hand, he thrust him through.
  The sword then drawn away,
When long the body had upheld
  itself in doubtful stay

170 Gange] of the Ganges     181 points] determines
185 skills] matters     197 leese] lose

Which way to fall, at length upon
  the uncle down it falls.
And then to th'altars cruelly
  Philisthenes he tralls,
And on his brother throws, and straight
  his neck off cutteth he.          210
The carcass headlong falls to ground;
  a piteous thing to see,
The mourning head with murmur yet
  uncertain doth complain.
*Chor.* What, after double death, doth he,
  and slaughter, then, of twain?
Spares he the child?  Or guilt on guilt
  again yet heepeth he?
*Mess.* As long-man'd lion fierce, amid
  the wood of Armenie          220
The drove pursues, and conquest makes
  of slaughter many one,
Though now defiled be his jaws
  with blood, and hunger gone,
Yet slaketh not his ireful rage,
  with blood of bulls so great,
But slothful now, with weary tooth,
  the lesser calves doth threat:
None otherwise doth Atreus rage,
  and swells with anger strain'd,    230
And, holding now the sword in hand
  with double slaughter stain'd,
Regarding not where fell his rage,
  with cursed hand unmild
He strake it through his body quite.
  at bosom of the child
The blade go'th in, and at the back
  again out went the same.
He falls, and quenching with his blood
  the altar's sacred flame,        240
Of either wound at length he dieth.
       208 tralls] drags

*Chor.*     Oh heinous hateful act!

*Mess.*  Abhor ye this? Ye hear not yet
  the end of all the fact;
 There follows more.

*Chor.*     A fiercer thing
 or worse than this to see
Could nature bear?

*Mess.*     Why, think ye this
 of guilt the end to be?
It is but part.

*Chor.*   What could he more?
 To cruel beasts, he cast,    250
Perhaps, their bodies to be torn,
 and kept from fires at last.

*Mess.*  Would God he had! That never tomb
 the dead might overhide,
Nor flames dissolve, though them for food
 to fowls in pastures wide
He had out-thrown, or them for prey
 to cruel beasts would fling!
That which the worst was wont to be
 were here a wished thing,   260
That them their father saw untomb'd.
 But oh, more cursed crime,
Uncredible, the which deny
 will men of aftertime!
From bosoms yet alive out-drawn
 the trembling bowels shake,
The veins yet breathe, the fearful heart
 doth yet both pant and quake,
But he the strings doth turn in hand,
 and destinies behold,   270
And of the guts the signs each one
 doth view, not fully cold.
When him the sacrifice had pleas'd,
 his diligence he puts

244 fact] deed  252 fires] *sc.* cremation

To dress his brother's banquet now,
  and straight asunder cuts
The bodies into quarters all,
  and by the stumps anon
The shoulders wide, and brawns of arms,
  he strikes off everichone.      280
He lays abroad their naked limbs,
  and cuts away the bones.
The only heads he keeps, and hands
  to him committed ones.
Some of the guts are broach'd, and in
  the fires that burn full slow
They drop; the boiling liquor some
  doth tumble to and fro
In mourning cauldron; from the flesh
  that overstands aloft      290
The fire doth fly, and scatter out,
  and into chimney oft
Up-heap'd again, and there constrain'd
  by force to tarry yet,
Unwilling burns; the liver makes
  great noise upon the spit,
Nor eas'ly wot I if the flesh
  or flames they be that cry,
But cry they do; the fire like pitch
  it fumeth by and by.      300
Nor yet the smoke itself, so sad,
  like filthy mist in sight,
Ascendeth up as wont it is,
  nor takes his way upright,
But even the Gods and house it doth
  with filthy fume defile.
O patient Phoebus, though from hence
  thou backward flee the while,
And in the midst of heaven above
  dost drown the broken day,      310

281 abroad] spread out    305 the Gods] Lares,
household gods

Thou fleest too late! The father eats
    his children welaway!
And limbs to which he once gave life
    with cursed jaw doth tear.
He shines with ointment shed full sweet
    all round about his hair,
Replete with wine, and oftentimes
    so cursed kind of food
His mouth hath held, that would not down.
    But yet this one thing good          320
In all thy ills, Thyestes, is:
    that them thou dost not know.
And yet shall that not long endure,
    though Titan backward go
And chariots turn against himself
    to meet the ways he went,
And heavy night so heinous deed
    to keep from sight be sent,
And out of time from east arise
    so foul a fact to hide,          330
Yet shall the whole at length be seen:
    thy ills shall all be spied.


### Chorus.

Which way, o Prince of lands and Gods on high,
    At whose uprise eftsoons of shadow'd night
All beauty fleeth, which way turn'st thou awry,
    And draw'st the day in midst of heaven to flight?
Why dost thou, Phoebus, hide from us thy sight?
    Not yet the watch that later hour brings in,
Doth Vesper warn the stars to kindle light.
    Not yet doth turn of Hesper's wheel begin
To loose thy chare his well-deserved way.
    The trumpet third not yet hath blown his blast, 10
While toward the night begins to yield the day.
    Great wonder hath of sudden supper's haste

        9 loose thy chare] unharness thy chariot

The plowman, yet whose oxen are untir'd.
　From wonted course of heaven what draws thee
　　back?
What causes have from certain race conspir'd
　To turn thy horse?  Do yet from dungeon black
Of hollow Hell the conquer'd giants prove
　A fresh assault?  Doth Tityus yet essay
With trenched heart and wounded womb to move
　The former ires?  Or from the hill away　　　20
Hath now Typhoeus wound his side by might?
　Is up to Heaven the way erected high
Of Phlegrey foes by mountains set upright?
　And now doth Ossa Pelion overlie?
The wonted turns are gone, of day and night.
　The rise of sun, nor fall, shall be no more.
Aurora, dewish mother of the light,
　That wonts to send the horses out before,
Doth wonder much, again return'd to see
　Her dawning light.  She wots not how to ease　30
The weary wheels, nor manes that smoking be
　Of horse with sweat, to bathe amid the seas.
Himself, unwonted there to lodge, likewise,
　Doth setting sun again the morning see,
And now commands the darkness up to rise
　Before the night to come prepared be.
About the Pole yet glow'th no fire in sight,
　Nor light of moon the shades doth comfort yet.
What-so it be, God grant it be the night!
　Our hearts do quake, with fear oppressed gret,　40
And dreadful are, lest heaven and earth and all,
　With fatal ruin shaken, shall decay;
And lest on Gods again, and men, shall fall
　Disfigur'd Chaos; and the land away,
The seas, and fires, and of the glorious skies
　The wand'ring lamps, lest Nature yet shall hide.

17 prove] try　　　　　　23 Phlegrey] Phlegraean
(sc. the Giants)　　　40 gret] great　　44 Disfigur'd]
formless

Now shall no more, with blaze of his uprise,
   The lord of stars, that leads the world so wide,
Of summer both, and winter, give the marks.
   Nor yet the moon, with Phoebus flames that burns,
Shall take from us by night the dreadful carks,     51
   With swifter course o'er-pass her brothers turns,
While compass less she fets in crooked race.
   The gods on heaps shall out of order fall,
And each with other mingled be in place.
   The wried way of holy planets all,
With path aslope that doth divide the zones,
   That bears the Signs, and years in course doth
      bring,
Shall see the stars fall down with him at ones.
   And he that first, not yet with gentle Spring,     60
The temperate gale doth give to sails, the Ram,
   Shall headlong fall a-down to seas again,
Through which he once with fearful Helen swam.
   Next him the Bull, that doth with horn sustain
The Sisters Seven, with him shall overturn
   The Twins, and arms of crooked Cancer all.
The Lion hot, that wonts the soil to burn,
   Of Hercules, again from Heaven shall fall.
To lands once left the Virgin shall be thrown,
   And level'd peise of balance sway a-low,     70
And draw with them the stinging Scorpion down.
   So likewise he that holds in Thessal bow
His swift well-feather'd arrows, Chiron old,
   Shall break the same, and eke shall leese his shot.
And Capricorn, that brings the winter cold,
   Shall overturn, and break thy water pot,
Who-so thou be. And down with thee to ground,
   The last of all the signs, shall Pisces fall.

51 carks] cares     53 fets] fetches     56 wried]
crooked (*referring to the curved course of their apparent motion*)
58 Signs] Sc. of the Zodiac, enumerated in the following
twenty lines.     59 ones] once     70 peise] weight
74 leese] lose

And monsters eke, in seas yet never drown'd,
 The water gulf shall overwhelm them all.     80
And he which doth between each Ursa glide
 Like crooked flood, the slipper serpent twin'd,
And lesser Bear by greater Dragon's side,
 Full cold with frost congealed hard by kind,
And Carter dull, that slowly guides his Wain,
 Unstable shall Boötes fall from high.
We are thought meet, of all men, whom again
 Should hugy heap of chaos overlie,
And world oppress with overturned mass.
 The latest age now falleth us upon.     90
With evil hap we are begot, alas,
 If, wretches, we have lost the sight of sun,
Or him by fault enforced have to fly.
 Let our complaints yet go, and fear be past:
He greedy is of life, that will not die
 When all the world shall end with him at last.


## The Fifth Act.

### Atreus *alone.*

Now equal with the stars I go,
 beyond each other wight;
With haughty head the heavens above,
 and highest pole I smite.
The Kingdom now and seat I hold
 where once my father reign'd.
I now let go the Gods, for all
 my will I have obtain'd.
Enough and well! Yea, even enough
 for me I am acquit.     10
But why enough? I will proceed,
 and fill the father yet

82 slipper] slippery          90 latest] last, *sc. the end of the world.*

With blood of his. Lest any shame
   should me restrain at all,
The day is gone. Go to, therefore,
   while thee the Heaven doth call!
Would God I could against their wills
   yet hold the Gods that flee,
And of revenging dish constrain
   them witnesses to be!        20
But yet, which well enough is wrought,
   let it the father see!
In spite of all the drowned day
   I will remove from thee.
The darkness all, in shade whereof
   do lurk thy miseries.
And guest at such a banquet now
   too long he careless lies
With merry face! Now eat and drunk
   enough he hath! At last        30
'Tis best himself should know his ills.
   Ye servants all, in haste
Undo the Temple doors, and let
   the House be open all.
Fain would I see, when look upon
   his children's heads he shall,
What countenance he then would make;
   or in what words break out
Would first his grief; or how would quake
   his body round about        40
With sprite amazed sore: of all
   my work the fruit were this.
I would not him a miser see,
   but while so made he is.
Behold the Temple opened now
   doth shine with many a light.
In glitt'ring gold and purple seat
   he sits himself upright,

     41 sprite] spirit        43 miser] wretch

And, staying up his heavy head
   with wine, upon his hand,         50
He belcheth out.  Now, chief of Gods,
   in highest place I stand,
And king of kings!  I have my wish,
   and more than I could think.
He filled is, he now the wine
   in silver bowl doth drink.
And spare it not!  There yet remains
   a worser draught for thee,
That sprung out of the bodies late
   of sacrifices three,         60
Which wine shall hide.  Let therewithal
   the boards be taken up.
The father, mingled with the wine,
   his children's blood shall sup,
That would have drunk of mine.
   Behold, he now begins to strain
His voice, and sings, nor yet for joy
   His mind he may refrain.


## The Second Scene.

### Thyestes *alone*.

O beaten bosoms, dull'd so long with woe,
   Lay down your cares!  At length your griefs relent!
Let sorrow pass, and all your dread let go,
   And, fellow eke of fearful banishment,
Sad poverty, and ill in misery,
   The shame of cares.  More whence thy fall thou
     haste
Than whither, skills.  Great hap to him, from high
   That falls, it is in surety to be plac'd
Beneath.  And great it is to him again
   That, press'd with storm, of evils feels the smart,  10

    62 boards] tables (*sc.* let the feast be ended)
   7 skills] it matters

Of Kingdom lost the peises to sustain
    With neck unbow'd: nor yet deject of **heart**
Nor overcome, his heavy hap always
    To bear upright. But now of careful carks
Shake off the show'rs, and of thy wretched **days**
    Away with all the miserable marks!
To joyful state return thy cheerful face!
    Put fro thy mind the old Thyestes hence.
It is the wont of wight in woeful case
    In state of joy to have no confidence.                    20
Though better haps to them returned be,
    Th'afflicted yet to joy it irketh sore.
Why call'st thou me aback, and hind'rest **me**
    This happy day to celebrate? Wherefore
Bidst thou me, Sorrow, weep without a cause?
    Who doth me let with flowers so fresh and gay
To deck my hairs? It lets, and me withdraws.
    Down from my head the roses fall away;
My moisted hair with ointment overall,
    With sudden maze stands up in wondrous wise. 30
From face that would not weep, the streams do fall,
    And howling cries amid my words arise.
My sorrow yet th'accustom'd tears doth love,
    And wretches still delight to weep and cry.
Unpleasant plaints it pleaseth them to move,
    And flourish'd fair it likes with Tyrian dye
Their robes to rent; to wail it likes them still.
    For sorrow sends, in sign that woes draw nigh,
The mind, that wots before of after ill.
    The sturdy storms the shipmen overlie         40
When void of wind th'assuaged seas do rest.
    What tumult, yet, or countenance to see,
Mak'st thou mad man? At length a trustful breast
    To brother give, whatever now it be,

11 peises] weight        14 carks] cares        26 let]
hinder        30 maze] amazement        36, 37 likes]
pleases        37 rent] rend

Causeless, or else too late thou art a-dread.
  I, wretch, would not so fear; but yet me draws
A trembling terror.  Down mine eyes do shed
  Their sudden tears, and yet I know no cause.
Is it a grief, or fear?  Or else hath tears
  Great joy itself?                                    50


## The Third Scene.

### Atreus.   Thyestes.

*Atr.*   Let us this day with one consent,
             o brother, celebrate!
         This day my sceptres may confirm
             and stablish my estate,
         And faithful bond of peace and love
             between us ratify.

*Thy.*   Enough with meat and eke with wine
             now satisfi'd am I.
         But yet, of all my joys it were
             a great increase to me                    10
         If now about my side I might
             my little children see.

*Atr.*   Believe that here, even in thine arms,
             thy children present be.
         For here they are, and shall be here;
             no part of them fro thee
         Shall be withheld.  Their loved looks
             now give to thee I will,
         And with the heap of all his babes
             the father fully fill.                     20
         Thou shalt be glutted, fear thou not!
             They, with my boys, as yet
         The joyful sacrifices make
             at board where children sit.
         They shall be call'd.  The friendly cup
             now take, of courtesy,
         With wine up-fill'd.

*Thy.*                          Of brother's feast
            I take full willingly
        The final gift; shed some to Gods
            of this, our fathers' land,                    30
        Then let the rest be drunk.  What's this?
            In no wise will my hand
        Obey!  The peise increaseth sore,
            and down mine arm doth sway,
        And from my lips the wafting wine
            itself doth fly away,
        And in deceived mouth, about
            my jaws it runneth round!
        The table, too, itself doth shake,
            and leap from trembling ground.              40
        Scant burns the fire.  The air itself
            with heavy cheer, to sight
        Forsook of sun, amazed is
            between the day and night.
        What meaneth this?  Yet more and more
            of backward-beaten sky
        The compass falls, and thicker mist
            the world doth overlie
        Than blackest darkness, and the night
            in night itself doth hide.                    50
        All stars be fled.  What-so it be,
            my brother, God provide,
        And sons to spare!  The Gods so grant
            that all this tempest fall
        On this vile head!  But now restore
            to me my children all.
*Atr.*    I will; and never day again
            shall them from thee withdraw.
*Thy.*    What tumult tumbleth so my guts
            and doth my bowels gnaw?                      60
        What quakes within?  With heavy peise
            I feel myself oppress'd,

33. 61 peise] weight          37 deceived] disappointed

And with another voice than mine
  bewails my doleful breast.
Come near, my sons, for you now doth
  th'unhappy father call!
Come near, for, you once seen, this grief
  would soon assuage and fall.
Whence murmur they?

*Atr.*               With father's arms
  embrace them quickly now!        70
For here they are, lo, come to thee!
  Dost thou thy children know?

*Thy.* I know, my brother.  Such a guilt
  yet canst thou suffer well,
O earth, to bear?  Nor yet from hence
  to Stygian lake of Hell
Dost thou both drown thyself and us?
  Nor yet with broken ground
Dost thou these Kingdoms and their King
  with chaos rude confound?       80
Nor yet, uprenting from the soil
  the bowers of wicked land,
Dost thou Mycenas overturn?
  With Tantalus to stand,
And ancestors of ours (if there
  in Hell be any one),
Now ought we both.  Now from the frames
  on either side anon
Of ground, all here and there rent up,
  out of thy bosom deep       90
Thy dens and dungeons set abroad,
  and us enclosed keep
In bottom low of Acheront.
  Above our heads aloft
Let wander all the guilty ghosts.
  With burning fret full oft

---

72] *Here Atreus shows Thyestes the heads of his sons.*   81 up-
renting] tearing up      96 fret] torrent

Let fiery Phlegethon, that drives
   his sands both to and fro,
To our confusion over-run,
   and violently flow.           100
O slothful soil, unshaken peise,
   unmoved yet art thou?
The Gods are fled.

*Atr.*                But take to thee
   with joy thy children now,
And rather them embrace! At length
   thy children all, of thee
So long wish'd for (for no delay
   there standeth now in me)
Enjoy and kiss! Embracing arms
   divide thou unto three!        110

*Thy.*  Is this thy league? May this thy love
   and faith of brother be?
And dost thou so repose thy hate?
   The father doth not crave
His sons alive—which might have been
   without the guilt—to have,
And eke without thy hate—but this
   doth brother brother pray:
That them he may entomb, restore,
   whom see thou shalt straightway    120
Be burnt. The father nought requires
   of thee that have he shall,
But soon forgo.

*Atr.*             Whatever part
   yet of thy children all
Remains, here shalt thou have; and what
   remaineth not, thou hast.

*Thy.*  Lie they in fields, a food out-flung
   for fleeing fowls to waste?
Or are they kept a prey for wild
   and brutish beasts to eat?      130

128 fleeing] flying (*sc. birds of the air*)

Atr.  Thou hast devour'd thy sons, and fill'd
         thyself with wicked meat.

Thy.  Oh, this it is that sham'd the Gods,
         and day from hence did drive
      Turn'd back to east.  Alas, I, wretch,
         what wailings may I give,
      Or what complaints?  What woefull words
         may be enough for me?
      Their heads cut off and hands off-torn
         I from their bodies see,                        140
      And wrenched feet from broken thighs
         I here behold again.
      'Tis this that greedy father could
         not suffer to sustain.
      In belly roll my bowels round,
         and closed crime so gret
      Without a passage strives within,
         and seeks away to get.
      Thy sword, o brother, lend to me!
         Much of my blood alas                           150
      It hath!  Let us therewith make way
         for all my sons to pass.
      Is yet the sword fro me withheld?
         Thyself thy bosoms tear,
      And let thy breasts resound with strokes!
         Yet, wretch, thy hand forbear,
      And spare the dead.  Who ever saw
         such mischief put in proof?
      What rude Heniochus, that dwells
         by ragged coasts aloof                          160
      Of Caucasus, unapt for men!
         Or fear to Athens, who
      Procrustes wild!  The father I
         oppress my children do,
      And am oppress'd.  Is any mean
         of guilt or mischief yet?


      146 gret] great       159 Heniochus] pirate

*Atr.*   A mean in mischief ought to be
        when guilt thou dost commit,
     Not when thou quit'st; for yet even this
        too little seems to me.      170
     The blood yet warm even from the wound
        I should, in sight of thee,
     Even in thy jaws have shed, that thou
        the blood of them might drink
     That lived yet. But while too much
        to haste my hate I think,
     My wrath beguiled is. Myself
        with sword the wounds them gave.
     I strake them down. The sacred fires
        with slaughter vow'd I have      180
     Well pleas'd. The carcase cutting then,
        and lifeless limbs, on ground
     I have in little parcels chopp'd;
        and some of them I drown'd
     In boiling cauldrons, some to fires
        that burn'd full slow I put
     And made to drop. Their sinews all
        and limbs, a-two I cut,
     Even yet alive, and on the spit
        that thrust was through the same      190
     I heard the liver wail and cry,
        and with my hand the flame
     I oft kept in. But every whit
        the father might of this
     Have better done, but now my wrath
        too lightly ended is.
     He rent his sons with wicked gum,
        himself, yet, wotting nought,
     Nor they, thereof.

*Thy.*                 O ye, enclos'd
     with bending banks about,      200
     All seas, me hear! and to this guilt,
        ye Gods, now hearken well,

169 quit'st] requitest      179 strake] struck

Whatever place ye fled are to!
  Hear, all ye sprites of Hell!
And hear, ye lands, and night so dark
  that them dost overlie
With cloud so black, to my complaints
  do thou thyself apply.
To thee now left I am; thou dost
  alone me miser see,      210
And thou art left without thy stars!
  I will not make for me
Petitions yet, nor ought for me
  require—may ought yet be
That me should vail?—for you shall all
  my wishes now foresee.
Thou Guider great of skies above,
  and Prince of highest might,
Of heavenly place, now all with clouds
  full horrible to sight      220
Enwrap the world, and let the winds
  on every side break out,
And send the dreadful thunder-clap
  through all the world about.
Not with what hand thou guiltless house
  and undeserved wall
With lesser bolt art wont to beat,
  but with the which did fall
The three up-heaped mountains once,
  and, which to hills in height      230
Stood equal up, the Giants huge:
  throw out such weapons straight,
And fling thy fires, and therewithal
  revenge the drowned day.
Let flee thy flames! The light thus lost
  and hid from heaven away
Let flashes fill! The cause—lest long
  thou shouldst doubt whom to hit—

210 miser] wretch       215 vail] avail, benefit

Of each of us is ill.  If not,
    at least let mine be it!          240
Me strike!  With triple-edged tool
    thy brand of flaming fire
Beat through this breast!  If father I
    my children do desire
To lay in tomb, or corpses cast
    to fire, as doth behove,
I must be burnt.  If nothing now
    the gods to wrath may move,
Nor power from skies with thunderbolt
    none strikes the wicked men,          250
Let yet eternal night remain
    and hide with darkness then
The world about.  I, Titan, nought
    complain, as now it stands,
If still thou hide thee thus away.

*Atr.*    Now praise I well my hands!
Now have I got the palm!  I had
    been overcome of thee,
Except thou sorrow'dst so.  But now
    even children born to me          260
I count, and now of bride-bed chaste
    the faith I do repair.

*Thy.* In what offended have my sons?
*Atr.*    In that, that thine they were.
*Thy.* Set'st thou the sons for father's food?
*Atr.*    I do, and, which is best,
The certain sons!
*Thy.*               The Gods that guide
    all infants I protest.
*Atr.* What wedlock Gods?
*Thy.*              Who would the guilt
    with guilt so quite again?          270
*Atr.* I know thy grief: prevented now
    with wrong, thou dost complain!

269 what] *sc.* why not    270 quite] requite    271 pre-
vented] forestalled

Nor this thee irks, that fed thou art
    with food of cursed kind,
But that thou hac'st not it prepar'd;
    for so it was thy mind
Such meats as these to set before
    thy brother wotting nought,
And by the mother's help to have
    likewise my children caught,     280
And them with such-like death to slay.
    This one thing letted thee:
Thou thought'st them thine.

*Thy.*              The Gods shall all
    of this revengers be.
And unto them for vengeance due
    my vows thee render shall.

*Atr.*   But vex'd to be I thee the while
    give to thy children all.


### The Fourth Scene,
### Added to the Tragedy
### by the Translator.

Thyestes *alone.*

O King of Dytis' dungeon dark,
    and grisly ghosts of Hell,
That in the deep and dreadful dens
    of blackest Tartar dwell,
Where lean and pale diseases lie,
    where fear and famine are,
Where Discord stands with bleeding brows,
    where every kind of care,
Where Furies fight in beds of steel,
    and hairs of crawling snakes,     10
Where Gorgon grim, where Harpies are,
    and loathsome Limbo lakes,

1 Dytis] Zeus's

Where most prodigious ugly things
  the hollow Hell doth hide,
If yet a monster more mis-shap'd
  than all there do abide,
That makes his brood his cursed food,
  ye all abhor to see,
Nor yet the deep Avern itself
  may bide to cover me,                              20
Now grisly gates of Pluto's place
  yet dare themselves to spread,
Nor gaping ground to swallow him
  whom Gods and day have fled:
Yet break ye out from cursed seats
  and here remain with me;
Ye need not now to be affray'd
  the air and heaven to see.
Nor, triple-headed Cerberus,
  thou needst not be affright                        30
The day unknown to thee to see,
  or else the loathsome light.
They both be fled; and now doth dwell
  none other count'nance here
Than doth beneath the foulest face
  of hateful Hell appear.
Come, see a meetest match for thee,
  a more than monstrous womb,
That is of his unhappy brood
  become a cursed tomb.                              40
Flock here, ye foulest fiends of Hell,
  and thou, o Grandsire great,
Come, see the glutted guts of mine,
  with such a kind of meat
As thou didst once for Gods prepare.
  Let torments all of Hell
now fall upon this hateful head,
  that hath deserv'd them well.

20 bide] abide, endure        42–5] *See note on I Chorus l. 26*

Ye all be plagued wrongfully,
    your guilts be small, in sight      50
Of mine, and meet it were your pangs
    on me alone should light.
Now thou, o Grandsire, guiltless art,
    and meeter were for me
With fleeing flood to be beguil'd,
    and fruit of fickle tree.
Thou slew'st thy son, but I my sons,
    alas, have made my meat.
I could thy famine better bear,
    my paunch is now replete      60
with food, and with my children three
    my belly is extent.
O filthy fowls and gnawing gripes
    that Tityus' bosom rent,
Behold a fitter prey for you
    to fill yourselves upon
Than are the growing guts of him:
    four wombs at once in one!
This paunch at once shall fill you all!
    If ye abhor the food,      70
Nor may yourselves abide to bathe
    in such a cursed blood,
Yet lend to me your clinching claws,
    your prey awhile forbear,
And with your talons suffer me
    this monstrous maw to tear.
Or whirling wheels, with swinge of which
    Ixion still is roll'd,
Your hooks upon this glutted gorge
    would catch a surer hold.      80
Thou filthy flood of Limbo lake,
    and Stygian pool so dire,
From choked channel belch abroad.
    Thou fearful fret of fire,

50–1 in sight Of] in comparison with    62 extent]
extended      63 gripes] vultures    84 fret] torrent

Spew out thy flames, o Phlegethon,
  and over-shed the ground.
With vomit of thy fiery stream
  let me and earth be drown'd.
Break up, thou soil, from bottom deep,
  and give thou room to Hell,          90
That night where day, that ghosts where Gods
  were wont to reign may dwell.
Why gap'st thou not?  Why do you not,
  o gates of Hell, unfold?
Why do ye thus th'infernal fiends
  so long from hence withhold?
Are you likewise affray'd to see
  and know so wretched wight,
From whom the Gods have wry'd their looks,
  and turned are to flight?          100
O hateful head, whom heaven and hell
  have shunn'd and left alone!
The sun, the stars, the light, the day,
  the Gods, the ghosts be gone.
Yet turn again ye skies, awhile,
  ere quite ye go fro me!
Take vengeance first on him whose fault
  enforceth you to flee!
If needs ye must your flight prepare,
  and may no longer bide,          110
But roll ye must with you forthwith
  the Gods and sun aside,
Yet slowly flee!  That I at length
  may you yet overtake,
While wand'ring ways I after you
  and speedy journey make.
By seas, by lands, by woods, by rocks,
  in dark I wander shall,
And on your wrath, for right reward
  to due deserts, will call.          120

        99 wry'd] turned away

Ye scape not fro me so, ye Gods!
  still after you I go,
And vengeance ask, on wicked wight
  your thunderbolt to throw.

**FINIS**

# GORBODUC

## BY

## THOMAS NORTON

### AND

## THOMAS SACKVILLE

# THOMAS NORTON (1532–84)
## and
# THOMAS SACKVILLE (1536–1608)

## *Gorboduc*

Acted in 1561; printed in 1565 in a bad text, revised edition in 1570.

[In *Early English Classical Tragedies*, ed. J. W. Cunliffe, Oxford, 1912. The title-page reproduced here is that of the revised edition, which gives the play its alternative name of *Ferrex and Porrex* instead of the more familiar *Gorboduc*.]

¶ The Tragidie of Ferrex
and Porrex,
ſet forth without addition or alte-
ration but altogether as the ſame was ſhewed
on ſtage before the Queenes Maieſtie,
about nine yeares paſt, *vz.* the
xviij. day of Ianuarie. 1561.
by the gentlemen of the
Inner Temple.

Seen and allowed. &c.

Imprinted at London by
Iohn Daye, dwelling ouer
Alderſgate.

# The Argument of the Tragedy.

Gorboduc, King of Britain, divided his realm in his lifetime to his sons, Ferrex and Porrex. The sons fell to dissension. The younger killed the elder. The mother, that more dearly loved the elder, for revenge killed the younger. The people, moved with the cruelty of the fact, rose in rebellion and slew both father and mother. The nobility assembled and most terribly destroyed the rebels. And afterwards, for want of issue of the Prince, whereby the succession of the crown became uncertain, they fell to civil war, in which both they and many of their issues were slain, and the land for a long time almost desolate and miserably wasted.

## The Names of the Speakers.

*Gorboduc*, King of Great Britain.
*Videna*, Queen, and wife to King Gorboduc.
*Ferrex*, Elder son to King Gorboduc.
*Porrex*, Younger son to King Gorboduc.
*Clotyn*, Duke of Cornwall.
*Fergus*, Duke of Albany.
*Mandud*, Duke of Loegris.
*Gwenard*, Duke of Cumberland.
*Eubulus*, Secretary to the King.
*Arostus*, a Counsellor to the King.
*Dordan*, a Counsellor assigned by the King to his eldest son, *Ferrex*;
*Philander*, a Counsellor assigned by the King to his youngest son, Porrex;
    Both being of the old king's council before.
*Hermon*, a Parasite remaining with Ferrex.
*Tyndar*, a Parasite remaining with Porrex.
*Nuntius*, a Messenger of the elder brother's death.
*Nuntius*, a Messenger of Duke Fergus rising in arms.
*Marcella*, a Lady of the Queen's privy chamber.
*Chorus*, four ancient and sage men of Britain.

Arg. 6 fact] deed

## ¶ The order of the dumb show before the first act, and the signification thereof

First the music of violins began to play, during which came in upon the stage six wild men, clothed in leaves. Of whom the first bare in his neck a fagot of small sticks, which they all, both severally and together, assayed with all their strengths to break, but it could not be broken by them. At the length one of them plucked out one of the sticks and brake it: and the rest plucking out all the other sticks one after another did easily break them, the same being severed, which being conjoined they had before attempted in vain. After they had this done, they departed the stage, and the music ceased. Hereby was signified, that a state knit in unity doth continue strong against all force, but being divided, is easily destroyed; as befell upon Duke Gorboduc dividing his land to his two sons, which he before held in monarchy; and upon the dissension of the brethren, to whom it was divided.

## Actus primus.　Scaena prima.

*Videna.　Ferrex.*

*Vid.* The silent night, that brings the quiet pause,
　　From painful travails of the weary day,
　　Prolongs my careful thoughts, and makes me blame
　　The slow Aurore, that so for love or shame
　　Doth long delay to show her blushing face,
　　And now the day renews my griefful plaint.
*Fer.* My gracious lady, and my mother dear,
　　Pardon my grief for your so grieved mind
　　To ask what cause tormenteth so your heart.

dumb show 3 in] on

*Vid.* So great a wrong and so unjust despite,  10
    Without all cause, against all course of kind!
*Fer.* Such causeless wrong, and so unjust despite,
    May have redress, or at the least, revenge.
*Vid.* Neither, my son; such is the froward will,
    The person such, such my mishap and thine.
*Fer.* Mine know I none, but grief for your distress.
*Vid.* Yes; mine for thine, my son. A father? no:
    In kind a father, not in kindliness.
*Fer.* My father? why? I know nothing at all,
    Wherein I have misdone unto his grace.  20
*Vid.* Therefore, the more unkind to thee and me.
    For, knowing well, my son, the tender love
    That I have ever borne, and bear to thee,
    He, grieved thereat, is not content alone
    To spoil thee of my sight, my chiefest joy,
    But thee, of thy birth-right and heritage,
    Causeless, unkindly, and in wrongful wise,
    Against all law and right, he will bereave:
    Half of his kingdom he will give away.
*Fer.* To whom?
*Vid.*              Even to Porrex, his younger son;  30
    Whose growing pride I do so sore suspect,
    That, being raised to equal rule with thee,
    Methinks I see his envious heart to swell,
    Filled with disdain and with ambitious hope.
    The end the gods do know, (whose altars I
    Full oft have made in vain of cattle slain
    To send the sacred smoke to Heaven's throne,
    For thee, my son,) if things do so succeed,
    As now my jealous mind misdeemeth sore.
*Fer.* Madam, leave care and careful plaint for me.  40
    Just hath my father been to every wight:
    His first injustice he will not extend
    To me, I trust, that give no cause thereof:
    My brother's pride shall hurt himself, not me.

  10 despite] insult     11 kind] nature     20 misdone]
done wrong     39 misdeemeth] suspects

*Vid.* So grant the gods! But yet thy father so
  Hath firmly fixed his unmoved mind,
  That plaints and prayers can no whit avail—
  For those have I assayed—but even this day
  He will endeavour to procure assent
  Of all his council to his fond device.          50
*Fer.* Their ancestors from race to race have borne
  True faith to my forefathers and their seed:
  I trust they eke will bear the like to me.
*Vid.* There resteth all. But if they fail thereof,
  And if the end bring forth an ill success,
  On them and theirs the mischief shall befall,
  And so I pray the gods requite it them;
  And so they will, for so is wont to be,
  When lords and trusted rulers under kings,
  To please the present fancy of the prince,          60
  With wrong transpose the course of governance,
  Murders, mischief, or civil sword at length,
  Or mutual treason, or a just revenge,
  When right succeeding line returns again,
  By Jove's just judgment and deserved wrath,
  Brings them to cruel and reproachful death,
  And roots their names and kindreds from the earth.
*Fer.* Mother, content you, you shall see the end.
*Vid.* The end! thy end I fear: Jove end me first!
                         [*Exeunt.*

## Actus primus.    Scaena secunda.

*Gorboduc.  Arostus.  Philander.  Eubulus.*

*Gor.* My lords, whose grave advice and faithful aid
  Have long upheld my honour and my realm,
  And brought me to this age from tender years,
  Guiding so great estate with great renown:

  50 fond] foolish      53 eke] also      55 success]
outcome, result, *whether good or bad*

Now more importeth me, than erst, to use
Your faith and wisdom, whereby yet I reign;
That when by death my life and rule shall cease,
The kingdom yet may with unbroken course
Have certain prince, by whose undoubted right
Your wealth and peace may stand in quiet stay;   10
And eke that they whom nature hath prepar'd
In time to take my place in princely seat,
While in their father's time their pliant youth
Yields to the frame of skilful governance,
May so be taught and trained in noble arts,
As what their fathers, which have reigned before,
Have with great fame derived down to them,
With honour they may leave unto their seed;
And not be thought, for their unworthy life,
And for their lawless swerving out of kind,   20
Worthy to lose what law and kind them gave;
But that they may preserve the common peace,
The cause that first began and still maintains
The lineal course of kings' inheritance,
For me, for mine, for you, and for the state
Whereof both I and you have charge and care.
Thus do I mean to use your wonted faith
To me and mine, and to your native land.
My lords, be plain without all wry respect,
Or poisonous craft to speak in pleasing wise,   30
Lest as the blame of ill succeeding things
Shall light on you, so light the harms also.

*Aros.* Your good acceptance so, most noble king,
Of such our faithfulness as heretofore
We have employed in duties to your grace,
And to this realm, whose worthy head you are,
Well proves that neither you mistrust at all,
Nor we shall need in boasting wise to show

5 importeth] is important to   10 stay] settled
state   20, 21 kind] nature, natural inheritance   29
wry respect] crooked motive   31 succeeding] subsequent

Our truth to you, nor yet our wakeful care
For you, for yours, and for our native land.     40
Wherefore, o king, I speak as one for all,
Sith all as one do bear you equal faith:
Doubt not to use our counsels and our aids,
Whose honours, goods, and lives are whole avowed
To serve, to aid, and to defend your grace.
*Gor.* My lords, I thank you all. This is the case:
Ye know, the gods, who have the sovereign care
For kings, for kingdoms, and for common weals,
Gave me two sons in my more lusty age,
Who now, in my decaying years, are grown     50
Well towards riper state of mind and strength,
To take in hand some greater princely charge.
As yet they live and spend their hopeful days
With me and with their mother here in court.
Their age now asketh other place and trade,
And mine also doth ask another change,
Theirs to more travail, mine to greater ease.
When fatal death shall end my mortal life,
My purpose is to leave unto them twain,
The realm divided into two sundry parts:     60
The one Ferrex mine elder son shall have,
The other shall the younger Porrex rule.
That both my purpose may more firmly stand,
And eke that they may better rule their charge,
I mean forthwith to place them in the same;
That in my life they may both learn to rule,
And I may joy to see their ruling well.
This is, in sum, what I would have ye weigh:
First, whether ye allow my whole device,
And think it good for me, for them, for you,     70
And for our country, mother of us all:
And if ye like it and allow it well,
Then, for their guiding and their governance,
Show forth such means of circumstance,

42 Sith] since     64 eke] also     69 allow] approve

D

As ye think meet to be both known and kept.
Lo, this is all; now tell me your advice.
*Aros.* And this is much, and asketh great advice:
But for my part, my sovereign lord and king,
This do I think: Your majesty doth know,
How under you, in justice and in peace,      80
Great wealth and honour long we have enjoyed:
So as we cannot seem with greedy minds
To wish for change of prince or governance:
But if we like your purpose and device,
Our liking must be deemed to proceed
Of rightful reason, and of heedful care,
Not for ourselves, but for the common state,
Sith our own state doth need no better change.
I think in all as erst your grace hath said:
First, when you shall unload your aged mind      90
Of heavy care and troubles manifold,
And lay the same upon my lords, your sons,
Whose growing years may bear the burden long,
(And long I pray the gods to grant it so)
And in your life, while you shall so behold
Their rule, their virtues, and their noble deeds,
Such as their kind behighteth to us all,
Great be the profits that shall grow thereof;
Your age in quiet shall the longer last,
Your lasting age shall be their longer stay.      100
For cares of kings that rule as you have ruled,
For public wealth, and not for private joy,
Do waste man's life and hasten crooked age,
With furrowed face, and with enfeebled limbs,
To draw on creeping death a swifter pace.
They two, yet young, shall bear the parted reign
With greater ease than one, now old, alone
Can wield the whole, for whom much harder is
With lessened strength the double weight to bear.
Your eye, your counsel, and the grave regard      110

97 behighteth] promises          108 wield] govern

Of father, yea, of such a father's name,
Now at beginning of their sunder'd reign,
When is the hazard of their whole success,
Shall bridle so their force of youthful heats,
And so restrain the rage of insolence,
Which most assails the young and noble minds,
And so shall guide and train in temper'd stay
Their yet green bending wits with reverent awe,
As now inured with virtues at the first,
Custom, o king, shall bring delightfulness,          120
By use of virtue, vice shall grow in hate.
But if you so dispose it, that the day
Which ends your life, shall first begin their reign,
Great is the peril what will be the end,
When such beginning of such liberties,
Void of such stays as in your life do lie,
Shall leave them free to random of their will,
An open prey to traitorous flattery,
The greatest pestilence of noble youth:
Which peril shall be past, if in your life,          130
Their temper'd youth with aged father's awe
Be brought in ure of skilful stayedness;
And in your life, their lives disposed so
Shall length your noble life in joyfulness.
Thus think I that your grace hath wisely thought,
And that your tender care of common weal
Hath bred this thought, so to divide your land,
And plant your sons to bear the present rule,
While you yet live to see their ruling well,
That you may longer live by joy therein.          140
What furder means behooveful are and meet,
At greater leisure may your grace devise,
When all have said, and when we be agreed
If this be best, to part the realm in twain,
And place your sons in present government.

119 inured with] accustomed to          132 ure] custom
use          134 length] lengthen

Whereof, as I have plainly said my mind,
So would I hear the rest of all my lords.
*Phil.* In part I think as hath been said before,
  In part, again, my mind is otherwise.
  As for dividing of this realm in twain,       150
  And lotting out the same in equal parts
  To either of my lords, your grace's sons,
  That think I best for this your realm's behoof,
  For profit and advancement of your sons,
  And for your comfort and your honour eke.
  But so to place them while your life do last,
  To yield to them your royal governance,
  To be above them only in the name
  Of father, not in kingly state also,
  I think not good for you, for them, nor us.    160
  This kingdom, since the bloody civil field
  Where Morgan slain did yield his conquered part
  Unto his cousin's sword in Camberland,
  Containeth all that whilom did suffice
  Three noble sons of your forefather Brute.
  So your two sons it may suffice also,
  The moe the stronger, if they gree in one.
  The smaller compass that the realm doth hold,
  The easier is the sway thereof to wield,
  The nearer justice to the wronged poor,    170
  The smaller charge, and yet enough for one.
  And when the region is divided so
  That brethren be the lords of either part,
  Such strength doth nature knit between them both,
  In sundry bodies by conjoined love,
  That not as two, but one of doubled force,
  Each is to other as a sure defence.

162 Morgan] *a legendary character, son of Lear's daughter Goneril, who divided the kingdom with Regan's son after deposing his aunt Cordelia, but later quarrelled with his cousin and was slain by him.*     163 Camberland] *Cambria, Wales* 165 Brute] *Brutus, the mythical Trojan founder of Britain.* 167 moe] *more*     gree] *agree*

The nobleness and glory of the one
Doth sharp the courage of the other's mind,
With virtuous envy to contend for praise.      180
And such an equalness hath nature made
Between the brethren of one father's seed,
As an unkindly wrong it seems to be,
To throw the brother subject under feet
Of him, whose peer he is by course of kind;
And Nature, that did make this equalness,
Oft so repineth at so great a wrong,
That oft she raiseth up a grudging grief
In younger brethren at the elder's state:
Whereby both towns and kingdoms have been
    rased,      190
And famous stocks of royal blood destroyed:
The brother, that should be the brother's aid,
And have a wakeful care for his defence,
Gapes for his death, and blames the lingering years
That draw not forth his end with faster course;
And oft impatient of so long delays,
With hateful slaughter he prevents the fates,
And heaps a just reward for brother's blood
With endless vengeance on his stock for aye.
Such mischiefs here are wisely met withal;      200
If equal state may nourish equal love,
Where none hath cause to grudge at other's good.
But now the head to stoop beneath them both,
Ne kind, ne reason, ne good order bears.
And oft it hath been seen, where nature's course
Hath been perverted in disordered wise,
When fathers cease to know that they should rule,
The children cease to know they should obey;
And often over-kindly tenderness
Is mother of unkindly stubbornness.      210
I speak not this in envy or reproach,

179 sharp] sharpen        courage] vigour (*as in* I. ii.
290, *and commonly*)      197 prevents] forestalls      204
Ne . . . ne . . . ne] neither . . . nor . . . nor

As if I grudged the glory of your sons,
Whose honour I beseech the gods increase:
Nor yet as if I thought there did remain
So filthy cankers in their noble breasts,
Whom I esteem (which is their greatest praise)
Undoubted children of so good a king.
Only I mean to show by certain rules,
Which kind hath graft within the mind of man,
That Nature hath her order and her course,     220
Which being broken doth corrupt the state
Of minds and things, even in the best of all.
My lords, your sons, may learn to rule of you.
Your own example in your noble court
Is fittest guider of their youthful years.
If you desire to see some present joy
By sight of their well ruling in your life,
See them obey, so shall you see them rule:
Who so obeyeth not with humbleness
Will rule with outrage and with insolence.     230
Long may they rule, I do beseech the gods,
But long may they learn, ere they begin to rule.
If kind and fates would suffer, I would wish
Them aged princes, and immortal kings.
Wherefore, most noble king, I well assent
Between your sons that you divide your realm,
And as in kind, so match them in degree.
But while the gods prolong your royal life,
Prolong your reign; for thereto live you here,
And therefore have the gods so long forborne     240
To join you to themselves, that still you might
Be prince and father of our common weal.
They, when they see your children ripe to rule,
Will make them room, and will remove you hence,
That yours, in right ensuing of your life,
May rightly honour your immortal name.
*Eub.* Your wonted true regard of faithful hearts

219 kind] nature     graft] grafted

Makes me, o king, the bolder to presume
To speak what I conceive within my breast;
Although the same do not agree at all          250
With that which other here my lords have said,
Nor which yourself have seemed best to like.
Pardon I crave, and that my words be deemed
To flow from hearty zeal unto your grace,
And to the safety of your common weal.
To part your realm unto my lords, your sons,
I think not good for you, ne yet for them,
But worst of all for this our native land.
Within one land, one single rule is best:
Divided reigns do make divided hearts,          260
But peace preserves the country and the prince.
Such is in man the greedy mind to reign,
So great is his desire to climb aloft,
In worldly stage the stateliest parts to bear,
That faith and justice, and all kindly love,
Do yield unto desire of sovereignty,
Where equal state doth raise an equal hope
To win the thing that either would attain.
Your grace rememb'reth how in passed years,
The mighty Brute, first prince of all this land,          270
Possessed the same, and ruled it well in one:
He, thinking that the compass did suffice
For his three sons three kingdoms eke to make,
Cut it in three, as you would now in twain.
But how much British blood hath since been spilt,
To join again the sunder'd unity!
What princes slain before their timely hour!
What waste of towns and people in the land!
What treasons heaped on murders and on spoils!
Whose just revenge even yet is scarcely ceased,          280
Ruthful remembrance is yet raw in mind.
The gods forbid the like to chance again:
And you, o king, give not the cause thereof.

257 ne] nor          270 Brute] *See note on* I. ii. 165.

My lord Ferrex, your elder son, perhaps
(Whom kind and custom gives a rightful hope
To be your heir, and to succeed your reign)
Shall think that he doth suffer greater wrong
Than he perchance will bear, if power serve.
Porrex, the younger, so upraised in state,
Perhaps in courage will be raised also.     290
If flattery then, which fails not to assail
The tender minds of yet unskilful youth,
In one shall kindle and increase disdain,
And envy in the other's heart inflame,
This fire shall waste their love, their lives, their land,
And ruthful ruin shall destroy them both.
I wish not this, o king, so to befall,
But fear the thing, that I do most abhor.
Give no beginning to so dreadful end.
Keep them in order and obedience:     300
And let them both by now obeying you,
Learn such behaviour as beseems their state;
The elder, mildness in his governance,
The younger, a yielding contentedness.
And keep them near unto your presence still,
That they, restrained by the awe of you,
May live in compass of well temper'd stay,
And pass the perils of their youthful years.
Your aged life draws on to feebler time,
Wherein you shall less able be to bear     310
The travails that in youth you have sustained,
Both in your person's and your realm's defence.
If, planting now your sons in furder parts,
You send them furder from your present reach,
Less shall you know how they themselves demean:
Traitorous corrupters of their pliant youth
Shall have unspied a much more free access,
And if ambition and inflamed disdain
Shall arm the one, the other, or them both,

290 courage] ambition    296 ruthful] pitiful    307 stay]
settled state               313, 314 furder] further

To civil war, or to usurping pride,     320
Late shall you rue that you ne recked before.
Good is I grant of all to hope the best,
But not to live still dreadless of the worst:
So trust the one that the other be foreseen.
Arm not unskilfulness with princely power.
But you that long have wisely ruled the reins
Of royalty within your noble realm,
So hold them, while the gods, for our avails,
Shall stretch the thread of your prolonged days.
Too soon he clamb into the flaming car,     330
Whose want of skill did set the earth on fire.
Time, and example of your noble Grace,
Shall teach your sons both to obey and rule.
When time hath taught them, time shall make them
    place,
The place that now is full: and so I pray
Long it remain, to comfort of us all.
*Gor.* I take your faithful hearts in thankful part.
But sith I see no cause to draw my mind
To fear the nature of my loving sons,
Or to misdeem that envy or disdain     340
Can there work hate, where nature planteth love;
In one self purpose do I still abide.
My love extendeth equally to both,
My land sufficeth for them both also.
Humber shall part the marches of their realms:
The southern part the elder shall possess,
The northern shall Porrex, the younger, rule.
In quiet I will pass mine aged days,
Free from the travail, and the painful cares,
That hasten age upon the worthiest kings.     350
But lest the fraud, that ye do seem to fear,
Of flattering tongues, corrupt their tender youth,

321 ne recked] did not heed     330 clamb] climbed,
*referring to Phaeton, who failed to guide the sun chariot of his
father, Apollo (cf. Chorus,* 16–18).     340 misdeem] suspect
345 marches] borders

And writhe them to the ways of youthful lust,
To climbing pride, or to revenging hate,
Or to neglecting of their careful charge,
Lewdly to live in wanton recklessness,
Or to oppressing of the rightful cause,
Or not to wreak the wrongs done to the poor,
To tread down truth, or favour false deceit:
I mean to join to either of my sons          360
Some one of those, whose long-approved faith,
And wisdom tried, may well assure my heart
That mining fraud shall find no way to creep
Into their fenced ears, with grave advice.
This is the end; and so I pray you all
To bear my sons the love and loyalty
That I have found within your faithful breasts.
*Aros.* You, nor your sons, my sovereign lord, shall want
Our faith and service while our hearts do last.
                                        [*Exeunt.*


*Chorus.* When settled stay doth hold the royal throne
In steadfast place, by known and doubtless right,
And chiefly when descent on one alone
Makes single and unparted reign to light;
Each change of course unjoints the whole estate,
And yields it thrall to ruin by debate.
The strength that, knit by fast accord in one,
Against all foreign power of mighty foes
Could of itself defend itself alone,
Disjoined once, the former force doth lose.          10
The sticks, that sunder'd brake so soon in twain,
In fagot bound attempted were in vain.
Oft tender mind that leads the partial eye
Of erring parents in their children's love,
Destroys the wrongly loved child thereby.
This doth the proud son of Apollo prove,

353 writhe] twist      358 wreak] avenge      chorus 1
stay] settled state      16 son of Apollo] *see note on* I. ii.
330.

Who, rashly set in chariot of his sire,
Inflamed the parched earth with heaven's fire.
And this great king, that doth divide his land,
And change the course of his descending crown,    20
And yields the reign into his children's hand,
From blissful state of joy and great renown,
A mirror shall become to princes all,
To learn to shun the cause of such a fall.

¶ The order and signification of the dumb show before the second act

First the music of cornets began to play, during which came in upon the stage a king accompanied with a number of his nobility and gentlemen. And after he had placed himself in a chair of estate prepared for him, there came and kneeled before him a grave and aged gentleman, and offer'd up a cup unto him of wine in a glass, which the king refused. After him comes a brave and lusty young gentleman, and presents the king with a cup of gold filled with poison, which the king accepted, and drinking the same, immediately fell down dead upon the stage, and so was carried thence away by his lords and gentlemen, and then the music ceased. Hereby was signified, that as glass by nature holdeth no poison, but is clear and may easily be seen through, ne boweth by any art; so a faithful counsellor holdeth no treason, but is plain and open, ne yieldeth to any undiscreet affection, but giveth wholesome counsel, which the ill-advised prince refuseth. The delightful gold filled with poison betokeneth flattery, which under fair seeming of pleasant words beareth deadly poison, which destroyed the prince that receiveth it. As befel in the two brethren, Ferrex and Porrex, who, refusing the

dumb show 4 estate] state       15 boweth] is bent

wholesome advice of grave counsellors, credited these
young parasites, and brought to themselves death and
destruction thereby.

## Actus secundus.    Scaena prima.

*Ferrex.   Hermon.   Dordan.*

*Fer.* I marvel much what reason led the king,
　　My father, thus, without all my desert,
　　To reave me half the kingdom, which by course
　　Of law and nature should remain to me.
*Her.* If you with stubborn and untamed pride
　　Had stood against him in rebelling wise,
　　Or if with grudging mind you had envied
　　So slow a sliding of his aged years,
　　Or sought before your time to haste the course
　　Of fatal death upon his royal head,　　　　　　10
　　Or stained your stock with murder of your kin:
　　Some face of reason might perhaps have seemed
　　To yield some likely cause to spoil ye thus.
*Fer.* The wreakful gods pour on my cursed head
　　Eternal plagues and never-dying woes,
　　The hellish prince adjudge my damned ghost
　　To Tantal's thirst, or proud Ixion's wheel,
　　Or cruel Gripe to gnaw my growing heart,
　　To during torments and unquenched flames,
　　If ever I conceived so foul a thought,　　　　20
　　To wish his end of life, or yet of reign.
*Dor.* Ne yet your father, o most noble prince,
　　Did ever think so foul a thing of you.
　　For he, with more than father's tender love,
　　While yet the fates do lend him life to rule,
　　(Who long might live to see your ruling well)

　　8 sliding] passing　　　14 wreakful] avenging　　17
Tantal] Tantalus　　　18 Gripe] vulture, *referring to the*
*punishment of Prometheus.*　　　26 might] *sc.* may he

To you, my lord, and to his other son,
Lo, he resigns his realm and royalty;
Which never would so wise a prince have done,
If he had once misdeemed that in your heart    30
There ever lodged so unkind a thought.
But tender love, my lord, and settled trust
Of your good nature, and your noble mind,
Made him to place you thus in royal throne,
And now to give you half this realm to guide;
Yea, and that half which, in abounding store
Of things that serve to make a wealthy realm,
In stately cities, and in fruitful soil,
In temperate breathing of the milder heaven,
In things of needful use, which friendly sea    40
Transports by traffic from the foreign parts,
In flowing wealth, in honour, and in force,
Doth pass the double value of the part
That Porrex hath allotted to his reign.
Such is your case, such is your father's love.
*Fer.* Ah love, my friends! Love wrongs not whom he
    loves.
*Dor.* Ne yet he wrongeth you, that giveth you
So large a reign, ere that the course of time
Bring you to kingdom by descended right,
Which time perhaps might end your time before.   50
*Fer.* Is this no wrong, say you, to reave from me
My native right of half so great a realm?
And thus to match his younger son with me
In equal power, and in as great degree?
Yea, and what son? The son whose swelling pride
Would never yield one point of reverence,
When I the elder and apparent heir
Stood in the likelihood to possess the whole;
Yea, and that son which from his childish age
Envieth mine honour, and doth hate my life.    60
What will he now do, when his pride, his rage,

---

30 misdeemed] suspected      31 unkind] unnatural

The mindful malice of his grudging heart
Is armed with force, with wealth, and kingly state?
*Her.* Was this not wrong, yea, ill advised wrong,
To give so mad a man so sharp a sword?
To so great peril of so great mishap,
Wide open thus to set so large a way?
*Dor.* Alas, my lord, what griefful thing is this,
That of your brother you can think so ill?
I never saw him utter likely sign,     70
Whereby a man might see or once misdeem
Such hate of you, ne such unyielding pride.
Ill is their counsel, shameful be their end,
That raising such mistrustful fear in you,
Sowing the seed of such unkindly hate,
Travail by treason to destroy you both.
Wise is your brother, and of noble hope,
Worthy to wield a large and mighty realm.
So much a stronger friend have you thereby,
Whose strength is your strength if you gree in one. 80
*Her.* If Nature and the Gods had pinched so
Their flowing bounty, and their noble gifts
Of princely qualities, from you, my lord,
And pour'd them all at once in wasteful wise
Upon your father's younger son alone;
Perhaps there be, that in your prejudice
Would say that birth should yield to worthiness.
But sith in each good gift and princely art
Ye are his match, and in the chief of all
In mildness and in sober governance     90
Ye far surmount; and sith there is in you
Sufficing skill and hopeful towardness
To wield the whole, and match your elder's praise;
I see no cause why ye should lose the half.
Ne would I wish you yield to such a loss,
Lest your mild sufferance of so great a wrong,
Be deemed cowardish and simple dread,

78 wield] rule      80 gree] agree

Which shall give courage to the fiery head
Of your young brother to invade the whole.
While yet therefore sticks in the people's mind　100
The loathed wrong of your disheritance,
And ere your brother have by settled power,
By guileful cloak of an alluring show,
Got him some force and favour in the realm,
And while the noble queen, your mother, lives,
To work and practise all for your avail;
Attempt redress by arms, and wreak yourself
Upon his life that gaineth by your loss,
Who now to shame of you, and grief of us,
In your own kingdom triumphs over you.　　110
Show now your courage meet for kingly state,
That they which have avowed to spend their goods,
Their lands, their lives and honours in your cause,
May be the bolder to maintain your part,
When they do see that coward fear in you
Shall not betray, ne fail their faithful hearts.
If once the death of Porrex end the strife,
And pay the price of his usurped reign,
Your mother shall persuade the angry king,
The lords, your friends, eke shall appease his
　　rage.　　120
For they be wise, and well they can foresee,
That ere long time your aged father's death
Will bring a time when you shall well requite
Their friendly favour, or their hateful spite,
Yea, or their slackness to advance your cause.
"Wise men do not so hang on passing state
"Of present princes, chiefly in their age,
"But they will further cast their reaching eye,
"To view and weigh the times and reigns to come.
Ne is it likely, though the king be wroth,　　130

106 practise] scheme　　112 avowed] vowed　　126-9]
*Inverted commas at the beginnings of the lines were used to
mark an emphatic and sententious passage; cf. ll. 146-51, and
elsewhere.*

That he yet will, or that the realm will bear,
Extreme revenge upon his only son.
Or, if he would, what one is he that dare
Be minister to such an enterprise?
And here you be now placed in your own,
Amid your friends, your vassals, and your strength:
We shall defend and keep your person safe,
Till either counsel turn his tender mind,
Or age or sorrow end his weary days.
But if the fear of gods, and secret grudge      140
Of nature's law, repining at the fact,
Withhold your courage from so great attempt,
Know ye, that lust of kingdoms hath no law.
The gods do bear, and well allow in kings,
The things that they abhor in rascal routs.
"When kings on slender quarrels run to wars,
"And then in cruel and unkindly wise
"Command thefts, rapes, murders of innocents,
"The spoil of towns, ruins of mighty realms;
"Think you such princes do suppose themselves      150
"Subject to laws of kind, and fear of gods?
Murders and violent thefts in private men
Are heinous crimes, and full of foul reproach;
Yet none offence, but deck'd with glorious name
Of noble conquests, in the hands of kings.
But if you like not yet so hot device,
Ne list to take such vantage of the time,
But, though with peril of your own estate,
You will not be the first that shall invade:
Assemble yet your force for your defence,      160
And for your safety stand upon your guard.
*Dor.* O heaven! was there ever heard or known
So wicked counsel to a noble prince?
Let me, my lord, disclose unto your grace
This heinous tale, what mischief it contains:
Your father's death, your brother's, and your own,

140 grudge] scruple          156 hot device] impetuous
plan          157 list] wish

Your present murder, and eternal shame.
Hear me, o king, and suffer not to sink
So high a treason in your princely breast.

*Fer.* The mighty gods forbid that ever I          170
Should once conceive such mischief in my heart.
Although my brother hath bereft my realm,
And bear, perhaps, to me an hateful mind,
Shall I revenge it with his death therefore?
Or shall I so destroy my father's life
That gave me life? The gods forbid, I say.
Cease you to speak so any more to me.
Ne you, my friend, with answer once repeat
So foul a tale. In silence let it die.
What lord or subject shall have hope at all,          180
That under me they safely shall enjoy
Their goods, their honours, lands, and liberties,
With whom, neither one only brother dear,
Ne father dearer, could enjoy their lives?
But, sith I fear my younger brother's rage,
And sith, perhaps, some other man may give
Some like advice, to move his grudging head
At mine estate, which counsel may perchance
Take greater force with him, than this with me,
I will in secret so prepare myself,          190
As if his malice or his lust to reign
Break forth in arms or sudden violence,
I may withstand his rage and keep mine own.
          [*Exeunt* Ferrex *and* Hermon.
*Dor.* I fear the fatal time now draweth on,
When civil hate shall end the noble line
Of famous Brute, and of his royal seed.
Great Jove, defend the mischiefs now at hand!
O that the secretary's wise advice
Had erst been heard, when he besought the king
Not to divide his land, nor send his sons          200
To further parts, from presence of his court,

187 grudging] envious          197 defend] ward off

Ne yet to yield to them his governance.
Lo, such are they now in the royal throne
As was rash Phaeton in Phœbus' car;
Ne then the fiery steeds did draw the flame
With wilder random through the kindled skies,
Than traitorous counsel now will whirl about
The youthful heads of these unskilful kings.
But I hereof their father will inform.
The reverence of him perhaps shall stay          210
The growing mischiefs, while they yet are green.
If this help not, then woe unto themselves,
The prince, the people, the divided land!    [*Exit.*

## Actus secundus.    Scaena secunda.

#### *Porrex. Tyndar. Philander.*

*Por.* And is it thus? and doth he so prepare
Against his brother as his mortal foe?
And now, while yet his aged father lives?
Neither regards he him, nor fears he me?
War would he have? and he shall have it so.
*Tyn.* I saw, myself, the great prepared store
Of horse, of armour, and of weapon there:
Ne bring I to my lord reported tales
Without the ground of seen and searched truth.
Lo, secret quarrels run about his court,          10
To bring the name of you, my lord, in hate.
Each man, almost, can now debate the cause,
And ask a reason of so great a wrong,
Why he, so noble and so wise a prince,
Is, as unworthy, reft his heritage,
And why the king, misled by crafty means,
Divided thus his land from course of right.
The wiser sort hold down their griefful heads;
Each man withdraws from talk and company

204 Phaeton] *See note on* I. ii. 330.

Of those that have been known to favour you.   20
To hide the mischief of their meaning there,
Rumours are spread of your preparing here.
The rascal numbers of unskilful sort
Are filled with monstrous tales of you and yours.
In secret, I was counselled by my friends
To haste me thence, and brought you, as you know,
Letters from those that both can truly tell,
And would not write unless they knew it well.

*Phil.* My lord, yet ere you move unkindly war,
  Send to your brother, to demand the cause.    30
  Perhaps some traitorous tales have filled his ears
  With false reports against your noble grace;
  Which, once disclosed, shall end the growing strife,
  That else, not stayed with wise foresight in time,
  Shall hazard both your kingdoms and your lives.
  Send to your father eke, he shall appease
  Your kindled minds, and rid you of this fear.

*Por.* Rid me of fear? I fear him not at all;
  Ne will to him, ne to my father send.
  If danger were for one to tarry there,      40
  Think ye it safety to return again?
  In mischiefs, such as Ferrex now intends,
  The wonted courteous laws to messengers
  Are not observed, which in just war they use.
  Shall I so hazard any one of mine?
  Shall I betray my trusty friends to him,
  That have disclosed his treason unto me?
  Let him entreat that fears, I fear him not.
  Or shall I to the king, my father, send?
  Yea, and send now, while such a mother lives,   50
  That loves my brother, and that hateth me?
  Shall I give leisure, by my fond delays,
  To Ferrex to oppress me all unware?
  I will not, but I will invade his realm,
  And seek the traitor prince within his court.

29 unkindly] unnatural      40 danger were] it were
dangerous     52 fond] foolish

Mischief for mischief is a due reward.
His wretched head shall pay the worthy price
Of this his treason and his hate to me.
Shall I abide, and treat, and send, and pray,
And hold my yielden throat to traitor's knife,    60
While I, with valiant mind and conquering force,
Might rid myself of foes, and win a realm?
Yet rather, when I have the wretch's head,
Then to the king, my father, will I send.
The bootless case may yet appease his wrath:
If not, I will defend me as I may.

                    [*Exeunt* Porrex *and* Tyndar.

*Phil.* Lo, here the end of these two youthful kings,
The father's death, the ruin of their realms.
"O most unhappy state of counsellors,
"That light on so unhappy lords and times,    70
"That neither can their good advice be heard,
"Yet must they bear the blames of ill success.
But I will to the king, their father, haste,
Ere this mischief come to the likely end;
That, if the mindful wrath of wreakful gods
(Since mighty Ilion's fall not yet appeased
With these poor remnants of the Trojan name)
Have not determined by unmoved fate,
Out of this realm to raze the British line,
By good advice, by awe of father's name,    80
By force of wiser lords, this kindled hate
May yet be quenched, ere it consume us all. [*Exit.*

*Chorus.* When youth, not bridled with a guiding stay,
Is left to random of their own delight,
And wields whole realms by force of sovereign sway,
Great is the danger of unmaster'd might,
Lest skilless rage throw down, with headlong fall,
Their lands, their states, their lives, themselves and
        all.

60 yielden] yielded      72 success] outcome      76
Ilion's fall] *cf. note on* 1. ii. 165. Ilion = Troy

When growing pride doth fill the swelling breast,
And greedy lust doth raise the climbing mind,
Oh, hardly may the peril be repress'd.
Ne fear of angry gods, ne lawes kind,          10
Ne country's care can fired hearts restrain,
When force hath armed envy and disdain.
When kings of foresight will neglect the rede
Of best advice, and yield to pleasing tales
That do their fancies' noisome humour feed,
Ne reason, nor regard of right avails.
Succeeding heaps of plagues shall teach, too late,
To learn the mischiefs of misguided state.
Foul fall the traitor false, that undermines
The love of brethren, to destroy them both.          20
Woe to the prince, that pliant ear inclines,
And yields his mind to poisonous tale that floweth
From flattering mouth! And woe to wretched land,
That wastes itself with civil sword in hand!
Lo thus it is, poison in gold to take,
And wholesome drink in homely cup forsake.


¶ The order and signification of the dumb
show before the third act

First the music of flutes began to play, during
which came in upon the stage a company of mourners
all clad in black, betokening death and sorrow to
ensue upon the ill-advised misgovernment and dissension of brethren, as befel upon the murder of Ferrex
by his younger brother. After the mourners had passed
thrice about the stage, they departed, and then the
music ceased.

chorus 10 lawes kind] natural law; *the metre requires the
old pronunciation* lawes.          13 rede] counsel, opinion
25–6] *alluding to the dumb show before act II.*

## Actus tertius    Scaena prima.

*Gorboduc. Eubulus. Arostus. Philander. Nuntius.*

*Gor.* O cruel fates, o mindful wrath of gods,
    Whose vengeance, neither Simois' stained streams
    Flowing with blood of Trojan princes slain,
    Nor Phrygian fields made rank with corpses dead
    Of Asian kings and lords, can yet appease;
    Ne slaughter of unhappy Priam's race,
    Nor Ilion's fall, made level with the soil,
    Can yet suffice: but still continued rage
    Pursues our lives, and from the farthest seas
    Doth chase the issues of destroyed Troy.       10
    "Oh, no man happy till his end be seen.
    If any flowing wealth and seeming joy
    In present years might make a happy wight,
    Happy was Hecuba, the woefullest wretch
    That ever lived, to make a mirror of;
    And happy Priam, with his noble sons;
    And happy I, till now, alas! I see
    And feel my most unhappy wretchedness.
    Behold, my lords, read ye this letter here;
    Lo, it contains the ruin of our realm,       20
    If timely speed provide not hasty help.
    Yet, o ye gods! if ever woeful king
    Might move ye, kings of kings, wreak it on me
    And on my sons, not on this guiltless realm:
    Send down your wasting flames from wrathful skies,
    To reave me and my sons the hateful breath.
    Read, read, my lords: this is the matter why
    I called ye now, to have your good advice.

Heading] *All the characters who appear during the scene are
announced at its head, although the last two do not appear until
lines* 58 *and* 154 *respectively.*    2 Simois] *the stream that
flows by Troy.*    11] *See note on* II. i. 126–9.

¶ The letter from *Dordan*, the Counsellor of the elder
        Prince.
                *Eubulus* readeth the letter.

My sovereign lord, what I am loath to write,
But loathest am to see, that I am forced          30
By letters now to make you understand.
My lord Ferrex, your eldest son, misled
By traitorous fraud of young untemper'd wits,
Assembleth force against your younger son,
Ne can my counsel yet withdraw the heat
And furious pangs of his inflamed head.
Disdain, saith he, of his disheritance
Arms him to wreak the great pretended wrong,
With civil sword upon his brother's life.
If present help do not restrain this rage,          40
This flame will waste your sons, your land, and you.

            Your Majesty's faithful, and most
                        humble subject, Dordan.


*Aros.* O king, appease your grief, and stay your plaint;
        Great is the matter, and a woeful case,
        But timely knowledge may bring timely help.
        Send for them both unto your presence here:
        The reverence of your honour, age, and state,
        Your grave advice, the awe of father's name,
        Shall quickly knit again this broken peace.
        And if in either of my lords, your sons,
        Be such untamed and unyielding pride,          50
        As will not bend unto your noble hests;
        If Ferrex, the elder son, can bear no peer,
        Or Porrex, not content, aspires to more
        Than you him gave above his native right:
        Join with the juster side, so shall you force
        Them to agree, and hold the land in stay.
*Eub.* What meaneth this? Lo, yonder comes in haste
        Philander from my lord your younger son.

            51 hests] orders          56 stay] settled state

*Enter* Philander.

*Gor.* The gods send joyful news!
*Phil.*                          The mighty Jove
  Preserve your majesty, o noble king.                    60
*Gor.* Philander, welcome: but how doth my son?
*Phil.* Your son, sir, lives, and healthy I him left.
  But yet, o king, the want of lustful health
  Could not be half so griefful to your grace,
  As these most wretched tidings that I bring.
*Gor.* O heavens, yet more? no end of woes to me?
*Phil.* Tyndar, o king, came lately from the court
  Of Ferrex, to my lord your younger son,
  And made report of great prepared store
  For war, and saith that it is wholly meant         70
  Against Porrex, for high disdain that he
  Lives now a king, and equal in degree
  With him that claimeth to succeed the whole,
  As by due title of descending right.
  Porrex is now so set on flaming fire,
  Partly with kindled rage of cruel wrath,
  Partly with hope to gain a realm thereby,
  That he in haste prepareth to invade
  His brother's land, and with unkindly war
  Threatens the murder of your elder son;            80
  Ne could I him persuade that first he should
  Send to his brother to demand the cause,
  Nor yet to you to stay this hateful strife.
  Wherefore sith there no more I can be heard,
  I come myself now to inform your grace,
  And to beseech you, as you love the life
  And safety of your children and your realm,
  Now to employ your wisdom and your force
  To stay this mischief ere it be too late.
*Gor.* Are they in arms? would he not send to me? 90
  Is this the honour of a father's name?
  In vain we travail to assuage their minds,

79 unkindly] unnatural

As if their hearts, whom neither brother's love,
Nor father's awe, nor kingdom's cares, can move,
Our counsels could withdraw from raging heat.
Jove slay them both, and end the cursed line.
For though perhaps fear of such mighty force
As I, my lords, joined with your noble aids,
May yet raise, shall repress their present heat,
The secret grudge and malice will remain.     100
The fire not quenched, but kept in close restraint,
Fed still within, breaks forth with double flame.
Their death and mine must pease the angry gods.
*Phil.* Yield not, o king, so much to weak despair:
Your sons yet live, and long, I trust, they shall.
If fates had taken you from earthly life,
Before beginning of this civil strife,
Perhaps your sons in their unmastered youth,
Loose from regard of any living wight,
Would run on headlong, with unbridled race,     110
To their own death, and ruin of this realm.
But sith the gods, that have the care for kings,
Of things and times dispose the order so
That in your life this kindled flame breaks forth,
While yet your life, your wisdom, and your power,
May stay the growing mischief, and repress
The fiery blaze of their enkindled heat;
It seems, and so ye ought to deem thereof,
That loving Jove hath temper'd so the time
Of this debate to happen in your days,     120
That you yet living may the same appease,
And add it to the glory of your latter age,
And they your sons may learn to live in peace.
Beware, o king, the greatest harm of all,
Lest, by your wailful plaints, your hastened death
Yield larger room unto their growing rage.
Preserve your life, the only hope of stay.
And if your highness herein list to use

103 pease] pacify        127 stay] settled state

Wisdom or force, counsel or knightly aid,
Lo we, our persons, powers, and lives are yours;  130
Use us till death, o king, we are your own.
*Eub.*  Lo, here the peril that was erst foreseen,
When you, o king, did first divide your land,
And yield your present reign unto your sons.
But now, o noble prince, now is no time
To wail and plain, and waste your woeful life;
Now is the time for present good advice.
Sorrow doth dark the judgment of the wit.
"The heart unbroken and the courage free
"From feeble faintness of bootless despair,      140
"Doth either rise to safety or renown
"By noble valour of unvanquish'd mind,
"Or yet doth perish in more happy sort.
Your grace may send to either of your sons
Some one both wise and noble personage,
Which with good counsel, and with weighty name
Of father, shall present before their eyes
Your hest, your life, your safety, and their own,
The present mischief of their deadly strife.
And in the while, assemble you the force      150
Which your commandment and the speedy haste
Of all my lords here present can prepare.
The terror of your mighty power shall stay
The rage of both, or yet of one at least.

*Enter* Nuntius.

*Nun.*  O king, the greatest grief that ever prince did
      hear,
That ever woeful messenger did tell,
That ever wretched land hath seen before,
I bring to you: Porrex your younger son,
With sudden force, invaded hath the land
That you to Ferrex did allot to rule,      160

138 dark] darken          139 courage] vigour, energy
143 sort] way

And with his own most bloody hand he hath
His brother slain, and doth possess his realm.
*Gor.* O heavens, send down the flames of your
    revenge!
Destroy, I say, with flash of wreakful fire
The traitor son, and then the wretched sire!
But let us go, that yet perhaps I may
Die with revenge, and pease the hateful gods.

                             *[Exeunt.*


*Chor.* The lust of kingdom knows no sacred faith,
No rule of reason, no regard of right,
No kindly love, no fear of heaven's wrath;
But with contempt of god's, and man's despite,
Through bloody slaughter, doth prepare the ways
To fatal sceptre and accursed reign.
The son so loathes the father's lingering days,
Ne dreads his hand in brother's blood to stain.
O wretched prince, ne dost thou yet record
The yet fresh murthers done within the land    10
Of thy forefathers, when the cruel sword
Bereft Morgan his life with cousin's hand?
Thus fatal plagues pursue the guilty race,
Whose murderous hand, imbrued with guiltless
    blood,
Asks vengeance still before the heavens' face,
With endless mischiefs on the cursed brood.
The wicked child thus brings to woeful sire
The mournful plaints to waste his very life.
Thus do the cruel flames of civil fire
Destroy the parted reign with hateful strife.    20
And hence doth spring the well from which doth
    flow
The dead black streams of mourning, plaints, and
    woe.

164 wreakful] avenging    chorus 12 Morgan] *See note*
*on* I. ii. 162.

## ¶ The order and signification of the dumb show before the fourth act

First the music of hautboys began to play, during which there came forth from under the stage, as though out of hell, three furies, Alecto, Megaera, and Tisiphone, clad in black garments sprinkled with blood and flames, their bodies girt with snakes, their heads spread with serpents instead of hair, the one bearing in her hand a snake, the other a whip, and the third a burning firebrand: each driving before them a king and a queen which, moved by furies, unnaturally had slain their own children. The names of the kings and queens were these: Tantalus, Medea, Athamas, Ino, Cambyses, Althea. After that the furies and these had passed about the stage thrice, they departed, and then the music ceased. Hereby was signified the unnatural murders to follow, that is to say: Porrex slain by his own mother, and of king Gorboduc and queen Viden, killed by their own subjects.    17

## Actus quartus. Scaena prima.

*Videna sola.*

*Vid.* Why should I live, and linger forth my time
In longer life to double my distress?
O me, most woeful wight, whom no mishap
Long ere this day could have bereaved hence,
Mought not these hands, by fortune or by fate,
Have pierc'd this breast, and life with iron reft?
Or in this palace here, where I so long
Have spent my days, could not that happy hour
Once, once have happ'd, in which these hugy frames
With death by fall might have oppressed me?    10

5, 41, &c. Mought] might          9 frames] building

Or should not this most hard and cruel soil,
So oft where I have press'd my wretched steps,
Sometime had ruth of mine accursed life,
To rend in twain, and swallow me therein?
So had my bones possessed now in peace
Their happy grave within the closed ground,
And greedy worms had gnawn this pined heart
Without my feeling pain: so should not now
This living breast remain the ruthful tomb,
Wherein my heart yielden to death is graved;   20
Nor dreary thoughts, with pangs of pining grief,
My doleful mind had not afflicted thus.
O my beloved son! O my sweet child!
My dear Ferrex, my joy, my life's delight!
Is my beloved son, is my sweet child,
My dear Ferrex, my joy, my life's delight,
Murdered with cruel death? O hateful wretch!
O heinous traitor both to heaven and earth!
Thou, Porrex, thou, this damned deed hast wrought;
Thou, Porrex, thou, shalt dearly bye the same.   30
Traitor to kin and kind, to sire and me,
To thine own flesh, and traitor to thyself:
The gods on thee in hell shall wreak their wrath,
And here in earth this hand shall take revenge
On thee, Porrex, thou false and caitiff wight.
If after blood so eager were thy thirst,
And murderous mind had so possessed thee,
If such hard heart of rock and stony flint
Lived in thy breast, that nothing else could like
Thy cruel tyrant's thought but death and blood:   40
Wild savage beasts, mought not their slaughter serve
To feed thy greedy will, and in the midst
Of their entrails to stain thy deadly hands
With blood deserved, and drink thereof thy fill?
Or if nought else but death and blood of man
Mought please thy lust, could none in Britain land,

30 bye] suffer for

Whose heart betorn out of his panting breast
With thine own hand, or work what death thou
    would'st,
Suffice to make a sacrifice to pease
That deadly mind and murderous thought in
    thee,                                              50
But he who in the selfsame womb was wrapped,
Where thou in dismal hour receivedst life?
Or if needs, needs thy hand must slaughter make,
Moughtest thou not have reached a mortal wound,
And with thy sword have pierced this cursed womb
That the accursed Porrex brought to light,
And given me a just reward therefore?
So Ferrex yet sweet life mought have enjoyed,
And to his aged father comfort brought,
With some young son in whom they both might
    live.                                              60
But whereunto waste I this ruthful speech,
To thee that hast thy brother's blood thus shed?
Shall I still think that from this womb thou sprung?
That I thee bare? or take thee for my son?
No, traitor, no; I thee refuse for mine:
Murderer, I thee renounce; thou art not mine.
Never, o wretch, this womb conceived thee,
Nor never bode I painful throes for thee.
Changeling to me thou art, and not my child,
Nor to no wight that spark of pity knew.            70
Ruthless, unkind, monster of nature's work,
Thou never suck'd the milk of woman's breast,
But, from thy birth, the cruel tiger's teats
Have nursed thee, nor yet of flesh and blood
Form'd is thy heart, but of hard iron wrought,
And wild and desert woods bred thee to life.
But canst thou hope to scape my just revenge?
Or that these hands will not be wroke on thee?
Dost thou not know that Ferrex' mother lives,

47 betorn] torn      68 bode] suffered      77 scape]
escape      78 wroke] wreaked, avenged

That loved him more dearly than herself?    80
And doth she live, and is not venged on thee?


### Actus quartus.    Scaena secunda.

*Gorboduc. Arostus. Eubulus. Porrex. Marcella.*

*Gor.* We marvel much whereto this ling'ring stay
    Falls out so long: Porrex unto our court,
    By order of our letters, is returned;
    And Eubulus received from us behest,
    At his arrival here, to give him charge
    Before our presence straight to make repair,
    And yet we have no word whereof he stays.
*Aros.* Lo where he comes, and Eubulus with him.


*Enter* Eubulus *and* Porrex.

*Eub.* According to your highness' hest to me,
    Here have I Porrex brought, even in such sort    10
    As from his wearied horse he did alight,
    For that your grace did will such haste therein.
*Gor.* We like and praise this speedy will in you,
    To work the thing that to your charge we gave.
    Porrex, if we so far should swerve from kind,
    And from those bounds which law of nature sets,
    As thou hast done by vile and wretched deed
    In cruel murder of thy brother's life,
    Our present hand could stay no longer time,
    But straight should bathe this blade in blood of
        thee,    20
    As just revenge of thy detested crime.
    No: we should not offend the law of kind,
    If now this sword of ours did slay thee here:
    For thou hast murdered him, whose heinous death
    Even nature's force doth move us to revenge
    By blood again: and justice forceth us
    To measure death for death, thy due desert.

Yet sithens thou art our child, and sith as yet
In this hard case what word thou canst allege
For thy defence, by us hath not been heard,    30
We are content to stay our will for that
Which justice bids us presently to work,
And give thee leave to use thy speech at full,
If ought thou have to lay for thine excuse.

*Por.* Neither, o king, I can or will deny
But that this hand from Ferrex life hath reft,
Which fact how much my doleful heart doth wail;
Oh! would it mought as full appear to sight
As inward grief doth pour it forth to me.
So yet, perhaps, if ever ruthful heart    40
Melting in tears within a manly breast,
Through deep repentance of his bloody fact;
If ever grief, if ever woeful man
Might move regret with sorrow of his fault,
I think the torment of my mournful case,
Known to your grace as I do feel the same,
Would force even wrath herself to pity me.
But as the water, troubled with the mud,
Shows not the face which else the eye should see,
Even so your ireful mind with stirred thought    50
Can not so perfectly discern my cause.
But this unhap, amongst so many haps,
I must content me with, most wretched man,
That to myself I must reserve my woe,
In pining thoughts of mine accursed fact;
Since I may not show here my smallest grief,
Such as it is, and as my breast endures,
Which I esteem the greatest misery
Of all mishaps that fortune now can send.
Not that I rest in hope with plaint and tears    60
To purchase life, for to the gods I clepe
For true record of this my faithful speech:
Never this heart shall have the thoughtful dread

28 sithens, sith] since     37, 55 fact] deed     61
clepe] call

To die the death that by your grace's doom,
By just desert, shall be pronounced to me:
Nor never shall this tongue once spend the speech,
Pardon to crave, or seek by suit to live.
I mean not this as though I were not touch'd
With care of dreadful death, or that I held
Life in contempt: but that I know the mind    70
Stoops to no dread, although the flesh be frail.
And for my guilt, I yield the same so great
As in myself I find a fear to sue
For grant of life.

*Gor.*            In vain, o wretch, thou showest
A woeful heart; Ferrex now lies in grave,
Slain by thy hand.

*Por.*            Yet this, o father, hear;
And then I end.  Your majesty well knows
That when my brother Ferrex and myself
By your own hest were joined in governance
Of this your grace's realm of Britain land,    80
I never sought nor travailed for the same;
Nor by myself, nor by no friend I wrought,
But from your highness' will alone it sprung,
Of your most gracious goodness bent to me.
But how my brother's heart even then repined
With swollen disdain against mine equal rule,
Seeing that realm, which by descent should grow
Wholly to him, allotted half to me;
Even in your highness' court he now remains,
And with my brother then in nearest place,    90
Who can record what proof thereof was show'd,
And how my brother's envious heart appear'd.
Yet I that judged it my part to seek
His favour and good will, and loth to make
Your highness know the thing which should have
    brought
Grief to your grace, and your offence to him;
Hoping my earnest suit should soon have won
A loving heart within a brother's breast,

E

Wrought in that sort, that, for a pledge of love
And faithful heart, he gave to me his hand.     100
This made me think that he had banish'd quite
All rancour from his thought, and bare to me
Such hearty love as I did owe to him.
But after once we left your grace's court,
And from your highness' presence lived apart,
This equal rule still, still did grudge him so
That now those envious sparks which erst lay raked
In living cinders of dissembling breast,
Kindled so far within his heart disdain,
That longer could he not refrain from proof     110
Of secret practice to deprive me life
By poison's force; and had bereft me so,
If mine own servant hired to this fact,
And moved by truth with hate to work the same,
In time had not bewrayed it unto me.
When thus I saw the knot of love unknit,
All honest league and faithful promise broke,
The law of kind and troth thus rent in twain,
His heart on mischief set, and in his breast
Black treason hid; then, then did I despair     120
That ever time could win him friend to me.
Then saw I how he smiled with slaying knife
Wrapped under cloak, then saw I deep deceit
Lurk in his face and death prepared for me:
Even nature moved me then to hold my life
More dear to me than his, and bade this hand
(Since by his life my death must needs ensue,
And by his death my life to be preserved)
To shed his blood, and seek my safety so.
And wisdom willed me without protract     130
In speedy wise to put the same in ure.
Thus have I told the cause that moved me

103 owe] own, bear          106 grudge] vex          111
practice] scheme          118 kind and troth] nature
and honour     130 protract] delay     131 ure] practice

To work my brother's death; and so I yield
My life, my death, to judgment of your grace.
*Gor.* O cruel wight, should any cause prevail
  To make thee stain thy hands with brother's blood?
  But what of thee we will resolve to do
  Shall yet remain unknown.  Thou in the mean
  Shalt from our royal presence banish'd be,
  Until our princely pleasure furder shall          140
  To thee be showed.  Depart therefore our sight,
  Accursed child! [*Exit* Porrex.]  What cruel destiny,
  What froward fate hath sorted us this chance,
  That even in those where we should comfort find,
  Where our delight now in our aged days
  Should rest and be, even there our only grief
  And deepest sorrows to abridge our life,
  Most pining cares and deadly thoughts do grow!
*Aros.* Your grace should now, in these grave years of
    yours
  Have found ere this the price of mortal joys,          150
  How short they be, how fading here in earth,
  How full of change, how brittle our estate,
  Of nothing sure, save only of the death,
  To whom both man and all the world doth owe
  Their end at last; neither should nature's power
  In other sort against your heart prevail,
  Than as the naked hand whose stroke assays
  The armed breast, where force doth light in vain.
*Gor.* Many can yield right sage and grave advice
  Of patient sprite to others wrapped in woe,          160
  And can in speech both rule and conquer kind;
  Who, if by proof they might feel nature's force,
  Would show themselves men as they are indeed,
  Which now will needs be gods.  But what doth
    mean
  The sorry cheer of her that here doth come?

138 mean] meanwhile     143 sorted] allotted     **160**
sprite] spirit     165 cheer] aspect

*Enter* Marcella.

*Mar.* Oh where is ruth? or where is pity now?
    Whither is gentle heart and mercy fled?
    Are they exiled out of our stony breasts,
    Never to make return? is all the world
    Drowned in blood, and sunk in cruelty?    170
    If not in women mercy may be found,
    If not, alas, within the mother's breast,
    To her own child, to her own flesh and blood;
    If ruth be banished thence, if pity there
    May have no place, if there no gentle heart
    Do live and dwell, where should we seek it then?
*Gor.* Madam, alas, what means your woeful tale?
*Mar.* O silly woman I! why to this hour
    Have kind and fortune thus deferred my breath,
    That I should live to see this doleful day?    180
    Will ever wight believe that such hard heart
    Could rest within the cruel mother's breast,
    With her own hand to slay her only son?
    But out, alas! these eyes beheld the same:
    They saw the dreary sight, and are become
    Most ruthful records of the bloody fact.
    Porrex, alas, is by his mother slain,
    And with her hand, a woeful thing to tell,
    While slumb'ring on his careful bed he rests,
    His heart stabb'd in with knife is reft of life.    190
*Gor.* O Eubulus, oh draw this sword of ours,
    And pierce this heart with speed! O hateful light,
    O loathsome life, o sweet and welcome death!
    Dear Eubulus, work this we thee beseech!
*Eub.* Patient your grace; perhaps he liveth yet,
    With wound received, but not of certain death.
*Gor.* O let us then repair unto the place,
    And see if Porrex live, or thus be slain.

                  [*Exeunt* Gorboduc *and* Eubulus.

189 careful] full of care, unhappy    195 Patient]
quiet yourself

*Mar.* Alas, he liveth not! it is too true,
   That with these eyes, of him a peerless prince,  200
   Son to a king, and in the flower of youth,
   Even with a twink a senseless stock I saw.
*Aros.* O damned deed!
*Mar.*                   But hear his ruthful end:
   The noble prince, pierc'd with the sudden wound,
   Out of his wretched slumber hastely start,
   Whose strength now failing straight he overthrew,
   When in the fall his eyes, even new unclosed,
   Beheld the queen, and cried to her for help.
   We then, alas, the ladies which that time
   Did there attend, seeing that heinous deed,    210
   And hearing him oft call the wretched name
   Of mother, and to cry to her for aid,
   Whose direful hand gave him the mortal wound,
   Pitying, alas, (for nought else could we do)
   His ruthful end, ran to the woeful bed,
   Despoiled straight his breast, and all we might
   Wiped in vain with napkins next at hand,
   The sudden streams of blood that flushed fast
   Out of the gaping wound. O what a look,
   O what a ruthful steadfast eye methought    220
   He fix'd upon my face, which to my death
   Will never part fro me, when with a braid
   A deep-fet sigh he gave, and therewithal
   Clasping his hands, to heaven he cast his sight;
   And straight, pale death pressing within his face,
   The flying ghost his mortal corpse forsook.
*Aros.* Never did age bring forth so vile a fact.
*Mar.* O hard and cruel hap, that thus assigned
   Unto so worthy a wight so wretched end:
   But most hard cruel heart that could consent    230
   To lend the hateful destinies that hand,
   By which, alas, so heinous crime was wrought.

   202 with a twink] in a twinkling     205 hastely start]
quickly started up     216 Despoiled] laid bare     222
braid] start     223 deep-fet] deep-fetched

O queen of adamant! o marble breast!
If not the favour of his comely face,
If not his princely cheer and countenance,
His valiant active arms, his manly breast,
If not his fair and seemly personage,
His noble limbs in such proportion cast
As would have rapt a silly woman's thought:
If this mought not have moved thy bloody heart,  240
And that most cruel hand the wretched weapon
Even to let fall, and kiss'd him in the face,
With tears for ruth to reave such one by death:
Should nature yet consent to slay her son?
O mother, thou to murder thus thy child!
Even Jove with justice must with lightning flames
From heaven send down some strange revenge on
      thee.
Ah, noble prince, how oft have I beheld
Thee mounted on thy fierce and trampling steed,
Shining in armour bright before the tilt,          250
And with thy mistress' sleeve tied on thy helm,
And charge thy staff, to please thy lady's eye,
That bowed the head-piece of thy friendly foe!
How oft in arms on horse to bend the mace,
How oft in arms on foot to break the sword,
Which never now these eyes may see again!
*Aros.* Madam, alas, in vain these plaints are shed;
   Rather with me depart, and help to swage
   The thoughtful griefs that in the aged king
   Must needs by nature grow by death of this    260
   His only son, whom he did hold so dear.
*Mar.* What wight is that which saw that I did see,
   And could refrain to wail with plaint and tears?
   Not I, alas! that heart is not in me:
   But let us go, for I am grieved anew,
   To call to mind the wretched father's woe. [*Exeunt.*

235 cheer] aspect        239 silly] simple        252 charge
thy staff] level thy lance

*Chor.* When greedy lust in royal seat to reign
   Hath reft all care of gods and eke of men,
   And cruel heart, wrath, treason, and disdain,
   Within ambitious breast are lodged, then
   Behold how mischief wide herself displays,
   And with the brother's hand the brother slays.
   When blood thus shed doth stain the heaven's face,
   Crying to Jove for vengeance of the deed,
   The mighty god even moveth from his place,
   With wrath to wreak: then sends he forth with
     speed                                                                10
   The dreadful Furies, daughters of the night,
   With serpents girt, carrying the whip of ire,
   With hair of stinging snakes, and shining bright
   With flames and blood, and with a brand of fire.
   These, for revenge of wretched murder done,
   Do make the mother kill her only son.
   Blood asketh blood, and death must death requite:
   Jove, by his just and everlasting doom,
   Justly hath ever so requited it.
   The times before record, and times to come          20
   Shall find it true, and so doth present proof
   Present before our eyes for our behoof.
   O happy wight, that suffers not the snare
   Of murderous mind to tangle him in blood;
   And happy he, that can in time beware
   By other's harms, and turn it to his good.
   But woe to him that, fearing not to offend,
   Doth serve his lust, and will not see the end.


¶ The order and signification of the dumb
show before the fifth act

   First the drums and flutes began to sound, during
which there came forth upon the stage a company of
arquebusiers, and of armed men, all in order of

18 doom] judgement

battle. These, after their pieces discharged, and that the armed men had three times marched about the stage, departed, and then the drums and flutes did cease. Hereby was signified tumults, rebellions, arms, and civil wars to follow, as fell in the realm of Great Britain, which, by the space of fifty years and more, continued in civil war between the nobility after the death of king Gorboduc and of his issues, for want of certain limitation in succession of the crown, till the time of Dunwallo Molmutius, who reduced the land to monarchy.     14

## Actus quintus. Scaena prima.

*Clotyn. Mandud. Gwenard. Fergus. Eubulus.*

*Clot.* Did ever age bring forth such tyrant hearts?
  The brother hath bereft the brother's life,
  The mother, she hath dyed her cruel hands
  In blood of her own son; and now at last
  The people, lo, forgetting troth and love,
  Contemning quite both law and loyal heart,
  Even they have slain their sovereign lord and queen.
*Man.* Shall this their traitorous crime unpunished rest?
  Even yet they cease not, carried on with rage,
  In their rebellious routs, to threaten still     10
  A new bloodshed unto the prince's kin,
  To slay them all, and to uproot the race
  Both of the king and queen; so are they moved
  With Porrex' death, wherein they falsely charge
  The guiltless king, without desert at all;
  And traitorously have murdered him therefore,
  And eke the queen.
*Gwen.*            Shall subjects dare with force
  To work revenge upon their prince's fact?

Dumb Show 13 Dunwallo Molmutius] *son of Cloten, king of Cornwall, who reduced Great Britain to a single monarchy.*

Admit the worst that may, as sure in this
The deed was foul, the queen to slay her son,    20
Shall yet the subject seek to take the sword,
Arise against his lord, and slay his king?
O wretched state, where those rebellious hearts
Are not rent out even from their living breasts,
And with the body thrown unto the fowls,
As carrion food, for terror of the rest.

*Ferg.* There can no punishment be thought too great
For this so grievous crime: let speed therefore
Be used therein, for it behooveth so.

*Eub.* Ye all, my lords, I see, consent in one,    30
And I as one consent with ye in all.
I hold it more than need, with sharpest law
To punish this tumultuous bloody rage.
For nothing more may shake the common state,
Than sufferance of uproars without redress;
Whereby how some kingdoms of mighty power,
After great conquests made, and flourishing
In fame and wealth, have been to ruin brought:
I pray to Jove, that we may rather wail
Such hap in them than witness in ourselves.    40
Eke fully with the duke my mind agrees,
That no cause serves, whereby the subject may
Call to account the doings of his prince,
Much less in blood by sword to work revenge,
No more than may the hand cut off the head;
In act nor speech, no not in secret thought
The subject may rebel against his lord,
Or judge of him that sits in Cæsar's seat,
With grudging mind to damn those he mislikes.
Though kings forget to govern as they ought,    50
Yet subjects must obey as they are bound.
But now, my lords, before ye farder wade,
Or spend your speech, what sharp revenge shall fall
By justice' plague on these rebellious wights,

42–9 That no . . . mislikes] *These lines, printed in the first edition, were later omitted.*        52 farder] farther

Methinks ye rather should first search the way,
By which in time the rage of this uproar
Mought be repressed, and these great tumults ceased.
Even yet the life of Britain land doth hang
In traitors' balance of unequal weight.
Think not, my lords, the death of Gorboduc,    60
Nor yet Videna's blood, will cease their rage:
Even our own lives, our wives, and children dear,
Our country, dearest of all, in danger stands,
Now to be spoiled, now, now made desolate,
And by ourselves a conquest to ensue.
For, give once sway unto the people's lusts
To rush forth on, and stay them not in time,
And as the stream that rolleth down the hill,
So will they headlong run with raging thoughts
From blood to blood, from mischief unto moe,    70
To ruin of the realm, themselves, and all;
So giddy are the common people's minds,
So glad of change, more wavering than the sea.
Ye see, my lords, what strength these rebels have,
What hugy number is assembled still:
For though the traitorous fact, for which they rose,
Be wrought and done, yet lodge they still in field,
So that, how far their furies yet will stretch,
Great cause we have to dread.  That we may seek
By present battle to repress their power,    80
Speed must we use to levy force therefore.
For either they forthwith will mischief work,
Or their rebellious roars forthwith will cease.
These violent things may have no lasting long.
Let us, therefore, use this for present help:
Persuade by gentle speech, and offer grace
With gift of pardon, save unto the chief;
And that upon condition that forthwith
They yield the captains of their enterprise,
To bear such guerdon of their traitorous fact    90

57, 61 ceased, cease] ended, end          70 moe] more
90 guerdon of] reward for

As may be both due vengeance to themselves,
And wholesome terror to posterity.
This shall, I think, scatter the greatest part
That now are holden with desire of home,
Wearied in field with cold of winter's nights,
And some, no doubt, stricken with dread of law.
When this is once proclaimed, it shall make
The captains to mistrust the multitude,
Whose safety bids them to betray their heads;
And so much more, because the rascal routs,      100
In things of great and perilous attempts,
Are never trusty to the noble race.
And while we treat, and stand on terms of grace,
We shall both stay their fury's rage the while,
And eke gain time, whose only help sufficeth
Withouten war to vanquish rebels' power.
In the meanwhile, make you in readiness
Such band of horsemen as ye may prepare.
Horsemen, you know, are not the commons'
   strength,
But are the force and store of noble men;      110
Whereby the unchosen and unarmed sort
Of skilless rebels, whom none other power
But number makes to be of dreadful force,
With sudden brunt may quickly be oppress'd.
And if this gentle mean of proffered grace
With stubborn hearts cannot so far avail
As to assuage their desperate courages,
Then do I wish such slaughter to be made,
As present age, and eke posterity,
May be adrad with horror of revenge      120
That justly then shall on these rebels fall.
This is, my lords, the sum of mine advice.
*Clot.* Neither this case admits debate at large;
   And though it did, this speech that hath been said,
   Hath well abridged the tale I would have told.

94 holden] possessed          117 assuage . . . courages]
moderate their violent passions   120 adrad] frightened

Fully with Eubulus do I consent
In all that he hath said: and if the same
To you, my lords, may seem for best advice,
I wish that it should straight be put in ure.

*Man.* My lords, then let us presently depart,    130
And follow this that liketh us so well.

    [*Exeunt* Clotyn, Mandud, Gwenard, *and* Eubulus.

*Ferg.* If ever time to gain a kingdom here
Were offer'd man, now it is offer'd me.
The realm is reft both of their king and queen,
The offspring of the prince is slain and dead,
No issue now remains, the heir unknown,
The people are in arms and mutinies,
The nobles, they are busied how to cease
These great rebellious tumults and uproars,
And Britain land, now desert left alone    140
Amid these broils uncertain where to rest,
Offers herself unto that noble heart
That will or dare pursue to bear her crown.
Shall I, that am the Duke of Albany,
Descended from that line of noble blood,
Which hath so long flourished in worthy fame
Of valiant hearts, such as in noble breasts
Of right should rest above the baser sort,
Refuse to venture life to win a crown?
Whom shall I find en'mies that will withstand    150
My fact herein, if I attempt by arms
To seek the same now in these times of broil?
These dukes' power can hardly well appease
The people that already are in arms.
But if, perhaps, my force be once in field,
Is not my strength in power above the best
Of all these lords now left in Britain land?
And though they should match me with power of
    men,
Yet doubtful is the chance of battles joined.

    126 consent] agree    129 ure] practice    **138**
cease] end

If victors of the field we may depart,                    160
Ours is the sceptre then of Great Britain;
If slain amid the plain this body lie,
Mine enemies yet shall not deny me this,
But that I died giving the noble charge
To hazard life for conquest of a crown.
Forthwith, therefore, will I in post depart
To Albany, and raise in armour there
All power I can: and here my secret friends
By secret practice shall solicit still
To seek to win to me the people's hearts. [*Exit.* 170


### Actus quintus. Scaena secunda.

*Eubulus. Clotyn. Mandud. Gwenard. Arostus. Nuntius.*

*Eub.* O Jove, how are these people's hearts abus'd!
What blind fury thus headlong carries them?
That though so many books, so many rolls
Of ancient time, record what grievous plagues
Light on these rebels aye, and though so oft
Their ears have heard their aged fathers tell
What just reward these traitors still receive;
Yea, though themselves have seen deep death and
    blood,
By strangling cord, and slaughter of the sword,
To such assigned, yet can they not beware,        10
Yet cannot stay their lewd rebellious hands;
But suff'ring, lo, foul treason to distain
Their wretched minds, forget their loyal heart,
Reject all truth, and rise against their prince.
A ruthful case, that those, whom duty's bond,
Whom grafted law, by nature, truth, and faith,

---

161 Britain] *here pronounced* Britaín, *but* Britain *in line* 157.
166 in post] post haste          v. ii. Heading] *Only Eubulus
is present at first, the rest entering later as directed. Cf. note on*
III. i. Heading.          7 still] always          11 lewd]
ignorant          12 distain] stain

Bound to preserve their country and their king,
Born to defend their commonwealth and prince,
Even they should give consent thus to subvert
Thee, Britain land, and from thy womb should
    spring,                       20
O native soil, those that will needs destroy
And ruin thee, and eke themselves in fine.
For lo, when once the dukes had offer'd grace
Of pardon sweet, the multitude, misled
By traitorous fraud of their ungracious heads,
One sort that saw the dangerous success
Of stubborn standing in rebellious war,
And knew the difference of prince's power
From headless number of tumultuous routs,
Whom common country's care, and private fear 30
Taught to repent the error of their rage,
Laid hands upon the captains of their band,
And brought them bound unto the mighty dukes:
And other sort, not trusting yet so well
The truth of pardon, or mistrusting more
Their own offence than that they could conceive
Such hope of pardon for so foul misdeed,
Or for that they their captains could not yield,
Who, fearing to be yielded, fled before,
Stale home by silence of the secret night:    40
The third unhappy and enraged sort
Of desperate hearts, who, stained in princes' blood,
From traitorous furor could not be withdrawn
By love, by law, by grace, ne yet by fear,
By proffered life, ne yet by threaten'd death,
With minds hopeless of life, dreadless of death,
Careless of country, and aweless of God,
Stood bent to fight, as furies did them move,
With violent death to close their traitorous life.
These all by power of horsemen were oppress'd, 50

22 in fine] in the end    26 &c. sort] lot, party    30
common country's care] common care for their country
40 stale] stole

And with revenging sword slain in the field,
Or with the strangling cord hang'd on the tree,
Where yet their carrion carcases do preach
The fruits that rebels reap of their uproars,
And of the murder of their sacred prince.
But lo, where do approach the noble dukes
By whom these tumults have been thus appeas'd.

*Enter* Clotyn, Mandud, Gwenard, *and* Arostus.

*Clot.* I think the world will now at length beware
And fear to put on arms against their prince.
*Man.* If not, those traitorous hearts that dare rebel, 6c
Let them behold the wide and hugy fields
With blood and bodies spread of rebels slain;
The lofty trees clothed with the corpses dead,
That strangled with the cord do hang thereon.
*Aros.* A just reward; such as all times before
Have ever lotted to those wretched folks.
*Gwen.* But what means he that cometh here so fast?

*Enter* Nuntius.

*Nun.* My lords, as duty and my troth doth move,
And of my country work a care in me,
That, if the spending of my breath availed    7
To do the service that my heart desires,
I would not shun to embrace a present death;
So have I now, in that wherein I thought
My travail mought perform some good effect,
Ventur'd my life to bring these tidings here.
Fergus, the mighty duke of Albany,
Is now in arms, and lodgeth in the field
With twenty thousand men: hither he bends
His speedy march, and minds to invade the crow
Daily he gathereth strength, and spreads abroad,
That to this realm no certain heir remains,
That Britain land is left without a guide,

66 lotted] allotted

That he the sceptre seeks, for nothing else
But to preserve the people and the land,
Which now remain as ship without a stern.
Lo, this is that which I have here to say.

*Clot.* Is this his faith? and shall he falsely thus
Abuse the vantage of unhappy times?
O wretched land, if his outrageous pride,
His cruel and untemper'd wilfulness,     90
His deep dissembling shows of false pretence,
Should once attain the crown of Britain land!
Let us, my lords, with timely force resist
The new attempt of this our common foe,
As we would quench the flames of common fire.

*Man.* Though we remain without a certain prince,
To wield the realm, or guide the wand'ring rule,
Yet now the common mother of us all,
Our native land, our country, that contains
Our wives, children, kindred, ourselves, and all 100
That ever is or may be dear to man,
Cries unto us to help ourselves and her.
Let us advance our powers to repress
This growing foe of all our liberties.

*Gwen.* Yea, let us so, my lords, with hasty speed.
And ye, o gods, send us the welcome death,
To shed our blood in field, and leave us not
In loathsome life to linger out our days,
To see the hugy heaps of these unhaps,
That now roll down upon the wretched land,   110
Where empty place of princely governance,
No certain stay now left of doubtless heir,
Thus leave this guideless realm an open prey
To endless storms and waste of civil war.

*Aros.* That ye, my lords, do so agree in one,
To save your country from the violent reign
And wrongfully usurped tyranny
Of him that threatens conquest of you all,

85 stern] rudder     97 wield] rule     109 unhaps]
misfortunes

To save your realm, and in this realm yourselves,
From foreign thraldom of so proud a prince,    120
Much do I praise; and I beseech the gods,
With happy honour to requite it you.
But, o my lords, sith now the heavens' wrath
Hath reft this land the issue of their prince;
Sith of the body of our late sovereign lord
Remains no moe, since the young kings be slain,
And of the title of descended crown
Uncertainly the divers minds do think
Even of the learned sort, and more uncertainly
Will partial fancy and affection deem;        130
But most uncertainly will climbing pride
And hope of reign withdraw to sundry parts
The doubtful right and hopeful lust to reign.
When once this noble service is achieved
For Britain land, the mother of ye all,
When once ye have with armed force repress'd
The proud attempts of this Albanian prince,
That threatens thraldom to your native land,
When ye shall vanquishers return from field,
And find the princely state an open prey      140
To greedy lust and to usurping power,
Then, then, my lords, if ever kindly care
Of ancient honour of your ancestors,
Of present wealth and nobless of your stocks,
Yea of the lives and safety yet to come
Of your dear wives, your children, and yourselves,
Might move your noble hearts with gentle ruth,
Then, then, have pity on the torn estate;
Then help to salve the well-near hopeless sore,
Which ye shall do, if ye yourselves withhold  150
The slaying knife from your own mother's throat.
Her shall you save, and you and yours in her,
If ye shall all with one assent forbear
Once to lay hand or take unto yourselves

126 moe] more      137 Albanian] Scottish      144
nobless] nobleness

The crown, by colour of pretended right,
Or by what other means soever it be,
Till first by common counsel of you all
In parliament, the regal diadem
Be set in certain place of governance;
In which your parliament, and in your choice,    160
Prefer the right, my lords, without respect
Of strength or friends, or whatsoever cause
That may set forward any other's part.
For right will last, and wrong cannot endure.
Right mean I his or hers, upon whose name
The people rest by mean of native line,
Or by the virtue of some former law,
Already made their title to advance.
Such one, my lords, let be your chosen king,
Such one so born within your native land;    170
Such one prefer, and in no wise admit
The heavy yoke of foreign governance:
Let foreign titles yield to public wealth.
And with that heart wherewith ye now prepare
Thus to withstand the proud invading foe,
With that same heart, my lords, keep out also
Unnatural thraldom of stranger's reign;
Ne suffer you, against the rules of kind,
Your mother land to serve a foreign prince.
*Eub.* Lo, here the end of Brutus' royal line,    180
And lo, the entry to the woeful wrack
And utter ruin of this noble realm.
The royal king and eke his sons are slain;
No ruler rests within the regal seat;
The heir, to whom the sceptre longs, unknown;
That to each force of foreign princes' power,
Whom vantage of our wretched state may move
By sudden arms to gain so rich a realm,
And to the proud and greedy mind at home,
Whom blinded lust to reign leads to aspire,    190

173 wealth] weal, well-being      185 longs] belongs

Lo, Britain realm is left an open prey,
A present spoil by conquest to ensue.
Who seeth not now how many rising minds
Do feed their thoughts with hope to reach a realm?
And who will not by force attempt to win
So great a gain, that hope persuades to have?
A simple colour shall for title serve.
Who wins the royal crown will want no right,
Nor such as shall display by long descent
A lineal race to prove him lawful king.                200
In the meanwhile these civil arms shall rage,
And thus a thousand mischiefs shall unfold,
And far and near spread thee, o Britain land;
All right and law shall cease, and he that had
Nothing today, tomorrow shall enjoy
Great heaps of gold, and he that flowed in wealth,
Lo, he shall be bereft of life and all;
And happiest he that then possesseth least.
The wives shall suffer rape, the maids deflowered,
And children fatherless shall weep and wail;        210
With fire and sword thy native folk shall perish,
One kinsman shall bereave another's life,
The father shall unwitting slay the son,
The son shall slay the sire and know it not.
Women and maids the cruel soldier's sword
Shall pierce to death, and silly children, lo,
That playing in the streets and fields are found,
By violent hand shall close their latter day.
Whom shall the fierce and bloody soldier
Reserve to life? whom shall he spare from death? 220
Even thou, o wretched mother, half alive,
Thou shalt behold thy dear and only child
Slain with the sword while he yet sucks thy breast.
Lo, guiltless blood shall thus each where be shed.
Thus shall the wasted soil yield forth no fruit,
But dearth and famine shall possess the land.

197 colour] pretence

The towns shall be consumed and burnt with fire,
The peopled cities shall wax desolate;
And thou, o Britain, whilom in renown,
Whilom in wealth and fame, shalt thus be torn,    230
Dismember'd thus, and thus be rent in twain,
Thus wasted and defaced, spoiled and destroyed.
These be the fruits your civil wars will bring.
Hereto it comes when kings will not consent
To grave advice, but follow wilful will.
This is the end, when in fond princes' hearts
Flattery prevails, and sage rede hath no place.
These are the plagues, when murder is the mean
To make new heirs unto the royal crown.
Thus wreak the gods, when that the mother's wrath    240
Nought but the blood of her own child may swage;
These mischiefs spring when rebels will arise
To work revenge and judge their prince's fact.
This, this ensues, when noble men do fail
In loyal troth, and subjects will be kings.
And this doth grow, when lo, unto the prince,
Whom death or sudden hap of life bereaves,
No certain heir remains, such certain heir,
As not all only is the rightful heir,
But to the realm is so made known to be;    250
And troth thereby vested in subjects' hearts,
To owe faith there where right is known to rest.
Alas, in parliament what hope can be,
When is of parliament no hope at all?
Which, though it be assembled by consent,
Yet is not likely with consent to end,
While each one for himself, or for his friend,
Against his foe, shall travail what he may.
While now the state, left open to the man
That shall with greatest force invade the same,    260

237 rede] advice      241 swage] assuage      249 all
only] alone, only      255, 256 consent] *pun:* (*a*) elected
by agreement, (*b*) unlikely to agree

Shall fill ambitious minds with gaping hope:
When will they once with yielding hearts agree?
Or in the while, how shall the realm be used?
No, no: then parliament should have been holden,
And certain heirs appointed to the crown,
To stay the title of established right,
And in the people plant obedience,
While yet the prince did live, whose name and power
By lawful summons and authority
Might make a parliament to be of force,          270
And might have set the state in quiet stay.
But now, o happy man, whom speedy death
Deprives of life, ne is enforced to see
These hugy mischiefs, and these miseries,
These civil wars, these murders, and these wrongs.
Of justice, yet must God in fine restore
This noble crown unto the lawful heir:
For right will always live, and rise at length,
But wrong can never take deep root to last.

¶ The end of the Tragedy of King Gorboduc.

276 in fine] in the end

# THE SPANISH TRAGEDY

### BY

# THOMAS KYD

# THOMAS KYD (1558–94)

## *The Spanish Tragedy*

Acted about 1589; printed without date perhaps in 1592; reprinted with additions in 1602

[*Works*, ed. F. S. Boas, Oxford, 1901. A type-facsimile of the edition of 1602 was issued by the Malone Society in 1925.]

THE

# SPANISH TRAGE-

die, Containing the lamentable
end of *Don Horatio*, and *Bel-imperia*:
with the pittifull death of
olde *Hieronimo*.

Newly corrected and amended of such grosse faults as
passed in the first impression.

AT LONDON
Printed by *Edward Allde*, for
Edward White.

# DRAMATIS PERSONAE

Ghost of Andrea, a Spanish nobleman, } *Chorus.*
Revenge,

*King of Spain.*
*Cyprian Duke of Castile*, his brother.
*Lorenzo*, the Duke's son.
*Bellimperia*, Lorenzo's sister.

*Viceroy of Portugal.*
*Balthazar*, his son.
*Don Pedro*, the Viceroy's brother.

*Hieronimo*, Marshal of Spain.
*Isabella*, his wife.
*Horatio*, their son.

Spanish General.
Deputy.
*Don Bazulto*, an old man.
Three Citizens.

Portuguese Ambassador.
*Alexandro*, } Portuguese Noblemen.
*Villuppo*,
Two Portuguese.

*Pedringano*, Bellimperia's servant.
*Christophil*, Bellimperia's custodian.
Lorenzo's Page.
*Serberine*, Balthazar's servant.
Isabella's Maid.
Messenger.
Hangman.
Three Kings and three Knights in the first dumb show.
Hymen and two torch-bearers in the second.

*Bazardo*, a Painter.
*Pedro* and *Jaques*, Hieronimo's servants.

Army. Banquet. Royal suites. Noblemen. Halberdiers.
Officers. Three Watchmen. Trumpets. Servants &c.

# THE SPANISH TRAGEDY

## ACTUS PRIMUS

### SCENE I

*Enter the* Ghost of Andrea, *and with him* Revenge.

*Ghost.* When this eternal substance of my soul
  Did live imprison'd in my wanton flesh,
  Each in their function serving other's need,
  I was a courtier in the Spanish court:
  My name was Don Andrea; my descent,
  Though not ignoble, yet inferior far
  To gracious fortunes of my tender youth.
  For there in prime and pride of all my years,
  By duteous service and deserving love,
  In secret I possess'd a worthy dame,    10
  Which hight sweet Bellimperia by name.
  But in the harvest of my summer joys
  Death's winter nipp'd the blossoms of my bliss,
  Forcing divorce betwixt my love and me.
  For in the late conflict with Portingal
  My valour drew me into danger's mouth,
  Till life to death made passage through my wounds.
  When I was slain, my soul descended straight
  To pass the flowing stream of Acheron;
  But churlish Charon, only boatman there,    20
  Said that, my rites of burial not perform'd,
  I might not sit amongst his passengers.
  Ere Sol had slept three nights in Thetis' lap,
  And slak'd his smoking chariot in her flood,
  By Don Horatio, our Knight Marshal's son,
  My funerals and obsequies were done.
  Then was the ferryman of hell content

15 Portingal] Portugal (*the usual form in this play*)

To pass me over to the slimy strond,
That leads to fell Avernus' ugly waves.
There, pleasing Cerberus with honey'd speech,    30
I pass'd the perils of the foremost porch.
Not far from hence, amidst ten thousand souls,
Sat Minos, Aeacus, and Rhadamanth,
To whom no sooner 'gan I make approach,
To crave a passport for my wandering ghost,
But Minos, in graven leaves of lottery,
Drew forth the manner of my life and death.
"This knight," quoth he, "both liv'd and died in
    love,
And for his love tried fortune of the wars,
And by war's fortune lost both love and life."    40
"Why then," said Aeacus, "convey him hence,
To walk with lovers in our fields of love,
And spend the course of everlasting time
Under green myrtle trees and cypress shades."
"No, no," said Rhadamanth, "it were not well,
With loving souls to place a martialist:
He died in war, and must to martial fields,
Where wounded Hector lives in lasting pain,
And Achilles' Myrmidons do scour the plain."
Then Minos, mildest censor of the three,    50
Made this device to end the difference:
"Send him," quoth he, "to our infernal king,
To doom him as best seems his majesty."
To this effect my passport straight was drawn.
In keeping on my way to Pluto's court,
Through dreadful shades of ever-glooming night,
I saw more sights than thousand tongues can tell,
Or pens can write, or mortal hearts can think.
Three ways there were: that on the right-hand side
Was ready way unto the foresaid fields,    60
Where lovers live and bloody martialists—
But either sort contain'd within his bounds.
The left-hand path, declining fearfully,

          28 strond] strand          53 doom] sentence

Was ready downfall to the deepest hell,
Where bloody Furies shake their whips of steel,
And poor Ixion turns an endless wheel;
Where usurers are chok'd with melting gold,
And wantons are embrac'd with ugly snakes,
And murderers groan with never-killing wounds,
And perjur'd wights scalded in boiling lead,      70
And all foul sins with torments overwhelm'd.
'Twixt these two ways I trod the middle path,
Which brought me to the fair Elysian green,
In midst whereof there stands a stately tower,
The walls of brass, the gates of adamant.
Here finding Pluto with his Proserpine,
I showed my passport, humbled on my knee;
Whereat fair Proserpine began to smile,
And begg'd that only she might give my doom.
Pluto was pleas'd, and seal'd it with a kiss.      80
Forthwith, Revenge, she rounded thee in th' ear,
And bade thee lead me through the gates of horn,
Where dreams have passage in the silent night.
No sooner had she spoke, but we were here,
I wot not how, in twinkling of an eye.
Revenge. Then know, Andrea, that thou art arriv'd
Where thou shalt see the author of thy death,
Don Balthazar, the prince of Portingal,
Depriv'd of life by Bellimperia.
Here sit we down to see the mystery,      90
And serve for Chorus in this tragedy.

## SCENE II

*Enter* Spanish King, General, Castile, Hieronimo.

King. Now say, Lord General, how fares our camp?
Gen. All well, my sovereign liege, except some few
That are deceas'd by fortune of the war.

77 humbled] bowing      81 rounded] whispered
82 horn] ivory

*King.* But what portends thy cheerful countenance,
   And posting to our presence thus in haste?
   Speak, man, hath fortune given us victory?
*Gen.* Victory, my liege, and that with little loss.
*King.* Our Portingals will pay us tribute then?
*Gen.* Tribute and wonted homage therewithal.
*King.* Then bless'd be heaven and guider of the
      heavens,                                    10
   From whose fair influence such justice flows.
*Cast.* *O multum dilecte Deo, tibi militat aether,*
   *Et conjuratae curvato poplite gentes*
   *Succumbunt; recti soror est victoria juris.*
*King.* Thanks to my loving brother of Castile.
   But, General, unfold in brief discourse
   Your form of battle and your war's success,
   That, adding all the pleasure of thy news
   Unto the height of former happiness,
   With deeper wage and greater dignity            20
   We may reward thy blissful chivalry.
*Gen.* Where Spain and Portingal do jointly knit
   Their frontiers, leaning on each other's bound,
   There met our armies in their proud array:
   Both furnish'd well, both full of hope and fear,
   Both meanacing alike with daring shows,
   Both vaunting sundry colours of device,
   Both cheerly sounding trumpets, drums, and fifes,
   Both raising dreadful clamours to the sky,
   That valleys, hills, and rivers made rebound,    30
   And heaven itself was frighted with the sound.
   Our battles both were pitch'd in squadron form,
   Each corner strongly fenc'd with wings of shot;
   But ere we join'd and came to push of pike,

12–14]
   O well-beloved of God, the heavens fight for thee,
   And spell-bound peoples fall on bended knee;
   For victory is sister of true right.
27 colours of device] standards    32, 47, 66, &c. battles]
main forces    34 push of pike] close quarters

I brought a squadron of our readiest shot
From out our rearward, to begin the fight:
They brought another wing to encounter us.
Meanwhile, our ordnance played on either side,
And captains strove to have their valours tried.
Don Pedro, their chief horsemen's Colonel,          40
Did with his cornet bravely make attempt
To break the order of our battle ranks:
But Don Rogero, worthy man of war,
March'd forth against him with our musketeers,
And stopp'd the malice of his fell approach.
While they maintain hot skirmish to and fro,
Both battles join, and fall to handy blows,
Their violent shot resembling th' ocean's rage,
When, roaring loud, and with a swelling tide,
It beats upon the rampires of huge rocks,          50
And gapes to swallow neighbour bounding lands.
Now while Bellona rageth here and there,
Thick storms of bullets ran like winter's hail,
And shivered lances dark the troubled air.
        *Pede pes et cuspide cuspis;*
*Arma sonant armis, vir petiturque viro.*
On every side drop captains to the ground,
And soldiers, some ill-maim'd, some slain outright:
Here falls a body sunder'd from his head,
There legs and arms lie bleeding on the grass,          60
Mingled with weapons and unbowell'd steeds,
That scattering overspread the purple plain.
In all this turmoil, three long hours and more,
The victory to neither part inclin'd,
Till Don Andrea, with his brave lanciers,
In their main battle made so great a breach,
That, half dismay'd, the multitude retir'd:

41 cornet] troop
55–6] Foot against foot, lance against lance is thrust,
        Arms clash on arms, man is attacked by man.
65 lanciers] lancers (*the spelling invites an accent on the second
syllable*)

But Balthazar, the Portingals' young prince,
Brought rescue, and encourag'd them to stay.
Here-hence the fight was eagerly renew'd,    70
And in that conflict was Andrea slain—
Brave man at arms, but weak to Balthazar.
Yet while the prince, insulting over him,
Breath'd out proud vaunts, sounding to our re-
    proach,
Friendship and hardy valour, join'd in one,
Prick'd forth Horatio, our Knight Marshal's son,
To challenge forth that prince in single fight.
Not long between these twain the fight endur'd,
But straight the prince was beaten from his horse,
And forc'd to yield him prisoner to his foe.    80
When he was taken, all the rest they fled,
And our carbines pursued them to the death,
Till, Phœbus waving to the western deep,
Our trumpeters were charg'd to sound retreat.

*King.* Thanks, good Lord General, for these good news;
And for some argument of more to come,
Take this and wear it for thy sovereign's sake.
                    [*Gives him his chain.*
But tell me now, hast thou confirm'd a peace?

*Gen.* No peace, my liege, but peace conditional,
That if with homage tribute be well paid,    90
The fury of your forces will be stay'd:
And to this peace their Viceroy hath subscrib'd,
                    [*Gives the* King *a paper.*
And made a solemn vow that, during life,
His tribute shall be truly paid to Spain.

*King.* These words, these deeds, become thy person
    well.
But now, Knight Marshal, frolic with thy king,
For 'tis thy son that wins this battle's prize.

*Hier.* Long may he live to serve my sovereign liege,
And soon decay unless he serve my liege.
                    [*A tucket afar off.*

82 carbines] mounted carabineers

*King.* Nor thou, nor he, shall die without reward.  100
  What means the warning of this trumpet's sound?
*Gen.* This tells me that your grace's men of war,
  Such as war's fortune hath reserv'd from death,
  Come marching on towards your royal seat,
  To show themselves before your majesty:
  For so I gave in charge at my depart.
  Whereby by demonstration shall appear,
  That all, except three hundred or few more,
  Are safe return'd, and by their foes enrich'd.

> *The Army enters;* Balthazar, *between* Lorenzo *and*
> Horatio, *captive.*

*King.* A gladsome sight!  I long to see them here.  110
> [*They enter and pass by.*
  Was that the warlike prince of Portingal,
  That by our nephew was in triumph led?
*Gen.* It was, my liege, the prince of Portingal.
*King.* But what was he that on the other side
  Held him by th' arm, as partner of the prize?
*Hier.* That was my son, my gracious sovereign;
  Of whom though from his tender infancy
  My loving thoughts did never hope but well,
  He never pleas'd his father's eyes till now,
  Nor fill'd my heart with over-cloying joys.    120
*King.* Go, let them march once more about these walls,
  That, staying them, we may confer and talk
  With our brave prisoner and his double guard.
  Hieronimo, it greatly pleaseth us
  That in our victory thou have a share,
  By virtue of thy worthy son's exploit. [*Enter again.*
  Bring hither the young prince of Portingal:
  The rest march on; but, ere they be dismiss'd,
  We will bestow on every soldier
  Two ducats, and on every leader ten,    130
  That they may know our largess welcomes them.
> [*Exeunt all but* Balthazar, Lorenzo, Horatio

F

Welcome, Don Balthazar! welcome, nephew!
And thou, Horatio, thou art welcome too.
Young prince, although thy father's hard misdeeds,
In keeping back the tribute that he owes,
Deserve but evil measure at our hands,
Yet shalt thou know that Spain is honourable.
*Bal.* The trespass that my father made in peace
Is now controll'd by fortune of the wars;
And cards once dealt, it boots not ask why so.  140
His men are slain, a weakening to his realm;
His colours seiz'd, a blot unto his name;
His son distress'd, a corsive to his heart:
These punishments may clear his late offence.
*King.* Ay, Balthazar, if he observe this truce,
Our peace will grow the stronger for these wars.
Meanwhile live thou, though not in liberty,
Yet free from bearing any servile yoke;
For in our hearing thy deserts were great,
And in our sight thyself art gracious.  150
*Bal.* And I shall study to deserve this grace.
*King.* But tell me—for their holding makes me
   doubt—
To which of these twain art thou prisoner?
*Lor.* To me, my liege.
*Hor.*                  To me, my sovereign.
*Lor.* This hand first took his courser by the reins.
*Hor.* But first my lance did put him from his horse.
*Lor.* I seiz'd his weapon, and enjoy'd it first.
*Hor.* But first I forc'd him lay his weapons down.
*King.* Let go his arm, upon our privilege.
                        [*They let him go.*
Say, worthy prince, to whether didst thou yield?  160
*Bal.* To him in courtesy, to this perforce:
He spake me fair, this other gave me strokes;
He promis'd life, this other threaten'd death;

      *Horatio*                      *Lorenzo*

139 controll'd] restrained      143 distress'd] taken
prisoner       corsive] corrosive     160 whether] which

He wan my love, this other conquered me,
And, truth to say, I yield myself to both.
*Hier.* But that I know your grace for just and wise,
And might seem partial in this difference,
Enforc'd by nature and by laws of arms
My tongue should plead for young **Horatio's** right:
He hunted well that was a lion's death,                170
Not he that in a garment wore his skin;
So hares may pull dead lions by the beard.
*King.* Content thee, Marshal, thou shalt have no
        wrong;
And for thy sake thy son shall want no right.
Will both abide the censure of my doom?
*Lor.* I crave no better than your grace awards.
*Hor.* Nor I, although I sit beside my right.
*King.* Then by my judgment thus your strife shall
        end:
You both deserve, and both shall have reward.
Nephew, thou took'st his weapon and his horse: 180
His weapons and his horse are thy reward.
Horatio, thou didst force him first to yield:
His ransom therefore is thy valour's fee;
Appoint the sum, as you shall both agree.
But, nephew, thou shalt have the prince in guard,
For thine estate best fitteth such a guest:
Horatio's house were small for all his train.
Yet, in regard thy substance passeth his,
And that just guerdon may befall desert,
To him we yield the armour of the prince.        190
How likes Don Balthazar of this device?
*Bal.* Right well, my liege, if this proviso **were,**
That Don Horatio bear us company,
Whom I admire and love for chivalry.
*King.* Horatio, leave him not that loves thee **so.**—
Now let us hence to see our soldiers paid,
And feast our prisoner as our friendly guest. [*Exeunt.*

164 wan] won       177 sit beside] stand upon, claim

## SCENE III

*Enter* Viceroy, Alexandro, Villuppo.

*Vic.* Is our ambassador despatch'd for Spain?
*Alex.* Two days, my liege, are past since his depart.
*Vic.* And tribute payment gone along with him?
*Alex.* Ay, my good lord.
*Vic.* Then rest we here awhile in our unrest,
And feed our sorrows with some inward sighs;
For deepest cares break never into tears.
But wherefore sit I in a regal throne?
This better fits a wretch's endless moan.
                              [*Falls to the ground.*
Yet this is higher than my fortunes reach,      10
And therefore better than my state deserves.
Ay, ay, this earth, image of melancholy,
Seeks him whom fates adjudge to misery.
Here let me lie; now am I at the lowest.
        *Qui jacet in terra, non habet unde cadat.*
    *In me consumpsit vires fortuna nocendo;*
        *Nil superest ut jam possit obesse magis.*
Yes, Fortune may bereave me of my crown:
Here, take it now;—let Fortune do her worst,
She will not rob me of this sable weed:         20
O no, she envies none but pleasant things.
Such is the folly of despiteful chance!
Fortune is blind, and sees not my deserts;
So is she deaf, and hears not my laments;
And could she hear, yet is she wilful mad,
And therefore will not pity my distress.
Suppose that she could pity me, what then?
What help can be expected at her hands
Whose foot is standing on a rolling stone,
And mind more mutable than fickle winds?        30

15–17] He who is prostrate hath no where to fall.
        Fortune hath spent her force for ill on me:
        Greater disaster cannot be in store.

Why wail I then, where's hope of no redress?
O yes, complaining makes my grief seem less.
My late ambition hath distain'd my faith;
My breach of faith occasion'd bloody wars;
Those bloody wars have spent my treasure;
And with my treasure my people's blood;
And with their blood, my joy and best beloved,
My best beloved, my sweet and only son.
O, wherefore went I not to war myself?
The cause was mine; I might have died for both: 40
My years were mellow, his but young and green;
My death were natural, but his was forced.
*Alex.* No doubt, my liege, but still the prince survives.
*Vic.* Survives! ay, where?
*Alex.* In Spain, a prisoner by mischance of war.
*Vic.* Then they have slain him for his father's fault.
*Alex.* That were a breach to common law of arms.
*Vic.* They reck no laws that meditate revenge.
*Alex.* His ransom's worth will stay from foul revenge.
*Vic.* No; if he lived, the news would soon be here. 50
*Alex.* Nay, evil news fly faster still than good.
*Vic.* Tell me no more of news, for he is dead.
*Vil.* My sovereign, pardon the author of ill news,
    And I'll bewray the fortune of thy son.
*Vic.* Speak on, I'll guerdon thee, whate'er it be:
    Mine ear is ready to receive ill news,
    My heart grown hard 'gainst mischief's battery.
    Stand up, I say, and tell thy tale at large.
*Vil.* Then hear that truth which these mine eyes have
        seen:
    When both the armies were in battle join'd,     60
    Don Balthazar, amidst the thickest troops,
    To win renown did wondrous feats of arms:
    Amongst the rest I saw him, hand to hand,
    In single fight with their Lord General;
    Till Alexandro, that here counterfeits

    33 distain'd] stained     51 still] always

Under the colour of a duteous friend,
Discharged his pistol at the prince's back,
As though he would have slain their general:
But therewithal Don Balthazar fell down;
And when he fell, then we began to fly:          70
But, had he lived, the day had sure been ours.
*Alex.* O wicked forgery! O traitorous miscreant!
*Vic.* Hold thou thy peace! But now, Villuppo, say,
Where then became the carcase of my son?
*Vil.* I saw them drag it to the Spanish tents.
*Vic.* Ay, ay, my nightly dreams have told me this.—
Thou false, unkind, unthankful, traitorous beast,
Wherein had Balthazar offended thee
That thou shouldst thus betray him to our foes?
Was't Spanish gold that bleared so thine eyes    80
That thou couldst see no part of our deserts?
Perchance, because thou art Terceira's lord,
Thou hadst some hope to wear this diadem,
If first my son and then myself were slain;
But thy ambitious thought shall break thy neck.
Ay, this was it that made thee spill his blood,
       [*Take the crown and put it on again.*
But I'll now wear it till thy blood be spilt.
*Alex.* Vouchsafe, dread sovereign, to hear me speak.
*Vic.* Away with him; his sight is second hell.
Keep him till we determine of his death:         90
If Balthazar be dead, he shall not live.
Villuppo, follow us for thy reward. [*Exit* Viceroy.
*Vil.* Thus have I with an envious, forged tale
Deceived the king, betray'd mine enemy,
And hope for guerdon of my villany.          [*Exit.*

66 colour] appearance          72, 93 forgery, forged]
invention, invented      77 unkind] unnatural

## SCENE IV

*Enter* Horatio *and* Bellimperia.

*Bel.* Signior Horatio, this is the place and hour,
Wherein I must entreat thee to relate
The circumstance of Don Andrea's death,
Who, living, was my garland's sweetest flower,
And in his death hath buried my delights.
*Hor.* For love of him and service to yourself,
I nill refuse this heavy doleful charge;
Yet tears and sighs, I fear, will hinder me.
When both our armies were enjoin'd in fight,
Your worthy chevalier amidst the thick'st,          10
For glorious cause still aiming at the fairest,
Was at the last by young Don Balthazar
Encounter'd hand to hand: their fight was long,
Their hearts were great, their clamours menacing,
Their strength alike, their strokes both dangerous.
But wrathful Nemesis, that wicked power,
Envying at Andrea's praise and worth,
Cut short his life, to end his praise and worth.
She, she herself, disguis'd in armour's mask,
(As Pallas was before proud Pergamus)          20
Brought in a fresh supply of halberdiers,
Which paunch'd his horse, and ding'd him to the
     ground.
Then young Don Balthazar with ruthless rage,
Taking advantage of his foe's distress,
Did finish what his halberdiers begun,
And left not till Andrea's life was done.
Then, though too late, incens'd with just remorse,
I with my band set forth against the prince,
And brought him prisoner from his halberdiers.
*Bel.* Would thou hadst slain him that so slew my love!  30
But then was Don Andrea's carcase lost?

7 nill] will not          9 enjoin'd] joined          22 ding'd]
hurled

*Hor.* No, that was it for which I chiefly strove,
Nor stepp'd I back till I recover'd him:
I took him up, and wound him in mine arms;
And welding him unto my private tent,
There laid him down, and dew'd him with my tears,
And sighed and sorrowed as became a friend.
But neither friendly sorrow, sighs, nor tears
Could win pale Death from his usurped right.
Yet this I did, and less I could not do:                    40
I saw him honoured with due funeral.
This scarf I pluck'd from off his lifeless arm,
And wear it in remembrance of my friend.
*Bel.* I know the scarf: would he had kept it still;
For had he lived he would have kept it still,
And worn it for his Bellimperia's sake:
For 'twas my favour at his last depart.
But now wear thou it both for him and me,
For after him thou hast deserved it best.
But for thy kindness in his life and death,              50
Be sure, while Bellimperia's life endures,
She will be Don Horatio's thankful friend.
*Hor.* And, madam, Don Horatio will not slack
Humbly to serve fair Bellimperia.
But now, if your good liking stand thereto,
I'll crave your pardon to go seek the prince,
For so the duke, your father, gave me charge.  [*Exit.*
*Bel.* Ay, go, Horatio, leave me here alone,
For solitude bests fits my cheerless mood.
Yet what avails to will Andrea's death,                  60
From whence Horatio proves my second love?
Had he not loved Andrea as he did,
He could not sit in Bellimperia's thoughts.
But how can love find harbour in my breast,
Till I revenge the death of my beloved?
Yes, second love shall further my revenge:
I'll love Horatio, my Andrea's friend,
The more to spite the prince that wrought his end.
35 welding] carrying        55 if ... thereto] if you approve

And where Don Balthazar, that slew my love,
Himself now pleads for favour at my hands,     70
He shall, in rigour of my just disdain,
Reap long repentance for his murderous deed.
For what was 't else but murderous cowardice,
So many to oppress one valiant knight,
Without respect of honour in the fight?
And here he comes that murder'd my delight.

*Enter* Lorenzo *and* Balthazar.

*Lor.* Sister, what means this melancholy walk?
*Bel.* That for a while I wish no company.
*Lor.* But here the prince is come to visit you.
*Bel.* That argues that he lives in liberty.     80
*Bal.* No, madam, but in pleasing servitude.
*Bel.* Your prison then, belike, is your conceit.
*Bal.* Ay, by conceit my freedom is enthrall'd.
*Bel.* Then with conceit enlarge yourself again.
*Bal.* What, if conceit have laid my heart to gage?
*Bel.* Pay that you borrowed, and recover it.
*Bal.* I die, if it return from whence it lies.
*Bel.* A heartless man, and live? A miracle!
*Bal.* Ay, lady, love can work such miracles.
*Lor.* Tush, tush, my lord! let go these ambages,     90
And in plain terms acquaint her with your love.
*Bel.* What boots complaint, when there's no remedy?
*Bal.* Yes, to your gracious self must I complain,
In whose fair answer lies my remedy;
On whose perfection all my thoughts attend;
On whose aspect mine eyes find beauty's bower;
In whose translucent breast my heart is lodg'd.
*Bel.* Alas, my lord, these are but words of course,
And but device to drive me from this place.

> [*She, in going in, lets fall her glove,*
> *which* Horatio, *coming out, takes up.*

69 where] whereas          82 conceit] fancy          90
ambages] round-about phrases          98 words of course]
ceremonial phrases

*Hor.* Madam, your glove.                                    100
*Bel.* Thanks, good Horatio, take it for thy pains.
*Bal.* Signior Horatio stoop'd in happy time!
*Hor.* I reap'd more grace than I deserv'd or hop'd.
*Lor.* My lord, be not dismay'd for what is past;
    You know that women oft are humorous:
    These clouds will overblow with little wind:
    Let me alone, I'll scatter them myself.
    Meanwhile, let us devise to spend the time
    In some delightful sports and revelling.
*Hor.* The king, my lords, is coming hither straight, 110
    To feast the Portingal ambassador;
    Things were in readiness before I came.
*Bal.* Then here it fits us to attend the king,
    To welcome hither our ambassador,
    And learn my father and my country's health.


## SCENE V

*Enter the Banquet, Trumpets, the* King, *and* Ambassador.

*King.* See, Lord Ambassador, how Spain entreats
    Their prisoner Balthazar, thy Viceroy's son:
    We pleasure more in kindness than in wars.
*Amb.* Sad is our king, and Portingal laments,
    Supposing that Don Balthazar is slain.
*Bal.* So am I slain, by beauty's tyranny.
    You see, my lord, how Balthazar is slain:
    I frolic with the Duke of Castile's son,
    Wrapp'd every hour in pleasures of the court,
    And grac'd with favours of his majesty.              10
*King.* Put off your greetings, till our feast be done;
    Now come and sit with us, and taste our cheer.
                        *[Sit to the banquet.*
    Sit down, young prince, you are our second guest;
    Brother, sit down; and, nephew, take your place.
    Signior Horatio, wait thou upon our cup;

    105 humorous] fanciful                    1 entreats] treats

For well thou hast deserved to be honoured.
Now, lordings, fall to; Spain is Portugal,
And Portugal is Spain: we both are friends;
Tribute is paid, and we enjoy our right.
But where is old Hieronimo, our Marshal?          20
He promised us, in honour of our guest,
To grace our banquet with some pompous jest.

*Enter* Hieronimo *with a drum, three knights, each his
scutcheon; then he fetches three kings, they take their crowns
and them captive.*

Hieronimo, this masque contents mine eye,
Although I sound not well the mystery.
*Hier.* The first arm'd knight, that hung his scutcheon
    up,
              *[He takes the scutcheon and gives it to the* King.
Was English Robert, Earl of Gloucester,
Who, when King Stephen bore sway in Albion,
Arrived with five and twenty thousand men
In Portingal, and by success of war
Enforced the king, then but a Saracen,          30
To bear the yoke of the English monarchy.
*King.* My lord of Portingal, by this you see
That which may comfort both your king and you,
And make your late discomfort seem the less.
But say, Hieronimo, what was the next?
*Hier.* The second knight, that hung his scutcheon up,
                  *[He doth as he did before.*
Was Edmond, Earl of Kent in Albion,
When English Richard wore the diadem.
He came likewise, and razed Lisbon walls,
And took the King of Portingal in fight;          40
For which and other such-like service done
He after was created Duke of York.
*King.* This is another special argument,

22 s.d. scutcheon] escutcheon, shield with armorial
bearings

That Portingal may deign to bear our yoke,
When it by little England hath been yok'd.
But now, Hieronimo, what were the last?
*Hier.* The third and last, not least in our account,

          *[Doing as before.*
Was, as the rest, a valiant Englishman,
Brave John of Gaunt, the Duke of Lancaster,
As by his scutcheon plainly may appear.   50
He with a puissant army came to Spain,
And took our King of Castile prisoner.
*Amb.* This is an argument for our Viceroy.
That Spain may not insult for her success,
Since English warriors likewise conquered Spain,
And made them bow their knees to Albion.
*King.* Hieronimo, I drink to thee for this device,
Which hath pleas'd both the ambassador and me:
Pledge me, Hieronimo, if thou love thy king.

        *[Takes the cup of* Horatio.
My lord, I fear we sit but over-long,   60
Unless our dainties were more delicate;
But welcome are you to the best we have.
Now let us in, that you may be despatch'd:
I think our council is already set.  *[Exeunt omnes.*


## SCENE VI

Ghost of Andrea, Revenge.

*Andrea.* Come we for this from depth of underground,
To see him feast that gave me my death's wound?
These pleasant sights are sorrow to my soul:
Nothing but league, and love, and banqueting.
*Revenge.* Be still, Andrea; ere we go from hence,
I'll turn their friendship into fell despite,
Their love to mortal hate, their day to night,
Their hope into despair, their peace to war,
Their joys to pain, their bliss to misery.

6 despite] hatred

## ACTUS SECUNDUS

### SCENE I

*Enter* Lorenzo *and* Balthazar.

*Lor.* My lord, though Bellimperia seem thus coy,
    Let reason hold you in your wonted joy:
    In time the savage bull sustains the yoke,
    In time all haggard hawks will stoop to lure,
    In time small wedges cleave the hardest oak,
    In time the flint is pierc'd with softest shower,
    And she in time will fall from her disdain,
    And rue the sufferance of your friendly pain.
*Bal.* No, she is wilder, and more hard withal,
    Than beast, or bird, or tree, or stony wall.    **10**
    But wherefore blot I Bellimperia's name?
    It is my fault, not she, that merits blame.
    My feature is not to content her sight,
    My words are rude, and work her no delight.
    The lines I send her are but harsh and ill,
    Such as do drop from Pan and Marsyas' quill.
    My presents are not of sufficient cost,
    And being worthless, all my labour's lost.
    Yet might she love me for my valiancy:
    Ay, but that's slander'd by captivity.    **20**
    Yet might she love me to content her sire:
    Ay, but her reason masters his desire.
    Yet might she love me as her brother's friend:
    Ay, but her hopes aim at some other end.
    Yet might she love me to uprear her state:
    Ay, but perhaps she hopes some nobler mate.
    Yet might she love me as her beauty's thrall:
    Ay, but I fear she cannot love at all.
*Lor.* My lord, for my sake leave this ecstasy,
    And doubt not but we'll find some remedy.    **30**

4 haggard] untamed

Some cause there is that lets you not be loved;
First that must needs be known, and then removed.
What, if my sister love some other knight?
*Bal.* My summer's day will turn to winter's night.
*Lor.* I have already found a stratagem,
To sound the bottom of this doubtful theme.
My lord, for once you shall be rul'd by me;
Hinder me not, whate'er you hear or see.
By force or fair means will I cast about
To find the truth of all this question out.　　　40
Ho, Pedringano!
*Ped.*　　　　　　*Signior!*
*Lor.*　　　　　　　　*Vien qui presto.*


*Enter* Pedringano.

*Ped.* Hath your lordship any service to command me?
*Lor.* Ay, Pedringano, service of import;
And, not to spend the time in trifling words,
Thus stands the case: It is not long, thou know'st,
Since I did shield thee from my father's wrath,
For thy conveyance in Andrea's love,
For which thou wert adjudg'd to punishment:
I stood betwixt thee and thy punishment,
And since, thou knowest how I have favoured thee. 50
Now to these favours will I add reward,
Not with fair words, but store of golden coin,
And lands and living join'd with dignities,
If thou but satisfy my just demand:
Tell truth, and have me for thy lasting friend.
*Ped.* Whate'er it be your lordship shall demand,
My bounden duty bids me tell the truth,
If case it lie in me to tell the truth.
*Lor.* Then, Pedringano, this is my demand:
Whom loves my sister Bellimperia?　　　　60

41 *Vien qui presto.*] Come here at once.　　44 trifling]
playing with　　47 conveyance] secret agency　　52
store] plenty

For she reposeth all her trust in thee.
Speak, man, and gain both friendship and reward:
I mean, whom loves she in Andrea's place?

*Ped.* Alas, my lord, since Don Andrea's death
I have no credit with her as before,
And therefore know not, if she love or no.

*Lor.* Nay, if thou dally, then I am thy foe,
　　　　　　　　　　　　[*Draws his sword.*
And fear shall force what friendship cannot win:
Thy death shall bury what thy life conceals;
Thou diest for more esteeming her than me.　70

*Ped.* O, stay, my lord.

*Lor.* Yet speak the truth, and I will guerdon thee,
And shield thee from whatever can ensue,
And will conceal whate'er proceeds from thee;
But if thou dally once again, thou diest.

*Ped.* If madam Bellimperia be in love——

*Lor.* What, villain! ifs and ands?　[*Offer to kill him.*

*Ped.* O, stay, my lord, she loves Horatio.
　　　　　　　　　　[Balthazar *starts back.*

*Lor.* What, Don Horatio, our Knight Marshal's son?

*Ped.* Even him, my lord.　　　　　　　　　80

*Lor.* Now say but how knowest thou he is her love,
And thou shalt find me kind and liberal:
Stand up, I say, and fearless tell the truth.

*Ped.* She sent him letters, which myself perus'd,
Full-fraught with lines and arguments of love,
Preferring him before Prince Balthazar.

*Lor.* Swear on this cross that what thou sayest is true;
And that thou wilt conceal what thou hast told.

*Ped.* I swear to both, by him that made us all.

*Lor.* In hope thine oath is true, here's thy reward:　90
But if I prove thee perjur'd and unjust,
This very sword, whereon thou took'st thine oath,
Shall be the worker of thy tragedy.

*Ped.* What I have said is true, and shall, for me,

87 this cross] *The hilt of his sword; see line* 92.　　94
for me] so far as I am concerned

Be still conceal'd from Bellimperia.
Besides, your honour's liberality
Deserves my duteous service, even till death.
*Lor.* Let this be all that thou shalt do for me:
   Be watchful, when and where these lovers meet,
   And give me notice in some secret sort.      100
*Ped.* I will, my lord.
*Lor.* Then shalt thou find that I am liberal.
   Thou know'st that I can more advance thy state
   Than she; be therefore wise, and fail me not.
   Go and attend her, as thy custom is,
   Lest absence make her think thou dost amiss.

                       [*Exit* Pedringano.

   Why so: *tam armis quam ingenio:*
   Where words prevail not, violence prevails;
   But gold doth more than either of them both.
   How likes Prince Balthazar this stratagem?    110
*Bal.* Both well and ill; it makes me glad and sad:
   Glad, that I know the hinderer of my love;
   Sad, that I fear she hates me whom I love.
   Glad, that I know on whom to be reveng'd;
   Sad, that she'll fly me, if I take revenge.
   Yet must I take revenge, or die myself,
   For love resisted grows impatient.
   I think Horatio be my destin'd plague:
   First, in his hand he brandished a sword,
   And with that sword he fiercely waged war,    120
   And in that war he gave me dangerous wounds,
   And by those wounds he forced me to yield,
   And by my yielding I became his slave.
   Now in his mouth he carries pleasing words,
   Which pleasing words do harbour sweet conceits,
   Which sweet conceits are lim'd with sly deceits,
   Which sly deceits smooth Bellimperia's ears,
   And through her ears dive down into her heart,
   And in her heart set him, where I should stand.

107 *tam . . . ingenio*] by force as well as wile  125, 126 & c.
conceits] fancies                         127 smooth] flatter

Thus hath he ta'en my body by his force,      130
And now by sleight would captivate my soul:
But in his fall I'll tempt the destinies,
And either lose my life, or win my love.

*Lor.* Let's go, my lord; your staying stays revenge.
Do you but follow me, and gain your love:
Her favour must be won by his remove.      [*Exeunt.*

## SCENE II

*Enter* Horatio *and* Bellimperia.

*Hor.* Now, madam, since by favour of your love
Our hidden smoke is turned to open flame,
And that with looks and words we feed our thoughts
(Two chief contents, where more cannot be had):
Thus, in the midst of love's fair blandishments,
Why show you sign of inward languishments?

Pedringano *showeth all to the* Prince *and*
Lorenzo, *placing them in secret.*

*Bel.* My heart, sweet friend, is like a ship at sea:
She wisheth port, where, riding all at ease,
She may repair what stormy times have worn,
And leaning on the shore, may sing with joy,      10
That pleasure follows pain, and bliss annoy.
Possession of thy love is th' only port,
Wherein my heart, with fears and hopes long toss'd,
Each hour doth wish and long to make resort,
There to repair the joys that it hath lost,
And, sitting safe, to sing in Cupid's choir
That sweetest bliss is crown of love's desire.

[Balthazar *and* Lorenzo *above.*

*Bal.* O sleep, mine eyes, see not my love profan'd;
Be deaf, my ears, hear not my discontent;
Die, heart: another joys what thou deservest.      20

136 remove] removal      6 s.d.] *Probably the con-*
*spirators enter here and proceed unseen by the lovers to the gallery,*
*where at line 17 they remain 'above', watching.*      20 joys] enjoys

*Lor.* Watch still, mine eyes, to see this love disjoin'd;
  Hear still, mine ears, to hear them both lament;
  Live, heart, to joy at fond Horatio's fall.
*Bel.* Why stands Horatio speechless all this while?
*Hor.* The less I speak, the more I meditate.
*Bel.* But whereon dost thou chiefly meditate?
*Hor.* On dangers past, and pleasures to ensue.
*Bal.* On pleasures past, and dangers to ensue.
*Bel.* What dangers and what pleasures dost thou mean?
*Hor.* Dangers of war, and pleasures of our love.   30
*Lor.* Dangers of death, but pleasures none at all.
*Bel.* Let dangers go, thy war shall be with me:
  But such a war, as breaks no bond of peace.
  Speak thou fair words, I'll cross them with fair
    words;
  Send thou sweet looks, I'll meet them with sweet
    looks;
  Write loving lines, I'll answer loving lines;
  Give me a kiss, I'll countercheck thy kiss:
  Be this our warring peace, or peaceful war.
*Hor.* But, gracious madam, then appoint the field,
  Where trial of this war shall first be made.   40
*Bal.* Ambitious villain, how his boldness grows!
*Bel.* Then be thy father's pleasant bower the field,
  Where first we vow'd a mutual amity;
  The court were dangerous, that place is safe.
  Our hour shall be, when Vesper 'gins to rise,
  That summons home distressful travailers.
  There none shall hear us but the harmless birds;
  Haply the gentle nightingale
  Shall carol us asleep, ere we be ware,
  And, singing with the prickle at her breast,   50
  Tell our delight and mirthful dalliance:
  Till then each hour will seem a year and more.
*Hor.* But, honey sweet and honourable love,
  Return we now into your father's sight:

46 distressful travailers] weary labourers   50 prickle]
thorn

Dangerous suspicion waits on our delight.
*Lor.* Ay, danger mix'd with jealous despite
  Shall send thy soul into eternal night.    [*Exeunt.*


## SCENE III

*Enter* King of Spain, Portingal Ambassador,
Don Cyprian, &c.

*King.* Brother of Castile, to the prince's love
  What says your daughter Bellimperia?
*Cyp.* Although she coy it, as becomes her kind,
  And yet dissemble that she loves the prince,
  I doubt not, I, but she will stoop in time.
  And were she froward, which she will not be,
  Yet herein shall she follow my advice,
  Which is to love him, or forgo my love.
*King.* Then, Lord Ambassador of Portingal,
  Advise thy king to make this marriage up,    10
  For strengthening of our late-confirmed league;
  I know no better means to make us friends.
  Her dowry shall be large and liberal:
  Besides that she is daughter and half-heir
  Unto our brother here, Don Cyprian,
  And shall enjoy the moiety of his land,
  I'll grace her marriage with an uncle's gift,
  And this it is: in case the match go forward,
  The tribute which you pay shall be releas'd,
  And if by Balthazar she have a son,    *LORENZO ??*    20
  He shall enjoy the kingdom after us.
*Amb.* I'll make the motion to my sovereign liege,
  And work it, if my counsel may prevail.
*King.* Do so, my lord, and if he give consent,
  I hope his presence here will honour us,
  In celebration of the nuptial day;
  And let himself determine of the time.

        3 kind] nature (*sc. as being a woman*)

*Amb.* Will't please your grace command me ought
　　beside?

*King.* Commend me to the king, and so farewell.
　　But where's Prince Balthazar to take his leave?　30

*Amb.* That is perform'd already, my good lord.

*King.* Amongst the rest of what you have in charge,
　　The prince's ransom must not be forgot:
　　That's none of mine, but his that took him prisoner,
　　And well his forwardness deserves reward.
　　It was Horatio, our Knight Marshal's son.

*Amb.* Between us there's a price already pitch'd,
　　And shall be sent with all convenient speed.

*King.* Then once again farewell, my lord.

*Amb.* Farewell, my Lord of Castile, and the rest. [*Exit.*

*King.* Now, brother, you must take some little pains　41
　　To win fair Bellimperia from her will:
　　Young virgins must be ruled by their friends.
　　The prince is amiable, and loves her well;
　　If she neglect him and forgo his love,
　　She both will wrong her own estate and ours.
　　Therefore, whiles I do entertain the prince
　　With greatest pleasure that our court affords,
　　Endeavour you to win your daughter's thought:
　　If she give back, all this will come to naught.　50
　　　　　　　　　　　　　　　　　[*Exeunt.*

## SCENE IV

*Enter* Horatio, Bellimperia, *and* Pedringano.

*Hor.* Now that the night begins with sable wings
　　To overcloud the brightness of the sun,
　　And that in darkness pleasures may be done,
　　Come, Bellimperia, let us to the bower,
　　And there in safety pass a pleasant hour.

*Bel.* I follow thee, my love, and will not back,
　　Although my fainting heart controls my soul.

　37 pitch'd] fixed　　50 give back] hold back　　**7**
controls] restrains, holds back

*Hor.* Why, make you doubt of Pedringano's faith?

*Bel.* No, he is as trusty as my second self.—

Go, Pedringano, watch without the gate,    10

And let us know if any make approach.

*Ped.* [*aside.*] Instead of watching, I'll deserve more gold

By fetching Don Lorenzo to this match.

                                 [*Exit* Pedringano.

*Hor.* What means my love?

*Bel.*                    I know not what myself;

And yet my heart foretells me some mischance.

*Hor.* Sweet, say not so; fair fortune is our friend,

And heavens have shut up day to pleasure us.

The stars, thou see'st, hold back their twinkling shine,

And Luna hides herself to pleasure us.

*Bel.* Thou hast prevail'd; I'll conquer my misdoubt, 20

And in thy love and counsel drown my fear.

I fear no more; love now is all my thoughts.

Why sit we not? for pleasure asketh ease.

*Hor.* The more thou sitt'st within these leafy bowers,

The more will Flora deck it with her flowers.

*Bel.* Ay, but if Flora spy Horatio here,

Her jealous eye will think I sit too near.

*Hor.* Hark, madam, how the birds record by night,

For joy that Bellimperia sits in sight.

*Bel.* No, Cupid counterfeits the nightingale,    30

To frame sweet music to Horatio's tale.

*Hor.* If Cupid sing, then Venus is not far;

Ay, thou art Venus, or some fairer star.

*Bel.* If I be Venus, thou must needs be Mars;

And where Mars reigneth, there must needs be wars.

*Hor.* Then thus begin our wars: put forth thy hand,

That it may combat with my ruder hand.

*Bel.* Set forth thy foot to try the push of mine.

*Hor.* But first my looks shall combat against thine.

       20 misdoubt] fear      28 record] sing

*Bel.* Then ward thyself: I dart this kiss at thee.    40
*Hor.* Thus I retort the dart thou threw'st at me.
*Bel.* Nay, then to gain the glory of the field,
  My twining arms shall yoke and make thee yield.
*Hor.* Nay, then my arms are large and strong withal:
  Thus elms by vines are compass'd, till they fall.
*Bel.* O, let me go; for in my troubled eyes
  Now may'st thou read that life in passion dies.
*Hor.* O, stay a while, and I will die with thee;
  So shalt thou yield, and yet have conquer'd me.
*Bel.* Who's there?  Pedringano! we are betray'd!  50


*Enter* Lorenzo, Balthazar, Serberine, Pedringano,
  *disguised.*

*Lor.* My lord, away with her, take her aside.—
  O, sir, forbear: your valour is already tried.
  Quickly despatch, my masters.
                    [*They hang him in the arbour.*
*Hor.*                What, will you murder me?
*Lor.* Ay, thus, and thus: these are the fruits of love.
                    [*They stab him.*
*Bel.* O, save his life, and let me die for him!
  O, save him, brother; save him, Balthazar:
  I loved Horatio; but he loved not me.
*Bal.* But Balthazar loves Bellimperia.
*Lor.* Although his life were still ambitious-proud,
  Yet is he at the highest now he is dead.    60
*Bel.* Murder! murder!  Help, Hieronimo, help!
*Lor.* Come, stop her mouth; away with her. [*Exeunt.*


## SCENE V

*Enter* Hieronimo *in his shirt, &c.*

*Hier.* What outcries pluck me from my naked bed,
  And chill my throbbing heart with trembling fear,

41 retort] throw back        Heading *shirt*] nightshirt

Which never danger yet could daunt before?
Who calls Hieronimo? speak, here I am.
I did not slumber; therefore 'twas no dream.
No, no, it was some woman cried for help,
And here within this garden did she cry,
And in this garden must I rescue her.—
But stay, what murd'rous spectacle is this?
A man hang'd up and all the murderers gone!   10
And in my bower, to lay the guilt on me!
This place was made for pleasure, not for death.
                    [*He cuts him down.*
Those garments that he wears I oft have seen:
Alas, it is Horatio, my sweet son!
O no, but he that whilom was my son!
O, was it thou that call'dst me from my bed?
O speak, if any spark of life remain:
I am thy father; who hath slain my son?
What savage monster, not of human kind,
Hath here been glutted with thy harmless blood,  20
And left thy bloody corpse dishonoured here,
For me, amidst these dark and deathful shades,
To drown thee with an ocean of my tears?
O heavens, why made you night to cover sin?
By day this deed of darkness had not been.
O earth, why didst thou not in time devour
The vild profaner of this sacred bower?
O poor Horatio, what hadst thou misdone,
To leese thy life, ere life was new begun?
O wicked butcher, whatsoe'er thou wert,      30
How could thou strangle virtue and desert?
Ay me most wretched, that have lost my joy,
In leesing my Horatio, my sweet boy!

                    *Enter* Isabella.

*Isab.* My husband's absence makes my heart to throb:—
    Hieronimo!

    **27** vild]vile        **29, 33** leese, leesing] lose, losing

*Hier.* Here, Isabella, help me to lament;
    For sighs are stopp'd, and all my tears are spent.
*Isab.* What world of grief! my son Horatio!
    O, where's the author of this endless woe?
*Hier.* To know the author were some ease of grief,    40
    For in revenge my heart would find relief.
*Isab.* Then is he gone? and is my son gone too?
    O, gush out, tears, fountains and floods of tears;
    Blow, sighs, and raise an everlasting storm;
    For outrage fits our cursed wretchedness.
*Hier.* Sweet lovely rose, ill pluck'd before thy time,
    Fair, worthy son, not conquer'd, but betray'd,
    I'll kiss thee now, for words with tears are
        stay'd.
*Isab.* And I'll close up the glasses of his sight,
    For once these eyes were only my delight.    50
*Hier.* See'st thou this handkercher besmear'd with
        blood?
    It shall not from me, till I take revenge.
    See'st thou those wounds that yet are bleeding
        fresh?
    I'll not entomb them, till I have reveng'd.
    Then will I joy amidst my discontent;
    Till then my sorrow never shall be spent.
*Isab.* The heavens are just, murder cannot be hid:
    Time is the author both of truth and right,
    And time will bring this treachery to light.
*Hier.* Meanwhile, good Isabella, cease thy plaints, 60
    Or, at the least, dissemble them awhile:
    So shall we sooner find the practice out,
    And learn by whom all this was brought about.
    Come, Isabel, now let us take him up,
                            [*They take him up.*
    And bear him in from out this cursed place.
    I'll say his dirge; singing fits not this case.

45–6] *Between these lines the First Addition was inserted in*
*1602; see p.* 229.    51 handkercher] handkerchief    62
practice] plot

*O aliquis mihi quas pulchrum ver educat herbas*
      [Hieronimo sets his breast unto his sword.
*Misceat, et nostro detur medicina dolori;*
*Aut, si qui faciunt annorum oblivia, succos*
*Praebeat; ipse metam magnum quaecunque per orbem*   70
*Gramina Sol pulchras effert in luminis oras;*
*Ipse bibam quicquid meditatur saga veneni,*
*Quicquid et herbarum vi caeca nenia nectit:*
*Omnia perpetiar, lethum quoque, dum semel omnis*
*Noster in extincto moriatur pectore sensus.—*
*Ergo tuos oculos nunquam, mea vita, videbo,*
*Et tua perpetuus sepelivit lumina somnus?*
*Emoriar tecum: sic, sic juvat ire sub umbras.—*
*At tamen absistam properato cedere letho,*
*Ne mortem vindicta tuam tam nulla sequatur.*    80
[Here he throws it from him and bears the body away.


## SCENE VI

### Ghost of Andrea, Revenge.

*Andrea.* Brought'st thou me hither to increase my pain?
    I look'd that Balthazar should have been slain:
    But 'tis my friend Horatio that is slain,
    And they abuse fair Bellimperia,

67–80] Compound for me all herbs that the fair spring
    Breeds forth, to serve as salve unto my pain;
    Or bring me blossoms of oblivion.
    Myself will garner all fell seeds the sun
    Draws to the shores of light, and I will drink
    All venoms any sorceress can devise,
    And all the fatal poisons herbs provide;
    I will essay all these, until at once
    All senses perish in my dying breast.—
    So then shall I ne'er see thy face, dear son,
    And shall eternal darkness cover thee?
    With thee I'll die: thus would I pass the bourne.—
    No, no! I will not yield my life so soon,
    Lest so thy death should lack its due revenge.

On whom I doted more than all the world,
Because she lov'd me more than all the world.
*Revenge.* Thou talkest of harvest, when the corn is
    green:
    The end is crown of every work well done;
    The sickle comes not, till the corn be ripe.
    Be still; and ere I lead thee from this place,     10
    I'll show thee Balthazar in heavy case.

## ACTUS TERTIUS

### SCENE I

*Enter* Viceroy of Portingal, Nobles, Alexandro,
Villuppo.

*Vic.* Infortunate condition of kings,
    Seated amidst so many helpless doubts!
    First we are plac'd upon extremest height,
    And oft supplanted with exceeding hate,
    But ever subject to the wheel of chance;
    And at our highest never joy we so,
    As we both doubt and dread our overthrow.
    So striveth not the waves with sundry winds,
    As Fortune toileth in the affairs of kings,
    That would be fear'd, yet fear to be beloved,    10
    Sith fear or love to kings is flattery.
    For instance, lordings, look upon your king,
    By hate deprived of his dearest son,
    The only hope of our successive line.
*Nob.* I had not thought that Alexandro's heart
    Had been envenom'd with such extreme hate;
    But now I see that words have several works,
    And there's no credit in the countenance.
*Vil.* No; for, my lord, had you beheld the train,

vi. 11 heavy case] sad plight        III. i. Heading.
Alexandro] *Though named here he does not enter until line 30.*
14 successive line] line of succession    19 train] deceitful
expression

That feigned love had coloured in his looks,      20
When he in camp consorted Balthazar,
Far more inconstant had you thought the sun,
That hourly coasts the centre of the earth,
Than Alexandro's purpose to the prince.
*Vic.* No more, Villuppo, thou hast said enough,
And with thy words thou slayest our wounded
      thoughts;
Nor shall I longer dally with the world,
Procrastinating Alexandro's death:
Go some of you, and fetch the traitor forth,
That, as he is condemned, he may die.      30

*Enter* Alexandro, *with a* Nobleman *and halberts.*

*Nob.* In such extremes will nought but patience serve.
*Alex.* But in extremes what patience shall I use?
Nor discontents it me to leave the world,
With whom there nothing can prevail but wrong.
*Nob.* Yet hope the best.
*Alex.*                          'Tis heaven is my hope:
As for the earth, it is too much infect
To yield me hope of any of her mould.
*Vic.* Why linger ye? bring forth that daring fiend,
And let him die for his accursed deed.
*Alex.* Not that I fear the extremity of death      40
(For nobles cannot stoop to servile fear)
Do I, O king, thus discontented live.
But this, O this, torments my labouring soul,
That thus I die suspected of a sin,
Whereof, as heavens have known my secret thoughts,
So am I free from this suggestion.
*Vic.* No more, I say! to the tortures! when!
Bind him, and burn his body in those flames,
                    [*They bind him to the stake.*

20 coloured] imitated          23 coasts] keeps close to
(*Boas*)          36 infect] infected, corrupt          47 when]
*An exclamation of impatience.*

That shall prefigure those unquenched fires
Of Phlegethon, prepared for his soul.                    50
*Alex.* My guiltless death will be aveng'd on thee,
   On thee, Villuppo, that hath malic'd thus,
   Or for thy meed hast falsely me accus'd.
*Vil.* Nay, Alexandro, if thou menace me,
   I'll lend a hand to send thee to the lake,
   Where those thy words shall perish with thy works:
   Injurious traitor! monstrous homicide!

### *Enter* Ambassador.

*Amb.* Stay, hold a while,
   And here, with pardon of his majesty,
   Lay hands upon Villuppo.
*Vic.*                          Ambassador,          60
   What news hath urg'd this sudden entrance?
*Amb.* Know, sovereign lord, that Balthazar doth live.
*Vic.* What sayest thou? liveth Balthazar our son?
*Amb.* Your highness' son, Lord Balthazar, doth live;
   And, well entreated in the court of Spain,
   Humbly commends him to your majesty.
   These eyes beheld, and these my followers;
   With these, the letters of the king's commends
                             [*Gives him letters.*
   Are happy witnesses of his highness' health.
            [*The King looks on the letters, and proceeds.*
*Vic. Thy son doth live, your tribute is receiv'd;*      70
   *Thy peace is made, and we are satisfied.*
   *The rest resolve upon as things propos'd*
   *For both our honours and thy benefit.*
*Amb.* These are his highness' farther articles.
                     [*He gives him more letters.*
*Vic.* Accursed wretch, to intimate these ills
   Against the life and reputation
   Of noble Alexandro! Come, my lord, unbind him:

52 malic'd] acted maliciously          53 meed] profit
55 lake] *sc. of Hell; see* III. xii. 11.    65 entreated] treated

Let him unbind thee, that is bound to death,
To make a quital for thy discontent.
                                        [*They unbind him.*

*Alex.* Dread lord, in kindness you could do no less, 80
Upon report of such a damned fact;
But thus we see our innocence hath sav'd
The hopeless life which thou, Villuppo, sought
By thy suggestions to have massacred.
*Vic.* Say, false Villuppo, wherefore didst thou thus
Falsely betray Lord Alexandro's life?
Him, whom thou knowest that no unkindness else,
But even the slaughter of our dearest son,
Could once have moved us to have misconceived.
*Alex.* Say, treacherous Villuppo, tell the king:    90
Wherein hath Alexandro used thee ill?
*Vil.* Rent with remembrance of so foul a deed,
My guilty soul submits me to thy doom:
For not for Alexandro's injuries,
But for reward and hope to be preferr'd,
Thus have I shamelessly hazarded his life.
*Vic.* Which, villain, shall be ransomed with thy death,
And not so mean a torment as we here
Devis'd for him who, thou said'st, slew our son,
But with the bitterest torments and extremes    100
That may be yet invented for thine end.
                        [Alexandro *seems to entreat.*
Entreat me not! go, take the traitor hence.
                                        [*Exit* Villuppo.
And, Alexandro, let us honour thee
With public notice of thy loyalty.
To end those things articulated here
By our great lord, the mighty King of Spain,
We with our Council will deliberate.
Come, Alexandro, keep us company.        [*Exeunt.*

    79 quital] requital        81 fact] deed

## SCENE II

*Enter* Hieronimo.

*Hier.* O eyes, no eyes, but fountains fraught with tears;
  O life, no life, but lively form of death;
  O world, no world, but mass of public wrongs,
  Confus'd and fill'd with murder and misdeeds!
  O sacred heavens! if this unhallowed deed,
  If this inhuman and barbarous attempt,
  If this incomparable murder thus
  Of mine, but now no more my son,
  Shall unreveal'd and unrevenged pass,
  How should we term your dealings to be just,    10
  If you unjustly deal with those that in your justice
    trust?
  The night, sad secretary to my moans,
  With direful visions wake my vexed soul,
  And with the wounds of my distressful son
  Solicits me for notice of his death.
  The ugly fiends do sally forth of hell,
  And frame my steps to unfrequented paths,
  And fear my heart with fierce inflamed thoughts.
  The cloudy day my discontents records,
  Early begins to register my dreams,    20
  And drive me forth to seek the murtherer.
  Eyes, life, world, heavens, hell, night, and day,
  See, search, show, send some man, some mean, that
    may—
                              [*A letter falleth.*
  What's here? a letter? tush! it is not so!—
  A letter written to Hieronimo!    [*Red ink.*
  *For want of ink, receive this bloody writ:*
  *Me hath my hapless brother hid from thee;*
  *Revenge thyself on Balthazar and him,*
  *For these were they that murdered thy son.*
  *Hieronimo, revenge Horatio's death,*    30

      18 fear] frighten        27 hapless] unhappy

*And better fare than Bellimperia doth.*
What means this unexpected miracle?
My son slain by Lorenzo and the prince!
What cause had they Horatio to malign?
Or what might move thee, Bellimperia,
To accuse thy brother, had he been the mean?
Hieronimo, beware!—thou art betray'd,
And to entrap thy life this train is laid.
Advise thee therefore, be not credulous:
This is devised to endanger thee,                    40
That thou, by this, Lorenzo shouldst accuse.
And he, for thy dishonour done, should draw
Thy life in question and thy name in hate.
Dear was the life of my beloved son,
And of his death behoves me be reveng'd:
Then hazard not thine own, Hieronimo,
But live t' effect thy resolution.
I therefore will by circumstances try
What I can gather to confirm this writ;
And, hearkening near the Duke of Castile's house, 50
Close, if I can, with Bellimperia,
To listen more, but nothing to bewray.

### *Enter* Pedringano.

Now, Pedringano!
*Ped.*                     Now, Hieronimo!
*Hier.* Where's thy lady?
*Ped.*                          I know not; here's my lord.

### *Enter* Lorenzo.

*Lor.* How now, who's this? Hieronimo?
*Hier.*                                      My lord.
*Ped.* He asketh for my lady Bellimperia.
*Lor.* What to do, Hieronimo?  The duke, my father,
    hath,
Upon some disgrace, awhile remov'd her hence;

34 malign] hate        51 Close . . . with] meet secretly

But if it be ought I may inform her of,
Tell me, Hieronimo, and I'll let her know it.    50
*Hier.* Nay, nay, my lord, I thank you; it shall not need.
I had a suit unto her, but too late,
And her disgrace makes me unfortunate.
*Lor.* Why so, Hieronimo, use me.
*Hier.* Oh no, my lord; I dare not; it must not be,
I humbly thank your lordship.
*Lor.*                                    Why then, farewell.
*Hier.* My grief no heart, my thoughts no tongue can
tell.                                        [*Exit.*
*Lor.* Come hither, Pedringano, see'st thou this?
*Ped.* My lord, I see it, and suspect it too.
*Lor.* This is that damned villain Serberine,    70
That hath, I fear, reveal'd Horatio's death.
*Ped.* My lord, he could not, 'twas so lately done;
And since, he hath not left my company.
*Lor.* Admit he have not, his condition's such,
As fear or flattering words may make him false.
I know his humour, and therewith repent
That e'er I us'd him in this enterprise.
But, Pedringano, to prevent the worst,
And 'cause I know thee secret as my soul,
Here, for thy further satisfaction, take thou this,    80
                        [*Gives him more gold.*
And hearken to me—thus it is devis'd:
This night thou must (and, prithee, so resolve)
Meet Serberine at Saint Luigi's Park—
Thou knowest 'tis here hard by behind the house—
There take thy stand, and see thou strike him sure;
For die he must, if we do mean to live.
*Ped.* But how shall Serberine be there, my lord?
*Lor.* Let me alone; I'll send to him to meet
The prince and me, where thou must do this deed.
*Ped.* It shall be done, my lord, it shall be done;    90

64 so] in that case        65–6] *For these lines the Second
Addition was substituted in 1602; see p.* 231.        74 condition]
station

And I'll go arm myself to meet him there.

*Lor.* When things shall alter, as I hope they will,
  Then shalt thou mount for this; thou knowest my
    mind.                              [*Exit* Pedringano.
  *Che le Ieron!*

*Enter* Page.

*Page.*             My lord?
*Lor.*                           Go, sirrah, to Serberine,
  And bid him forthwith meet the prince and me
  At Saint Luigi's Park, behind the house;
  This evening, boy!
*Page.*             I go, my lord.
*Lor.* But, sirrah, let the hour be eight o'clock:
  Bid him not fail.
*Page.*             I fly, my lord.             [*Exit.*
*Lor.* Now to confirm the complot thou hast cast   100
  Of all these practices, I'll spread the watch,
  Upon precise commandment from the king,
  Strongly to guard the place where Pedringano
  This night shall murder hapless Serberine.
  Thus must we work that will avoid distrust;
  Thus must we practise to prevent mishap,
  And thus one ill another must expulse.
  This sly enquiry of Hieronimo
  For Bellimperia breeds suspicion,
  And this suspicion bodes a further ill.          110
  As for myself, I know my secret fault,
  And so do they; but I have dealt for them:
  They that for coin their souls endangered,
  To save my life, for coin shall venture theirs;
  And better it's that base companions die,
  Than by their life to hazard our good haps.

94 *Che le Ieron*] '*An unintelligible expression, possibly a cor-
ruption of the page's name*' (*Boas*).        100 complot] con-
spiracy        101 practices] tricks        107 expulse]
expel        112 dealt for] provided against        115 base
companions] low fellows

Nor shall they live, for me to fear their faith:
I'll trust myself, myself shall be my friend;
For die they shall, slaves are ordain'd to no other
   end.                                    [*Exit.*

## SCENE III

*Enter* Pedringano *with a pistol.*

*Ped.* Now, Pedringano, bid thy pistol hold;
   And hold on, Fortune! once more favour me,
   Give but success to mine attempting spirit,
   And let me shift for taking of mine aim!
   Here is the gold, this is the gold propos'd;
   It is no dream that I adventure for,
   But Pedringano is possess'd thereof.
   And he that would not strain his conscience
   For him that thus his liberal purse hath stretch'd,
   Unworthy such a favour, may he fail,             10
   And, wishing, want, when such as I prevail.
   As for the fear of apprehension,
   I know, if need should be, my noble lord
   Will stand between me and ensuing harms:
   Besides, this place is free from all suspect.
   Here therefore will I stay and take my stand.

*Enter the* Watch.

1. I wonder much to what intent it is
   That we are thus expressly charg'd to watch.
2. 'Tis by commandment in the king's own name.
3. But we were never wont to watch and ward       20
   So near the duke, his brother's, house before.
2. Content yourself, stand close, there's somewhat
   in't.

*Enter* Serberine.

*Ser.* Here, Serberine, attend and stay thy pace,
   For here did Don Lorenzo's page appoint

   4 let me shift] trust me        22 close] concealed

That thou by his command should'st meet with him.
How fit a place, if one were so dispos'd,
Methinks this corner is to close with one.
*Ped.* Here comes the bird that I must seize upon;
Now, Pedringano, or never, play the man!
*Ser.* I wonder that his lordship stays so long,      30
Or wherefore should he send for me so late?
*Ped.* For this, Serberine!—and thou shalt ha't.

                        *[Shoots the dag.*
So, there he lies; my promise is perform'd.

### *The* Watch.

1. Hark, gentlemen, this is a pistol shot.
2. And here's one slain; stay the murderer.
*Ped.* Now by the sorrows of the souls in hell,
               *[He strives with the* Watch.
Who first lays hand on me, I'll be his priest.
3. Sirrah, confess, and therein play the priest,
   Why hast thou thus unkindly kill'd the man?
*Ped.* Why? because he walk'd abroad so late.      40
3. Come, sir, you had been better kept your bed,
Than have committed this misdeed so late.
2. Come, to the Marshal's with the murderer!
1. On to Hieronimo's! help me here
To bring the murder'd body with us too.
*Ped.* Hieronimo? carry me before whom you will:
Whate'er he be, I'll answer him and you;
And do your worst, for I defy you all.      *[Exeunt.*


### SCENE IV

#### *Enter* Lorenzo *and* Balthazar.

*Bal.* How now, my lord, what makes you rise so soon?
*Lor.* Fear of preventing our mishaps too late.

   27 close with] meet secretly      32 s.d. *dag*] pistol
39 unkindly] unnaturally, inhumanly

*Bal.* What mischief is it that we not mistrust?

*Lor.* Our greatest ills we least mistrust, my lord,
And unexpected harms do hurt us most.

*Bal.* Why, tell me, Don Lorenzo, tell me, man,
If ought concerns our honour and your own.

*Lor.* Nor you, nor me, my lord, but both in one:
For I suspect, and the presumption's great,
That by those base confederates in our fault,      10
Touching the death of Don Horatio,
We are betray'd to old Hieronimo.

*Bal.* Betray'd, Lorenzo? tush, it cannot be.

*Lor.* A guilty conscience, urged with the thought
Of former evils, easily cannot err:
I am persuaded, and dissuade me not,
That all's revealed to Hieronimo.
And therefore know that I have cast it thus—

*Enter* Page.

But here's the page. How now, what news with
thee?

*Page.* My lord, Serberine is slain.                20

*Bal.* Who? Serberine, my man?

*Page.* Your highness' man, my lord.

*Lor.* Speak, page, who murdered him?

*Page.* He that is apprehended for the fact.

*Lor.* Who?

*Page.* Pedringano.

*Bal.* Is Serberine slain, that lov'd his lord so well?
Injurious villain, murderer of his friend!

*Lor.* Hath Pedringano murdered Serberine?
My lord, let me entreat you to take the pains      30
To exasperate and hasten his revenge
With your complaints unto my lord the king.
This their dissension breeds a greater doubt.

*Bal.* Assure thee, Don Lorenzo, he shall die,

3, 4 mistrust] suspect      18 cast] schemed      24 fact]
deed      31 exasperate] make harsher

Or else his highness hardly shall deny.
Meanwhile I'll haste the Marshal-Sessions:
For die he shall for this his damned deed.

[*Exit* Balthazar.

*Lor.* Why so, this fits our former policy,
And thus experience bids the wise to deal.
I lay the plot: he prosecutes the point;        40
I set the trap: he breaks the worthless twigs,
And sees not that wherewith the bird was lim'd.
Thus hopeful men, that mean to hold their own,
Must look like fowlers to their dearest friends.
He runs to kill whom I have holp to catch,
And no man knows it was my reaching fatch.
'Tis hard to trust unto a multitude,
Or any one, in mine opinion,
When men themselves their secrets will reveal.

*Enter a* Messenger *with a letter.*

Boy!                                             50
*Page.* My lord?
*Lor.* What's he?
*Mes.*              I have a letter to your lordship.
*Lor.* From whence?
*Mes.*              From Pedringano that's imprisoned.
*Lor.* So he is in prison then?
*Mes.*                          Ay, my good lord.
*Lor.* What would he with us? He writes us here,
*To stand good lord, and help him in distress.*
Tell him I have letters, know his mind;
And what we may, let him assure him of.
Fellow, begone: my boy shall follow thee.

[*Exit* Messenger.

This works like wax; yet once more try thy wits. 60
Boy, go, convey this purse to Pedringano;
Thou knowest the prison, closely give it him,

35 hardly shall deny] shall find it hard to refuse    45
holp] helped      46 fatch] fetch, *i.e.* stratagem    62
closely] secretly

And be advis'd that none be there about:
Bid him be merry still, but secret;
And though the Marshal-Sessions be today,
Bid him not doubt of his delivery.
Tell him his pardon is already sign'd,
And thereon bid him boldly be resolved:
For, were he ready to be turned off—
As 'tis my will the uttermost be tried—      70
Thou with his pardon shalt attend him still.
Show him this box, tell him his pardon's in't;
But open't not, an if thou lovest thy life;
But let him wisely keep his hopes unknown:
He shall not want while Don Lorenzo lives.
Away!
*Page.*      I go, my lord, I run.
*Lor.* But, sirrah, see that this be cleanly done.
                                    [*Exit* Page.
Now stands our fortune on a tickle point,
And now or never ends Lorenzo's doubts.
One only thing is uneffected yet,      80
And that's to see the executioner.
But to what end? I list not trust the air
With utterance of our pretence therein,
For fear the privy whisp'ring of the wind
Convey our words amongst unfriendly ears,
That lie too open to advantages.
*E quel che voglio io, nessun lo sa;*
*Intendo io: quel mi basterà.*      [*Exit.*

## SCENE V

*Enter* Boy, *with the box.*

*Boy.* My master hath forbidden me to look in this box;
    and by my troth 'tis likely, if he had not warned

69 turned off] hanged (*so in* III. vi. 54, 110)      78
tickle] precarious, 'ticklish'
    87–8] What my intent is, that no man doth know;
        'Tis in my mind, and it is better so.

me, I should not have had so much idle time; for
we men's-kind, in our minority, are like women in
their uncertainty: that they are most forbidden,
they will soonest attempt: so I now.——By my
bare honesty, here's nothing but the bare empty
box: were it not sin against secrecy, I would say
it were a piece of gentlemanlike knavery.  I must
go to Pedringano, and tell him his pardon is in
this box; nay, I would have sworn it, had I not
seen the contrary.  I cannot choose but smile to
think how the villain will flout the gallows, scorn
the audience, and descant on the hangman, and
all presuming of his pardon from hence.  Will't
not be an odd jest for me to stand and grace every
jest he makes, pointing my finger at this box, as
who would say, "Mock on, here's thy warrant."
Is't not a scurvy jest that a man should jest himself to death?  Alas, poor Pedringano, I am in a
sort sorry for thee; but if I should be hanged with
thee, I cannot weep.                    [*Exit.* 22

## SCENE VI

*Enter* Hieronimo *and the* Deputy.

*Hier.* Thus must we toil in other men's extremes,
That know not how to remedy our own;
And do them justice, when unjustly we,
For all our wrongs, can compass no redress.
But shall I never live to see the day,
That I may come, by justice of the heavens,
To know the cause that may my cares allay?
This toils my body, this consumeth age,
That only I to all men just must be,
And neither gods nor men be just to me.          10
*Dep.* Worthy Hieronimo, your office asks
A care to punish such as do transgress.
*Hier.* So is't my duty to regard his death

Who, when he lived, deserved my dearest blood.
But come, for that we came for: let's begin;
For here lies that which bids me to be gone.

*Enter* Officers, Boy, *and* Pedringano, *with a letter in his hand, bound.*

*Dep.* Bring forth the prisoner, for the court is set.
*Ped.* Gramercy, boy, but it was time to come;
For I had written to my lord anew
A nearer matter that concerneth him,                    20
For fear his lordship had forgotten me.
But sith he hath remember'd me so well—
Come, come, come on, when shall we to this gear?
*Hier.* Stand forth, thou monster, murderer of men,
And here, for satisfaction of the world,
Confess thy folly, and repent thy fault;
For there's thy place of execution.
*Ped.* This is short work: well, to your Marshalship
First I confess, nor fear I death therefore,
I am the man, 'twas I slew Serberine.                   30
But, sir, then you think this shall be the place
Where we shall satisfy you for this gear?
*Dep.* Ay, Pedringano.
*Ped.*                    Now I think not so.
*Hier.* Peace, impudent, for thou shalt find it so:
For blood with blood shall, while I sit as judge,
Be satisfied, and the law discharg'd.
And though myself cannot receive the like,
Yet will I see that others have their right.
Despatch: the fault's approved and confess'd,
And by our law he is condemn'd to die.                  40
*Hangm.* Come on, sir, are you ready?
*Ped.* To do what, my fine, officious knave?
*Hangm.* To go to this gear.
*Ped.* O sir, you are too forward: thou wouldst fain fur-
nish me with a halter, to disfurnish me of my habit.

23, 32, 43 gear] business        45 habit] clothes (*which
became the hangman's perquisite*)

So I should go out of this gear, my raiment, into
that gear, the rope. But, hangman, now I spy your
knavery, I'll not change without boot, that's flat.

*Hangm.* Come, sir.

*Ped.* So, then, I must up?  50

*Hangm.* No remedy.

*Ped.* Yes, but there shall be for my coming down.

*Hangm.* Indeed, here's a remedy for that.

*Ped.* How? be turn'd off?

*Hangm.* Ay, truly; come, are you ready? I pray, sir,
despatch; the day goes away.

*Ped.* What, do you hang by the hour? if you do, I may
chance to break your old custom.

*Hangm.* Faith, you have reason; for I am like to break
your young neck.  60

*Ped.* Dost thou mock me, hangman? pray God, I be
not preserved to break your knave's pate for this.

*Hangm.* Alas, sir, you are a foot too low to reach it, and
I hope you will never grow so high while I am
in the office.

*Ped.* Sirrah, dost see yonder boy with the box in his
hand?

*Hangm.* What, he that points to it with his finger?

*Ped.* Ay, that, companion.

*Hangm.* I know him not; but what of him?  70

*Ped.* Dost thou think to live till his old doublet will
make thee a new truss?

*Hangm.* Ay, and many a fair year after, to truss up
many an honester man than either thou or he.

*Ped.* What hath he in his box, as thou think'st?

*Hangm.* Faith, I cannot tell, nor I care not greatly.
Methinks you should rather hearken to your soul's
health.

*Ped.* Why, sirrah hangman, I take it that that is good
for the body is likewise good for the soul: and it
may be, in that box is balm for both.  81

48 boot] profit        69 companion] low fellow

*Hangm.* Well, thou art even the merriest piece of man's
flesh that e'er groan'd at my office door!

*Ped.* Is your roguery become an office with a knave's
name?

*Hangm.* Ay, and that shall all they witness that see
you scal it with a thief's name.

*Ped.* I prithee, request this good company to pray
with me.

*Hangm.* Ay, marry, sir, this is a good motion: my
masters, you see here's a good fellow.                91

*Ped.* Nay, nay, now I remember me, let them alone
till some other time; for now I have no great need.

*Hier.* I have not seen a wretch so impudent!
O monstrous times, where murder's set so light,
And where the soul, that should be shrin'd in
heaven,
Solely delights in interdicted things,
Still wand'ring in the thorny passages,
That intercepts itself of happiness.
Murder! O bloody monster! God forbid         100
A fault so foul should 'scape unpunished.
Despatch, and see this execution done!—
This makes me to remember thee, my son.
                              [*Exit* Hieronimo.

*Ped.* Nay, soft, no haste.

*Dep.* Why, wherefore stay you? Have you hope of
life?

*Ped.* Why, ay!

*Hangm.* As how?

*Ped.* Why, rascal, by my pardon from the king.

*Hangm.* Stand you on that? then you shall off with this.
                              [*He turns him off.*

*Dep.* So, executioner;—convey him hence;         110
But let his body be unburied:
Let not the earth be choked or infect
With that which heaven contemns, and men neglect.
                              [*Exeunt.*

109 Stand] count, depend

## SCENE VII

*Enter* Hieronimo.

*Hier.* Where shall I run to breathe abroad my woes,
My woes, whose weight hath wearied the earth?
Or mine exclaims, that have surcharged the air
With ceaseless plaints for my deceased son?
The blust'ring winds, conspiring with my words,
At my lament have moved the leafless trees,
Disrob'd the meadows of their flower'd green,
Made mountains marsh with spring-tides of my
     tears,
And broken through the brazen gates of hell.
Yet still tormented is my tortured soul          10
With broken sighs and restless passions,
That winged mount, and, hovering in the air,
Beat at the windows of the brightest heavens,
Soliciting for justice and revenge:
But they are plac'd in those empyreal heights,
Where, countermur'd with walls of diamond,
I find the place impregnable; and they
Resist my woes, and give my words no way.

*Enter* Hangman *with a letter.*

*Hangm.* O lord, sir! God bless you, sir! the man, sir,
     Petergade, sir, he that was so full of merry
     conceits—                                    21
*Hier.* Well, what of him?
*Hangm.* O lord, sir, he went the wrong way; the fellow
     had a fair commission to the contrary. Sir, here is
     his passport; I pray you, sir, we have done him
     wrong.
*Hier.* I warrant thee, give it me.
*Hangm.* You will stand between the gallows and me?

3 exclaims] outcries          16 countermur'd] double-
walled        21 conceits] jests

*Hier.* Ay, ay.

*Hangm.* I thank your Lord Worship. [*Exit* Hangman.

*Hier.* And yet, though somewhat nearer me concerns,
    I will, to ease the grief that I sustain,    32
    Take truce with sorrow while I read on this.
    *My lord, I write as mine extremes requir'd,*
    *That you would labour my delivery;*
    *If you neglect, my life is desperate,*
    *And in my death I shall reveal the troth.*
    *You know, my lord, I slew him for your sake,*
    *And was confederate with the prince and you;*
    *Won by rewards and hopeful promises,*    40
    *I holp to murder Don Horatio too.*
    Holp he to murder mine Horatio?
    And actors in th' accursed tragedy
    Wast thou, Lorenzo, Balthazar and thou,
    Of whom my son, my son deserved so well?
    What have I heard, what have mine eyes beheld?
    O sacred heavens, may it come to pass
    That such a monstrous and detested deed,
    So closely smother'd, and so long conceal'd,
    Shall thus by this be venged or reveal'd!    50
    Now see I what I durst not then suspect,
    That Bellimperia's letter was not feign'd.
    Nor feigned she, though falsely they have wrong'd
    Both her, myself, Horatio, and themselves.
    Now may I make compare, 'twixt hers and this,
    Of every accident I ne'er could find
    Till now, and now I feelingly perceive
    They did what heaven unpunish'd would not leave.
    O false Lorenzo! are these thy flattering looks?
    Is this the honour that thou didst my son?    60
    And Balthazar, bane to thy soul and me,

41 holp] helped    49 smother'd] kept secret    52
feign'd] forged. *He is relieved of two doubts (see* III. ii. 1–52*),
whether or not Bellimperia really wrote the letter, and if so whether
or not she was telling the truth.*    56 accident] occurrence
find] understand

Was this the ransom he reserv'd thee for?
Woe to the cause of these constrained wars!
Woe to thy baseness and captivity!
Woe to thy birth, thy body and thy soul,
Thy cursed father, and thy conquered self!
And bann'd with bitter execrations be
The day and place where he did pity thee!
But wherefore waste I mine unfruitful words,
When naught but blood will satisfy my woes?      70
I will go plain me to my lord the king,
And cry aloud for justice through the court,
Wearing the flints with these my withered feet,
And either purchase justice by entreats,
Or tire them all with my revenging threats. [*Exit.*

### SCENE VIII

*Enter* Isabella *and her* Maid.

*Isab.* So that, you say, this herb will purge the eye,
   And this, the head?
   Ah, but none of them will purge the heart!
   No, there's no medicine left for my disease,
   Nor any physic to recure the dead.
                              [*She runs lunatic.*
   Horatio! O, where's Horatio?
*Maid.* Good madam, affright not thus yourself
   With outrage for your son Horatio:
   He sleeps in quiet in the Elysian fields.
*Isab.* Why, did I not give you gowns and goodly
      things,                                    10
   Bought you a whistle and a whipstalk too,
   To be revenged on their villainies?
*Maid.* Madam, these humours do torment my soul.
*Isab.* My soul—poor soul, thou talk'st of things

5 recure] cure      8 outrage] outcry      11 whipstalk]
whip-handle

Thou know'st not what—my soul hath silver wings,
That mounts me up unto the highest heavens;
To heaven: ay, there sits my Horatio,
Back'd with a troop of fiery Cherubins,
Dancing about his newly healed wounds,
Singing   sweet   hymns   and   chanting   heavenly
    notes:                                                    20
Rare harmony to greet his innocence,
That died, ay died, a mirror in our days.
But say, where shall I find the men, the murderers,
That slew Horatio? Whither shall I run
To find them out that murdered my son? [*Exeunt.*

## SCENE IX

#### Bellimperia *at a window.*

*Bel.* What means this outrage that is offered me?
    Why am I thus sequester'd from the court?
    No notice!—Shall I not know the cause
    Of these my secret and suspicious ills?
    Accursed brother, unkind murderer,
    Why bends thou thus thy mind to martyr me?
    Hieronimo, why writ I of thy wrongs,
    Or why art thou so slack in thy revenge?
    Andrea, O Andrea! that thou sawest
    Me for thy friend Horatio handled thus,          10
    And him for me thus causeless murdered!
    Well, force perforce, I must constrain myself
    To patience, and apply me to the time,
    Till heaven, as I have hoped, shall set me free.

#### *Enter* Christophil.

*Chris.* Come, madam Bellimperia, this may not be.
                                                    [*Exeunt.*

13 apply me] conform myself

## SCENE X

*Enter* Lorenzo, Balthazar, *and the* Page.

*Lor.* Boy, talk no further; thus far things go well.
　Thou art assur'd that thou sawest him dead?
*Page.* Or else, my lord, I live not.
*Lor.*　　　　　　　　　　　　That's enough.
　As for his resolution in his end,
　Leave that to him with whom he sojourns now.
　Here, take my ring and give it Christophil,
　And bid him let my sister be enlarg'd,
　And bring her hither straight.　　　[*Exit* Page.
　This that I did was for a policy,
　To smooth and keep the murder secret,　　　10
　Which, as a nine-days' wonder, being o'erblown,
　My gentle sister will I now enlarge.
*Bal.* And time, Lorenzo: for my lord the duke,
　You heard, enquired for her yester-night.
*Lor.* Why, and my lord, I hope you heard me say
　Sufficient reason why she kept away;
　But that's all one. My lord, you love her?
*Bal.*　　　　　　　　　　　　　　　　Ay.
*Lor.* Then in your love beware; deal cunningly:
　Salve all suspicions, only soothe me up;
　And if she hap to stand on terms with us,　　20
　As for her sweetheart and concealment so,
　Jest with her gently: under feigned jest
　Are things conceal'd that else would breed unrest.—
　But here she comes.

### *Enter* Bellimperia.

　　　　　　　Now, sister—
*Bel.*　　　　　　　　　　　　Sister?—No!
　Thou art no brother, but an enemy;

　10 smooth] hush up　　19 soothe me up] confirm what
I say　　　20 on terms] at distance

Else wouldst thou not have used thy sister so:
First, to affright me with thy weapons drawn,
And with extremes abuse my company;
And then to hurry me, like whirlwind's rage,
Amidst a crew of thy confederates,　　　　30
And clap me up where none might come at me,
Nor I at any, to reveal my wrongs.
What madding fury did possess thy wits?
Or wherein is't that I offended thee?

*Lor.* Advise you better, Bellimperia,
For I have done you no disparagement;
Unless, by more discretion than deserv'd,
I sought to save your honour and mine own.

*Bel.* Mine honour? why, Lorenzo, wherein is't
That I neglect my reputation so,　　　　40
As you, or any, need to rescue it?

*Lor.* His highness and my father were resolv'd
To come confer with old Hieronimo,
Concerning certain matters of estate,
That by the viceroy was determined.

*Bel.* And wherein was mine honour touch'd in that?

*Bal.* Have patience, Bellimperia; hear the rest.

*Lor.* Me, next in sight, as messenger they sent,
To give him notice that they were so nigh:
Now when I came, consorted with the prince,　50
And unexpected, in an arbour there,
Found Bellimperia with Horatio—

*Bel.* How then?

*Lor.* Why, then, remembering that old disgrace,
Which you for Don Andrea had endur'd,
And now were likely longer to sustain,
By being found so meanly accompanied,
Thought rather—for I knew no readier mean—
To thrust Horatio forth my father's way.

*Bal.* And carry you obscurely somewhere else,　60

28 with extremes abuse my company] use fatal violence
to my companion (*Boas*)　　　35 Advise you] Think
44 estate] state

Lest that his highness should have found you there.

*Bel.* Even so, my lord? And you are witness
 That this is true which he entreateth of?
 You, gentle brother, forged this for my sake,
 And you, my lord, were made his instrument:
 A work of worth, worthy the noting too!
 But what's the cause that you conceal'd me since?

*Lor.* Your melancholy, sister, since the news
 Of your first favourite Don Andrea's death,
 My father's old wrath hath exasperate.          70

*Bal.* And better was't for you, being in disgrace,
 To absent yourself, and give his fury place.

*Bel.* But why had I no notice of his ire?

*Lor.* That were to add more fuel to your fire,
 Who burnt like Ætna for Andrea's loss.

*Bel.* Hath not my father then enquir'd for me?

*Lor.* Sister, he hath, and thus excus'd I thee.

                    [*He whispereth in her ear.*

 But, Bellimperia, see the gentle prince;
 Look on thy love, behold young Balthazar,
 Whose passions by thy presence are increas'd;   80
 And in whose melancholy thou mayest see
 Thy hate, his love; thy flight, his following thee.

*Bel.* Brother, you are become an orator—
 I know not, I, by what experience—
 Too politic for me, past all compare,
 Since last I saw you; but content yourself:
 The prince is meditating higher things.

*Bal.* 'Tis of thy beauty then, that conquers kings;
 Of those thy tresses, Ariadne's twines,
 Wherewith my liberty thou hast surpris'd;        90
 Of that thine ivory front, my sorrow's map,
 Wherein I see no haven to rest my hope.

*Bel.* To love and fear, and both at once, my lord,
 In my conceit, are things of more import
 Than women's wits are to be busied with.

63 entreateth] treats, speaks    70 exasperate] made
harsher    91 front] forehead    94 conceit] judgement

*Bal.* 'Tis I that love.

*Bel.*                    Whom?

*Bal.*                              Bellimperia.

*Bel.* But I that fear.

*Bal.*                    Whom?

*Bel.*                              Bellimperia.

*Lor.* Fear yourself?

*Bel.*                    Ay, brother.

*Lor.*                              How?

*Bel.*                                        As those
That what they love are loath and fear to lose.

*Bal.* Then, fair, let Balthazar your keeper be.        100

*Bel.* No, Balthazar doth fear as well as we:
   *Et tremulo metui pavidum junxere timorem,*
    *Et vanum stolidae proditionis opus.*        [*Exit.*

*Lor.* Nay, an you argue things so cunningly,
We'll go continue this discourse at court.

*Bal.* Led by the loadstar of her heavenly looks,
Wends poor, oppressed Balthazar,
As o'er the mountains walks the wanderer,
Incertain to effect his pilgrimage.        [*Exeunt.*


## SCENE XI

*Enter two* Portingals, *and* Hieronimo *meets them.*

1. By your leave, sir.

*Hier.* Good leave have you: nay, I pray you go,
For I'll leave you, if you can leave me so.

2. Pray you, which is the next way to my lord the
duke's?

*Hier.* The next way from me.

1.                                        To his house, we mean.

102–3] They joined to trembling fright a quivering fear,
    A futile act of blockish self-betrayal.

1–2] *Between these lines the Third Addition was inserted in 1602;
see p.* 231.        4 next] shortest

*Hier.* O, hard by: 'tis yon house that you see.

2. You could not tell us if his son were there?

*Hier.* Who, my Lord Lorenzo?

1.                                            Ay, sir.

*He goeth in at one door and comes out at another.*

*Hier.*                                            O, forbear!

For other talk for us far fitter were.

But if you be importunate to know                    10

The way to him, and where to find him out,

Then list to me, and I'll resolve your doubt.

There is a path upon your left-hand side,

That leadeth from a guilty conscience

Unto a forest of distrust and fear,

A darksome place, and dangerous to pass:

There shall you meet with melancholy thoughts,

Whose baleful humours if you but uphold,

It will conduct you to Despair and Death:

Whose rocky cliffs when you have once beheld,    20

Within a hugy dale of lasting night,

That, kindled with the world's iniquities,

Doth cast up filthy and detested fumes:—

Not far from thence, where murderers have built

A habitation for their cursed souls,

There, in a brazen cauldron, fix'd by Jove,

In his fell wrath, upon a sulphur flame,

Yourselves shall find Lorenzo bathing him

In boiling lead and blood of innocents.

1. Ha, ha, ha!

*Hier.*              Ha, ha, ha!                    30

Why, Ha, ha, ha! Farewell, good Ha, ha, ha!

                                            [*Exit.*

2. Doubtless this man is passing lunatic,

Or imperfection of his age doth make him dote.

Come, let's away to seek my lord the duke.

                                            [*Exeunt.*


12 resolve] decide        32 passing] very

## SCENE XII

*Enter* Hicronimo, *with a poniard in one hand and a rope in the other.*

*Hier.* Now, sir, perhaps I come and see the king;
  The king sees me, and fain would hear my suit:
  Why, is not this a strange and seld seen thing,
  That standers-by with toys should strike me mute?
  Go to, I see their shifts, and say no more.
  Hieronimo, 'tis time for thee to trudge:
  Down by the dale that flows with purple gore,
  Standeth a fiery tower; there sits a judge
  Upon a seat of steel and molten brass,
  And 'twixt his teeth he holds a fire-brand,      10
  That leads unto the lake where hell doth stand.
  Away, Hieronimo! to him be gone:
  He'll do thee justice for Horatio's death.
  Turn down this path: thou shalt be with him
      straight;
  Or this, and then thou need'st not take thy breath:
  This way or that way!—Soft and fair, not so:
  For if I hang or kill myself, let's know
  Who will revenge Horatio's murther then?
  No, no! fie, no! pardon me, I'll none of that.
                    [*He flings away the dagger and halter.*
  This way I'll take, and this way comes the king:  20
                    [*He takes them up again.*
  And here I'll have a fling at him, that's flat;
  And, Balthazar, I'll be with thee to bring,
  And thee, Lorenzo! Here's the king—nay, stay;
  And here, ay here—there goes the hare away.

4 toys] trivial excuses (*by which Lorenzo keeps him from the King*)    14–15 this path . . . Or this] *The poniard or the rope.*    22 be with thee to bring] chastise you, bring you to reason (*Boas*)    24 there goes the hare away] '*A proverbial phrase meaning* here the matter ends' (*Boas*).

*Enter* King, Ambassador, Castile, *and* Lorenzo.

*King.* Now show, ambassador, what our Viceroy saith:
  Hath he receiv'd the articles we sent?
*Hier.* Justice, O, justice to Hieronimo.
*Lor.* Back! see'st thou not the king is busy?
*Hier.* O, is he so?
*King.* Who is he that interrupts our business?          30
*Hier.* Not I.  Hieronimo, beware! go by, go by!
*Amb.* Renowned King, he hath received and read
  Thy kingly proffers, and thy promis'd league;
  And, as a man extremely overjoy'd
  To hear his son so princely entertain'd,
  Whose death he had so solemnly bewail'd,
  This for thy further satisfaction,
  And kingly love, he kindly lets thee know:
  First, for the marriage of his princely son
  With Bellimperia, thy beloved niece,                40
  The news are more delightful to his soul,
  Than myrrh or incense to the offended heavens.
  In person, therefore, will he come himself,
  To see the marriage rites solemnized,
  And, in the presence of the court of Spain,
  To knit a sure inextricable band
  Of kingly love and everlasting league
  Betwixt the crowns of Spain and Portingal.
  There will he give his crown to Balthazar,
  And make a queen of Bellimperia.                    50
*King.* Brother, how like you this our Viceroy's love?
*Cast.* No doubt, my lord, it is an argument
  Of honourable care to keep his friend,
  And wondrous zeal to Balthazar his son;
  Nor am I least indebted to his grace,
  That bends his liking to my daughter thus.
*Amb.* Now last, dread lord, here hath his highness sent
  (Although he send not that his son return)
  His ransom due to Don Horatio.

  31 go by] go unobserved, *i.e.* be careful

*Hier.* Horatio! who calls Horatio?                                    60
*King.* And well remember'd: thank his majesty.
   Here, see it given to Horatio.
*Hier.* Justice, O, justice, justice, gentle king!
*King.* Who is that? Hieronimo?
*Hier.* Justice, O, justice! O my son, my son!
   My son, whom naught can ransom or redeem!
*Lor.* Hieronimo, you are not well-advis'd.
*Hier.* Away, Lorenzo, hinder me no more;
   For thou hast made me bankrupt of my bliss.
   Give me my son! you shall not ransom him!    70
   Away! I'll rip the bowels of the earth,
                        [*He diggeth with his dagger.*
   And ferry over to th' Elysian plains,
   And bring my son to show his deadly wounds.
   Stand from about me!
   I'll make a pickaxe of my poniard,
   And here surrender up my Marshalship;
   For I'll go marshal up the fiends in hell,
   To be avenged on you all for this.
*King.* What means this outrage?
   Will none of you restrain his fury?                80
*Hier.* Nay, soft and fair! you shall not need to strive:
   For needs must he go that the devils drive.    [*Exit.*
*King.* What accident hath happ'd Hieronimo?
   I have not seen him to demean him so.
*Lor.* My gracious lord, he is with extreme pride,
   Conceived of young Horatio his son,
   And covetous of having to himself
   The ransom of the young prince Balthazar,
   Distract, and in a manner lunatic.
*King.* Believe me, nephew, we are sorry for't:    90
   This is the love that fathers bear their sons!
   But, gentle brother, go give to him this gold,
   The prince's ransom; let him have his due.
   For what he hath, Horatio shall not want;

   79 outrage] outcry, violent language    89, 96 Distract]
distracted

Haply Hieronimo hath need thereof.
*Lor.* But if he be thus helplessly distract,
　'Tis requisite his office be resign'd,
　And given to one of more discretion.
*King.* We shall increase his melancholy so.
　'Tis best that we see further in it first,　　　　　100
　Till when ourself will exempt him the place.
　And, brother, now bring in the ambassador,
　That he may be a witness of the match
　'Twixt Balthazar and Bellimperia,
　And that we may prefix a certain time,
　Wherein the marriage shall be solemnized,
　That we may have thy lord the Viceroy here.
*Amb.* Therein your highness highly shall content
　His majesty, that longs to hear from hence.
*King.* On, then, and hear you, lord ambassador.  110
　　　　　　　　　　　　　　　　　　　　[*Exeunt.*

## SCENE XIII

*Enter* Hieronimo, *with a book in his hand.*

*Vindicta mihi!*
Ay, heaven will be revenged of every ill;
Nor will they suffer murder unrepaid.
Then stay, Hieronimo, attend their will:
For mortal men may not appoint their time.
*Per scelus semper tutum est sceleribus iter.*
Strike, and strike home, where wrong is offer'd thee;
For evils unto ills conductors be,
And death's the worst of resolution.

110] *Between this scene and the next the Fourth Addition,
forming scene* XIIA, *was inserted in 1602; see p.* 233.　　1]
Revenge is due to me!　　4 attend their will] await their
pleasure　　6] Through crime is ever the safe way for
crime.　　9 death's the worst of resolution] resolute
action can at the worst end in death (*Boas*)

For he that thinks with patience to contend    10
To quiet life, his life shall easily end.
*Fata si miseros juvant, habes salutem:*
*Fata si vitam negant, habes sepulchrum.*
If destiny thy miseries do ease,
Then hast thou health, and happy shalt thou be:
If destiny deny thee life, Hieronimo,
Yet shalt thou be assured of a tomb:
If neither, yet let this thy comfort be:
Heaven covereth him that hath no burial.
And to conclude, I will revenge his death!    20
But how? not as the vulgar wits of men,
With open, but inevitable ills,
As by a secret, yet a certain mean,
Which under kindship will be cloaked best.
Wise men will take their opportunity
Closely and safely, fitting things to time.
But in extremes advantage hath no time;
And therefore all times fit not for revenge.
Thus therefore will I rest me in unrest,
Dissembling quiet in unquietness,    30
Not seeming that I know their villainies,
That my simplicity may make them think,
That ignorantly I will let all slip;
For ignorance, I wot, and well they know,
*Remedium malorum iners est.*
Nor ought avails it me to menace them
Who, as a wintry storm upon a plain,
Will bear me down with their nobility.
No, no, Hieronimo, thou must enjoin
Thine eyes to observation, and thy tongue    40
To milder speeches than thy spirit affords,
Thy heart to patience, and thy hands to rest,

12–13] If Fates befriend a wretch, thou hast a refuge;
     If Fates deny thee life, thou hast a tomb.
24 kindship] kindness       26 Closely] With secrecy
35] It is an idle remedy for ills.

Thy cap to courtesy, and thy knee to bow,
Till to revenge thou know, when, where and how.
                              [*A noise within.*
How now, what noise? what coil is that you keep?

*Enter a* Servant.

*Serv.* Here are a sort of poor petitioners,
  That are importunate, an it shall please you, sir,
  That you should plead their cases to the king.
*Hier.* That I should plead their several actions?
  Why, let them enter, and let me see them.

*Enter three* Citizens *and an* Old Man.

1.                                  So, 50
  I tell you this: for learning and for law,
  There is not any advocate in Spain
  That can prevail, or will take half the pain
  That he will, in pursuit of equity.
*Hier.* Come near, you men, that thus importune me.—
  [*Aside.*] Now must I bear a face of gravity;
  For thus I us'd, before my Marshalship,
  To plead in causes as Corregidor.—
  Come on, sirs, what's the matter?
2.                              Sir, an action.
*Hier.* Of battery?
1.              Mine of debt.
*Hier.*                          Give place.      60
2. No, sir, mine is an action of the case.
3. Mine an *ejectione firmae* by a lease.
*Hier.* Content you, sirs; are you determined
  That I should plead your several actions?
1. Ay, sir, and here's my declaration.

45 coil] noise, disturbance      46 sort] band      61
action of the case] *Obsolete legal term for a case wherein the
plaintiff's complaint is set forth at length in the original writ.*
62 *ejectione firmae*] *A writ which lay to eject a tenant from his
holding (Boas).*

2. And here's my band.

3.                          And here's my lease.

                          [*They give him papers.*

*Hier.* But wherefore stands yon silly man so mute,
   With mournful eyes and hands to heaven uprear'd?
   Come hither, father, let me know thy cause.

*Senex.* O worthy sir, my cause, but slightly known,  70
   May move the hearts of warlike Myrmidons,
   And melt the Corsic rocks with ruthful tears.

*Hier.* Say, father, tell me what's thy suit?

*Senex.* No, sir; could my woes
   Give way unto my most distressful words,
   Then should I not in paper, as you see,
   With ink bewray what blood began in me.

*Hier.* What's here? *The humble supplication*
   *Of Don Bazulto for his murder'd son.*

*Senex.* Ay, sir.

*Hier.*            No, sir, it was my murder'd son:   80
   O my son, my son, O my son Horatio!
   But mine, or thine, Bazulto, be content.
   Here, take my handkercher, and wipe thine eyes,
   Whiles wretched I in thy mishaps may see
   The lively portrait of my dying self.

                    [*He draweth out a bloody napkin.*

   O no, not this; Horatio, this was thine;
   And when I dy'd it in thy dearest blood,
   This was a token 'twixt thy soul and me,
   That of thy death revenged I should be.
   But here, take this, and this—what, my purse?— 90
   Ay, this, and that, and all of them are thine;
   For all as one are our extremities.

1. O, see the kindness of Hieronimo!

2. This gentleness shows him a gentleman.

*Hier.* See, see, O see thy shame, Hieronimo;
   See here a loving father to his son!
   Behold the sorrows and the sad laments,

66 band] bond        72 Corsic] Corsican

That he delivereth for his son's decease!
If love's effects so strives in lesser things,
If love enforce such moods in meaner wits,        100
If love express such power in poor estates:
Hieronimo, when, as a raging sea
Toss'd with the wind and tide, o'erturnest thou,
The upper billows' course of waves to keep,
Whilst lesser waters labour in the deep:
Then shamest thou not, Hieronimo, to neglect
The sweet revenge of thy Horatio?
Though on this earth justice will not be found,
I'll down to hell, and in this passion
Knock at the dismal gates of Pluto's court,        110
Getting by force, as once Alcides did,
A troop of Furies and tormenting hags
To torture Don Lorenzo and the rest.
Yet lest the triple-headed porter should
Deny my passage to the slimy strond,
The Thracian poet thou shalt counterfeit.
Come on, old father, be my Orpheus,
And if thou canst no notes upon the harp,
Then sound the burden of thy sore heart's grief,
Till we do gain that Proserpine may grant        120
Revenge on them that murdered my son.
Then will I rent and tear them, thus and thus,
Shivering their limbs in pieces with my teeth.

> [*Tears the papers.*

1. O sir, my declaration!
> *Exit* Hieronimo, *and they after.*

101 express] reveal        102–5] *A difficult and probably
corrupt passage which has been variously emended and interpreted.
The gist seems to be that Hieronimo is ashamed of himself when
he compares his emotional outbursts with Bazulto's silent depth of
feeling.*        103 o'erturnest] *as the crest of a wave turns over,
to break in foam and noise* (?)        103 thou] *All early editions
read* then        104] to fluctuate like the sea's surface (?)
115 strond] strand        118 canst] knowest        122 rent]
rend

2. Save my bond!
                    *Enter* Hieronimo.
2. Save my bond!
3. Alas, my lease! it cost me ten pound, and you, my
    lord, have torn the same.
*Hier.* That cannot be, I gave it never a wound;
    Show me one drop of blood fall from the same:
    How is it possible I should slay it then?          130
    Tush, no; run after, catch me if you can.
                    *Exeunt all but the Old Man.*


        *Bazulto remains till* Hieronimo *enters again, who,
            staring him in the face, speaks.*

*Hier.* And art thou come, Horatio, from the depth,
    To ask for justice in this upper earth,
    To tell thy father thou art unreveng'd,
    To wring more tears from Isabella's eyes,
    Whose lights are dimm'd with over-long laments?
    Go back, my son, complain to Aeacus,
    For here's no justice; gentle boy, be gone,
    For justice is exiled from the earth:
    Hieronimo will bear thee company.                  140
    Thy mother cries on righteous Rhadamanth
    For just revenge against the murderers.
*Senex.* Alas, my lord, whence springs this troubled
    speech?
*Hier.* But let me look on my Horatio:
    Sweet boy, how art thou chang'd in death's black
    shade!
    Had Prosérpine no pity on thy youth,
    But suffered thy fair crimson-coloured spring
    With withered winter to be blasted thus?
    Horatio, thou art older than thy father:
    Ah, ruthless fate, that favour thus transforms!  150
*Baz.* Ah, my good lord, I am not your young son.
*Hier.* What, not my son? thou then a Fury art,

                150 favour] appearance

Sent from the empty kingdom of black night
To summon me to make appearance
Before grim Minos and just Rhadamanth,
To plague Hieronimo that is remiss,
And seeks not vengeance for Horatio's death.

*Baz.* I am a grieved man, and not a ghost,
That came for justice for my murdered son.

*Hier.* Ay, now I know thee, now thou namest thy
    son:                                160
Thou art the lively image of my grief;
Within thy face, my sorrows I may see.
Thy eyes are gumm'd with tears, thy cheeks are wan,
Thy forehead troubled, and thy mutt'ring lips
Murmur sad words abruptly broken off
By force of windy sighs thy spirit breathes;
And all this sorrow riseth for thy son:
And selfsame sorrow feel I for my son.
Come in, old man, thou shalt to Isabel;
Lean on my arm: I thee, thou me, shalt stay,  170
And thou, and I, and she will sing a song,
Three parts in one, but all of discords fram'd:—
Talk not of cords, but let us now be gone,
For with a cord Horatio was slain.     *[Exeunt.*

## SCENE XIV

*Enter* King of Spain, *the* Duke, Viceroy, *and* Lorenzo,
    Balthazar, Don Pedro, *and* Bellimperia.

*King.* Go, brother, it is the Duke of Castile's cause;
    Salute the Viceroy in our name.

*Cast.*                       I go.

*Vic.* Go forth, Don Pedro, for thy nephew's sake,
    And greet the Duke of Castile.

*Ped.*                   It shall be so.

*King.* And now to meet these Portaguise:

      5 Portaguise] Portuguese

For as we now are, so sometimes were these,
Kings and commanders of the western Indies.
Welcome, brave Viceroy, to the court of Spain,
And welcome all his honourable train:
'Tis not unknown to us for why you come,    10
Or have so kingly cross'd the seas:
Sufficeth it, in this we note the troth
And more than common love you lend to us.
So is it that mine honourable niece
(For it beseems us now that it be known)
Already is betroth'd to Balthazar:
And by appointment and our condescent
To-morrow are they to be married.
To this intent we entertain thyself,
Thy followers, their pleasure, and our peace.    20
Speak, men of Portingal, shall it be so?
If ay, say so; if not, say flatly no.
*Vic.* Renowmed King, I come not, as thou think'st,
With doubtful followers, unresolved men,
But such as have upon thine articles
Confirmed thy motion, and contented me.
Know, sovereign, I come to solemnize
The marriage of thy beloved niece,
Fair Bellimperia, with my Balthazar—
With thee, my son; whom sith I live to see,    30
Here take my crown, I give it her and thee;
And let me live a solitary life,
In ceaseless prayers,
To think how strangely heaven hath thee pre-
serve d.
*King.* See, brother, see, how nature strives in him!
Come, worthy Viceroy, and accompany
Thy friend with thine extremities:
A place more private fits this princely mood.
*Vic.* Or here, or where your highness thinks it good.
            [*Exeunt all but* Castile *and* Lorenzo.

17 condescent] consent      23 Renowmed] Renowned
37 extremities] unrestrained bursts of emotion (*Boas*)

*Cast.* Nay, stay, Lorenzo, let me talk with you.　　40
　　See'st thou this entertainment of these kings?
*Lor.* I do, my lord, and joy to see the same.
*Cast.* And knowest thou why this meeting is?
*Lor.* For her, my lord, whom Balthazar doth love,
　　And to confirm their promised marriage.
*Cast.* She is thy sister?
*Lor.*　　　　　　　　Who, Bellimperia? ay,
　　My gracious lord, and this is the day,
　　That I have long'd so happily to see.
*Cast.* Thou wouldst be loath that any fault of thine
　　Should intercept her in her happiness?　　50
*Lor.* Heavens will not let Lorenzo err so much.
*Cast.* Why then, Lorenzo, listen to my words:
　　It is suspected, and reported too,
　　That thou, Lorenzo, wrong'st Hieronimo,
　　And in his suits towards his majesty
　　Still keep'st him back, and seeks to cross his suit.
*Lor.* That I, my lord——?
*Cast.* I tell thee, son, myself have heard it said,
　　When, to my sorrow, I have been ashamed
　　To answer for thee, though thou art my son.　　6o
　　Lorenzo, knowest thou not the common love
　　And kindness that Hieronimo hath won
　　By his deserts within the court of Spain?
　　Or see'st thou not the king my brother's care
　　In his behalf, and to procure his health?
　　Lorenzo, shouldst thou thwart his passions,
　　And he exclaim against thee to the king,
　　What honour were 't in this assembly,
　　Or what a scandal were 't among the kings
　　To hear Hieronimo exclaim on thee?　　70
　　Tell me, and look thou tell me truly too,
　　Whence grows the ground of this report in court?
*Lor.* My lord, it lies not in Lorenzo's power
　　To stop the vulgar, liberal of their tongues:

　　　　66, 79 passions] passionate outbursts

A small advantage makes a water-breach,
And no man lives that long contenteth all.
*Cast.* Myself have seen thee busy to keep back
Him and his supplications from the king.
*Lor.* Yourself, my lord, hath seen his passions,
That ill beseem'd the presence of a king;        80
And, for I pitied him in his distress,
I held him thence with kind and courteous words,
As free from malice to Hieronimo
As to my soul, my lord.
*Cast.* Hieronimo, my son, mistakes thee then.
*Lor.* My gracious father, believe me, so he doth.
But what's a silly man, distract in mind
To think upon the murder of his son?
Alas, how easy is it for him to err!
But for his satisfaction and the world's,        90
'Twere good, my lord, that Hieronimo and I
Were reconcil'd, if he misconster me.
*Cast.* Lorenzo, thou hast said; it shall be so.
Go one of you, and call Hieronimo.

*Enter* Balthazar *and* Bellimperia.

*Bal.* Come, Bellimperia, Balthazar's content,
My sorrow's ease and sovereign of my bliss,
Sith heaven hath ordain'd thee to be mine:
Disperse those clouds and melancholy looks,
And clear them up with those thy sun-bright eyes,
Wherein my hope and heaven's fair beauty lies.   100
*Bel.* My looks, my lord, are fitting for my love,
Which, new begun, can show no brighter yet.
*Bal.* New kindled flames should burn as morning sun.
*Bel.* But not too fast, lest heat and all be done.
I see my lord my father.
*Bal.*                            Truce, my love;
I will go salute him.

81 for] because    87 silly] simple    92 misconster]
misconstrue, misinterpret

*Cast.*                          Welcome, Balthazar,
Welcome, brave prince, the pledge of Castile's
    peace.
And welcome, Bellimperia. How now, girl?
Why comest thou sadly to salute us thus?
Content thyself, for I am satisfied :                110
It is not now as when Andrea liv'd;
We have forgotten and forgiven that,
And thou art graced with a happier love.
But, Balthazar, here comes Hieronimo;
I'll have a word with him.

> *Enter* Hieronimo *and a* Servant.

*Hier.* And where's the duke?
*Serv.*                     Yonder.
*Hier.*                                Even so.—
What new device have they devised, trow?
*Pocas palabras!* mild as the lamb!
Is't I will be reveng'd? No, I am not the man.
*Cast.* Welcome, Hieronimo.                          120
*Lor.* Welcome, Hieronimo.
*Bal.* Welcome, Hieronimo.
*Hier.* My lords, I thank you for Horatio.
*Cast.* Hieronimo, the reason that I sent
    To speak with you, is this.
*Hier.*                        What, so short?
Then I'll be gone, I thank you for 't.
*Cast.* Nay, stay, Hieronimo!—go call him, son.
*Lor.* Hieronimo, my father craves a word with you.
*Hier.* With me, sir? why, my lord, I thought you had
    done.
*Lor.* [*aside*] No; would he had!
*Cast.*                           Hieronimo, I hear 130
You find yourself aggrieved at my son,
Because you have not access unto the king;
And say 'tis he that intercepts your suits.

117 device] plot      118 *Pocas palabras*] Few words

H

*Hier.* Why, is not this a miserable thing, my lord?
*Cast.* Hieronimo, I hope you have no cause,
   And would be loath that one of your deserts
   Should once have reason to suspect my son,
   Considering how I think of you myself.
*Hier.* Your son Lorenzo! whom, my noble lord?
   The hope of Spain, mine honourable friend?    140
   Grant me the combat of them, if they dare:
                        [*Draws out his sword.*
   I'll meet him face to face, to tell me so!
   These be the scandalous reports of such
   As love not me, and hate my lord too much.
   Should I suspect Lorenzo would prevent
   Or cross my suit, that loved my son so well?
   My lord, I am ashamed it should be said.
*Lor.* Hieronimo, I never gave you cause.
*Hier.* My good lord, I know you did not.
*Cast.*                 There then pause;
   And for the satisfaction of the world,    150
   Hieronimo, frequent my homely house,
   The Duke of Castile, Cyprian's ancient seat;
   And when thou wilt, use me, my son, and it:
   But here, before Prince Balthazar and me,
   Embrace each other, and be perfect friends.
*Hier.* Ay, marry, my lord, and shall.
   Friends, quoth he? see, I'll be friends with you all:
   Specially with you, my lovely lord;
   For divers causes it is fit for us
   That we be friends: the world is suspicious,    160
   And men may think what we imagine not.
*Bal.* Why, this is friendly done, Hieronimo.
*Lor.* And that I hope: old grudges are forgot?
*Hier.* What else? it were a shame it should not
   be so.
*Cast.* Come on, Hieronimo, at my request;
   Let us entreat your company to-day.    [*Exeunt.*

     150 for the satisfaction of] to satisfy, convince

*Hier.* Your lordship's to command.—Pah! keep your
    way:
    *Chi mi fa più carezze che non suole,*
    *Tradito mi ha, o tradir mi vuole.*        **[***Exit.*


## Scene XV

*Enter* Ghost *and* Revenge.

*Ghost.* Awake, Erichtho! Cerberus, awake!
  Solicit Pluto, gentle Proserpine!
  To combat, Acheron and Erebus!
  For ne'er, by Styx and Phlegethon in hell,
  O'er-ferried Charon to the fiery lakes
  Such fearful sights, as poor Andrea sees.
  Revenge, awake!
*Revenge.* Awake? for why?
*Ghost.* Awake, Revenge; for thou art ill-advis'd
  To sleep away what thou art warn'd to watch!  10
*Revenge.* Content thyself, and do not trouble me.
*Ghost.* Awake, Revenge, if love—as love hath had—
  Have yet the power or prevalence in hell!
  Hieronimo with Lorenzo is join'd in league,
  And intercepts our passage to revenge:
  Awake, Revenge, or we are woe-begone!
*Revenge.* Thus worldlings ground, what they have
    dream'd, upon.
  Content thyself, Andrea; though I sleep,
  Yet is my mood soliciting their souls.
  Sufficeth thee that poor Hieronimo      20
  Cannot forget his son Horatio.
  Nor dies Revenge, although he sleep awhile;
  For in unquiet, quietness is feign'd,
  And slumb'ring is a common worldly wile.
  Behold, Andrea, for an instance, how

168–9]  Who pays me court he was not wont to pay me,
      He has betrayed me, or would fain betray me.

Revenge hath slept, and then imagine thou,
What 'tis to be subject to destiny.

*Enter a Dumb Show.*

*Ghost.* Awake, Revenge; reveal this mystery.
*Revenge.* The two first the nuptial torches bore
　As brightly burning as the mid-day's sun;　　30
　But after them both Hymen hie as fast,
　Clothed in sable and a saffron robe,
　And blows them out, and quencheth them with blood,
　As discontent that things continue so.
*Ghost.* Sufficeth me; thy meaning's understood,
　And thanks to thee and those infernal powers,
　That will not tolerate a lover's woe.
　Rest thee, for I will sit to see the rest.
*Revenge.* Then argue not, for thou hast thy request.
　　　　　　　　　　　　　　　　*[Exeunt.*

# ACTUS QUARTUS

## SCENE 1

*Enter* Bellimperia *and* Hieronimo.

*Bel.* Is this the love thou bear'st Horatio?
　Is this the kindness that thou counterfeits?
　Are these the fruits of thine incessant tears?
　Hieronimo, are these thy passions,
　Thy protestations and thy deep laments,
　That thou wert wont to weary men withal?
　O unkind father! O deceitful world!
　With what excuses canst thou show thyself,
　With what dishonour and the hate of men,
　From this dishonour and the hate of men,　　10

7 unkind] unnatural　　9–10] *The text is corrupt. Most editors omit line* 9, *and Boas suggests* With what devices seek thyself to save *or some similar phrase; or perhaps line* 10 *is the offender.*

Thus to neglect the loss and life of him
Whom both my letters and thine own belief
Assures thee to be causeless slaughtered?
Hieronimo, for shame, Hieronimo,
Be not a history to after times
Of such ingratitude unto thy son:
Unhappy mothers of such children then,
But monstrous fathers to forget so soon
The death of those, whom they with care and cost
Have tender'd so, thus careless should be lost.    20
Myself, a stranger in respect of thee,
So loved his life, as still I wish their deaths.
Nor shall his death be unreveng'd by me,
Although I bear it out for fashion's sake:
For here I swear, in sight of heaven and earth,
Shouldst thou neglect the love thou shouldst retain,
And give it over, and devise no more,
Myself should send their hateful souls to hell,
That wrought his downfall with extremest death.
*Hier.* But may it be that Bellimperia       30
Vows such revenge as she hath deign'd to say?
Why, then I see that heaven applies our drift,
And all the saints do sit soliciting
For vengeance on those cursed murtherers.
Madam, 'tis true, and now I find it so,
I found a letter, written in your name,
And in that letter, how Horatio died.
Pardon, O pardon, Bellimperia,
My fear and care in not believing it;
Nor think I thoughtless think upon a mean      40
To let his death be unreveng'd at full.
And here I vow—so you but give consent,
And will conceal my resolution—
I will ere long determine of their deaths
That causeless thus have murdered my son.

18 so soon] *sc.* so soon, that *&c.*      21 respect of]
comparison with      32 applies our drift] favours our
design

*Bel.* Hieronimo, I will consent, conceal,
  And aught that may effect for thine avail,
  Join with thee to revenge Horatio's death.
*Hier.* On, then; whatsoever I devise,
  Let me entreat you, grace my practices;                    50
  For why the plot's already in mine head.
  Here they are.


                *Enter* Balthazar *and* Lorenzo.

*Bal.* How now, Hieronimo?  What, courting Bellim-
    peria?
*Hier.* Ay, my lord; such courting as, I promise
    you,
  She hath my heart, but you, my lord, have hers.
*Lor.* But now, Hieronimo, or never, we
  Are to entreat your help.
*Hier.*                    My help?
  Why, my good lords, assure yourselves of me;
  For you have given me cause; ay, by my faith have
    you!
*Bal.* It pleas'd you, at the entertainment of the
    ambassador,                                              60
  To grace the king so much as with a show:
  Now, were your study so well furnished,
  As for the passing of the first night's sport
  To entertain my father with the like,
  Or any such-like pleasing motion,
  Assure yourself, it would content them well.
*Hier.* Is this all?
*Bal.* Ay, this is all.
*Hier.* Why then, I'll fit you; say no more.
  When I was young, I gave my mind                           70
  And plied myself to fruitless poetry;

50 grace my practices] help my schemes        51 For
why] because        65 motion] show        69 fit] supply
(*but there is the sinister double meaning* outwit)

Which though it profit the professor naught,
Yet is it passing pleasing to the world.
*Lor.* And how for that?
*Hier.*                    Marry, my good lord, thus:
(And yet, methinks, you are too quick with us):—
When in Toledo there I studied,
It was my chance to write a tragedy:
See. here, my lords—        [*He shows them a book.*
Which, long forgot, I found this other day.
Now would your lordships favour me so much      80
As but to grace me with your acting it—
I mean each one of you to play a part—
Assure you it will prove most passing strange,
And wondrous plausible to that assembly.
*Bal.* What, would you have us play a tragedy!
*Hier.* Why, Nero thought it no disparagement,
And kings and emperors have ta'en delight
To make experience of their wits in plays.
*Lor.* Nay, be not angry, good Hieronimo;
The prince but asked a question.      90
*Bal.* In faith, Hieronimo, an you be in earnest,
I'll make one.
*Lor.* And I another.
*Hier.* Now, my good lord, could you entreat
Your sister Bellimperia to make one?
For what's a play without a woman in it!
*Bel.* Little entreaty shall serve me, Hieronimo;
For I must needs be employed in your play.
*Hier.* Why, this is well; I tell you, lordings,
It was determined to have been acted,      100
By gentlemen and scholars too,
Such as could tell what to speak.
*Bal.* And now it shall be play'd by princes and
courtiers,
Such as can tell how to speak:

84 plausible] worthy of applause      88 experience] trial
102 what to speak] *It appears below that they are to extemporize
words to fit the story and the characters assigned them.*

If, as it is our country manner,
You will but let us know the argument.
*Hier.* That shall I roundly.  The chronicles of Spain
Record this written of a knight of Rhodes:
He was betrothed, and wedded at the length,
To one Perseda, an Italian dame,                    110
Whose beauty ravished all that her beheld,
Especially the soul of Soliman,
Who at the marriage was the chiefest guest.
By sundry means sought Soliman to win
Perseda's love, and could not gain the same.
Then 'gan he break his passions to a friend,
One of his Bashaws, whom he held full dear;
Her had this Bashaw long solicited,
And saw she was not otherwise to be won
But by her husband's death, this knight of
    Rhodes,                                         120
Whom presently by treachery he slew.
She, stirr'd with an exceeding hate therefore,
As cause of this slew Soliman,
And, to escape the Bashaw's tyranny,
Did stab herself: and this the tragedy.
*Lor.* O excellent!
*Bel.*                    But say, Hieronimo,
What then became of him that was the Bashaw?
*Hier.* Marry, thus: moved with remorse of his mis-
    deeds,
Ran to a mountain-top and hung himself.
*Bal.* But which of us is to perform that part?    130
*Hier.* O, that will I, my lords, make no doubt of it:
I'll play the murderer, I warrant you,
For I already have conceited that.
*Bal.* And what shall I?
*Hier.* Great Soliman, the Turkish emperor.
*Lor.* And I?

105–6 our country manner] *The manner is more Italian than
Portuguese; compare* IV. i. 163–5.       107 roundly] readily
133 conceited] devised

*Hier.* Erastus, the knight of Rhodes.
*Bel.* And I?
*Hier.* Perseda, chaste and resolute.
    And here, my lords, are several abstracts drawn,  140
    For each of you to note your parts,
    And act it, as occasion's offer'd you.
    You must provide a Turkish cap,
    A black mustachio and a falchion;
                  [*Gives a paper to* Balthazar.
    You with a cross, like to a knight of Rhodes;
                  [*Gives another to* Lorenzo.
    And, madam, you must attire yourself
                  [*He giveth* Bellimperia *another.*
    Like Phœbe, Flora, or the Huntress,
    Which to your discretion shall seem best.
    And as for me, my lords, I'll look to one,
    And, with the ransom that the viceroy sent,  150
    So furnish and perform this tragedy,
    As all the world shall say, Hieronimo
    Was liberal in gracing of it so.
*Bal.* Hieronimo, methinks a comedy were better.
*Hier.* A comedy?
    Fie! comedies are fit for common wits:
    But to present a kingly troop withal,
    Give me a stately-written tragedy;
    *Tragedia cothurnata*, fitting kings,
    Containing matter, and not common things.  160
    My lords, all this must be performed,
    As fitting for the first night's revelling.
    The Italian tragedians were so sharp of wit,
    That in one hour's meditation
    They would perform anything in action.
*Lor.* And well it may; for I have seen the like
    In Paris 'mongst the French tragedians.

140–2 abstracts . . . as occasion's offer'd you] *See note on*
IV. i. 102.    157 present a kingly troop withal] offer to
a royal audience    159 *Tragedia cothurnata*] buskined,
lofty tragedy

*Hier.* In Paris? mass, and well remembered!
  There's one thing more that rests for us to do.
*Bal.* What's that, Hieronimo? forget not anything. 170
*Hier.* Each one of us
  Must act his part in unknown languagcs,
  That it may breed the more variety:
  As you, my lord, in Latin, I in Greek,
  You in Italian, and for because I know
  That Bellimperia hath practised the French,
  In courtly French shall all her phrases be.
*Bel.* You mean to try my cunning then, Hieronimo?
*Bal.* But this will be a mere confusion,
  And hardly shall we all be understood.     180
*Hier.* It must be so; for the conclusion
  Shall prove the invention and all was good:
  And I myself in an oration,
  And with a strange and wondrous show besides,
  That I will have there behind a curtain,
  Assure yourself, shall make the matter known:
  And all shall be concluded in one scene,
  For there's no pleasure ta'en in tediousncss.
*Bal.* How like you this?
*Lor.* Why, thus my lord:     190
  We must resolve to soothe his humours up.
*Bal.* On then, Hieronimo; farewell till soon.
*Hier.* You'll ply this gear?
*Lor.*             I warrant you.
          [*Exeunt all but* Hieronimo.
*Hier.*                  Why so:
  Now shall I see the fall of Babylon,
  Wrought by the heavens in this confusion.
  And if the world like not this tragedy,
  Hard is the hap of old Hieronimo.     [*Exit.*

191 soothe his humours up] satisfy his whims    193
ply this gear] be active in this matter

## SCENE II

*Enter* Isabella *with a weapon.*

*Isab.* Tell me no more:—O monstrous homicides!
Since neither piety nor pity moves
The king to justice or compassion,
I will revenge myself upon this place,
Where thus they murdered my beloved son.
                              [*She cuts down the arbour.*
Down with these branches and these loathsome
    boughs
Of this unfortunate and fatal pine:
Down with them, Isabella; rent them up,
And burn the roots from whence the rest is sprung.
I will not leave a root, a stalk, a tree,                    10
A bough, a branch, a blossom, nor a leaf,
No, not an herb within this garden-plot—
Accursed complot of my misery!
Fruitless for ever may this garden be,
Barren the earth, and blissful whosoever
Imagines not to keep it unmanur'd!
An eastern wind, commix'd with noisome airs,
Shall blast the plants and the young saplings;
The earth with serpents shall be pestered,
And passengers, for fear to be infect,                      20
Shall stand aloof, and, looking at it, tell:
"There, murder'd, died the son of Isabel."
Ay, here he died, and here I him embrace:
See, where his ghost solicits with his wounds
Revenge on her that should revenge his death.
Hieronimo, make haste to see thy son;
For sorrow and despair hath cited me
To hear Horatio plead with Rhadamanth:
Make haste, Hieronimo, to hold excus'd
Thy negligence in pursuit of their deaths                   30

16 unmanur'd] uncultivated          20 passengers]
travellers, passers-by

Whose hateful wrath bereav'd him of his breath.
Ah, nay, thou dost delay their deaths,
Forgives the murderers of thy noble son,
And none but I bestir me—to no end!
And as I curse this tree from further fruit,
So shall my womb be cursed for his sake;
And with this weapon will I wound the breast,
The hapless breast, that gave Horatio suck.

[*She stabs herself.*

## SCENE III

*Enter* Hieronimo; *he knocks up the curtain.*
*Enter the* Duke of Castile.

*Cast.* How now, Hieronimo, where's your fellows,
   That you take all this pain?
*Hier.* O sir, it is for the author's credit,
   To look that all things may go well.
   But, good my lord, let me entreat your grace,
   To give the king the copy of the play:
   This is the argument of what we show.
*Cast.* I will, Hieronimo.
*Hier.* One thing more, my good lord.
*Cast.* What's that?                                10
*Hier.* Let me entreat your grace
   That, when the train are pass'd into the gallery,
   You would vouchsafe to throw me down the key.
*Cast.* I will, Hieronimo.          [*Exit* Castile.
*Hier.* What, are you ready, Balthazar?
   Bring a chair and a cushion for the king.

*Enter* Balthazar, *with a chair.*

Well done, Balthazar! hang up the title:
Our scene is Rhodes:—what, is your beard on?

Heading *the curtain*] sc., *that which conceals Horatio's body.*
12 gallery] *The upper stage, whence they watch Hieronimo's play*
*on the main stage.*          17 title] *Placard announcing the name*
*of the play.*

*Bal.* Half on; the other is in my hand.

*Hier.* Despatch, for shame; are you so long?           20

[*Exit* Balthazar.

Bethink thyself, Hieronimo,
Recall thy wits, recount thy former wrongs
Thou hast received by murder of thy son,
And lastly, not least, how Isabel,
Once his mother and thy dearest wife,
All woe-begone for him, hath slain herself.
Behoves thee then, Hieronimo, to be reveng'd.
The plot is laid of dire revenge:
On, then, Hieronimo, pursue revenge;
For nothing wants but acting of revenge.           30

[*Exit* Hieronimo.


## SCENE IV

*Enter* Spanish King, Viceroy, *the* Duke of Castile,
*and their train.*

*King.* Now, Viceroy, shall we see the tragedy
Of Soliman, the Turkish emperor.
Perform'd of pleasure by your son the prince,
My nephew Don Lorenzo, and my niece.

*Vic.* Who? Bellimperia?

*King.* Ay, and Hieronimo, our Marshal,
At whose request they deign to do't themselves.
These be our pastimes in the court of Spain.
Here, brother, you shall be the bookkeeper:
This is the argument of that they show.           10

[*He giveth him a book.*

*Gentlemen, this play of* Hieronimo, *in sundry languages,
was thought good to be set down in English, more largely,
for the easier understanding to every public reader.*

Heading] *See note on* IV. iii. 12.           10 s.d. *a book*]
*See* IV. iii. 6.   *The anonymous tragedy* Soliman and Perseda *was
probably written after this play.*

*Enter* Balthazar, Bellimperia, *and* Hieronimo.

Bal. *Bashaw, that Rhodes is ours, yield heavens the honour,*
    *And holy Mahomet, our sacred prophet:*
    *And be thou grac'd with every excellence*
    *That Soliman can give, or thou desire.*
    *But thy desert in conquering Rhodes is less*
    *Than in reserving this fair Christian nymph,*
    *Perseda, blissful lamp of excellence,*
    *Whose eyes compel, like powerful adamant,*
    *The warlike heart of Soliman to wait.*
King. See, Viceroy, that is Balthazar, your son,    20
    That represents the emperor Soliman:
    How well he acts his amorous passion!
Vic. Ay, Bellimperia hath taught him that.
Cast. That's because his mind runs all on Bellimperia.
Hier. *Whatever joy earth yields, betide your majesty.*
Bal. *Earth yields no joy without Perseda's love.*
Hier. *Let then Perseda on your grace attend.*
Bal. *She shall not wait on me, but I on her:*
    *Drawn by the influence of her lights, I yield.*
    *But let my friend, the Rhodian knight, come forth,*    30
    *Erasto, dearer than my life to me,*
    *That he may see Perseda, my beloved.*

*Enter* Erasto.

King. Here comes Lorenzo: look upon the plot,
    And tell me, brother, what part plays he?
Bel. *Ah, my Erasto, welcome to Perseda.*
Lor. *Thrice happy is Erasto that thou livest;*
    *Rhodes' loss is nothing to Erasto's joy*
    *Sith his Perseda lives, his life survives.*
Bal. *Ah, bashaw, here is love betwixt Erasto*
    *And fair Perseda, sovereign of my soul.*    40
Hier. *Remove Erasto, mighty Soliman,*
    *And then Perseda will be quickly won.*

29 *lights*] eyes

Bal. *Erasto is my friend; and while he lives,*
  *Perseda never will remove her love.*
Hier. *Let not Erasto live to grieve great Soliman.*
Bal. *Dear is Erasto in our princely eye.*
Hier. *But if he be your rival, let him die.*
Bal. *Why, let him die!—so love commandeth me.*
  *Yet grieve I that Erasto should so die.*
Hier. *Erasto, Soliman saluteth thee,*                          50
  *And lets thee wit by me his highness' will,*
  *Which is, thou shouldst be thus employ'd.*    [*Stab him.*
Bel.                                    *Ay me!*
  *Erasto! see, Soliman, Erasto's slain!*
Bal. *Yet liveth Soliman to comfort thee.*
  *Fair queen of beauty, let not favour die,*
  *But with a gracious eye behold his grief,*
  *That with Perseda's beauty is increas'd,*
  *If by Perseda his grief be not releas'd.*
Bel. *Tyrant, desist soliciting vain suits;*
  *Relentless are mine ears to thy laments,*                    60
  *As thy butcher is pitiless and base,*
  *Which seiz'd on my Erasto, harmless knight.*
  *Yet by thy power thou thinkest to command,*
  *And to thy power Perseda doth obey:*
  *But, were she able, thus she would revenge*
  *Thy treacheries on thee, ignoble prince:*    [*Stab him.*
  *And on herself she would be thus reveng'd.* [*Stab herself.*
King. Well said!—Old Marshal, this was bravely done!
Hier. But Bellimperia plays Perseda well!
Vic. Were this in earnest, Bellimperia,                        70
  You would be better to my son than so.
King. But now what follows for Hieronimo?
Hier. Marry, this follows for Hieronimo:
  Here break we off our sundry languages,
  And thus conclude I in our vulgar tongue.
  Haply you think—but bootless are your thoughts—
  That this is fabulously counterfeit,

          51 *wit*] know

And that we do as all tragedians do:
To die to-day for (fashioning our scene)
The death of Ajax, or some Roman peer,                80
And in a minute starting up again,
Revive to please to-morrow's audience.
No, princes; know I am Hieronimo,
The hopeless father of a hapless son,
Whose tongue is tun'd to tell his latest tale,
Not to excuse gross errors in the play.
I see, your looks urge instance of these words;
Behold the reason urging me to this:
                        [*Shows his dead son.*
See here my show, look on this spectacle:
Here lay my hope, and here my hope hath end; 90
Here lay my heart, and here my heart was slain;
Here lay my treasure, here my treasure lost;
Here lay my bliss, and here my bliss bereft;
But hope, heart, treasure, joy, and bliss,
All fled, fail'd, died, yea, all decay'd with this.
From forth these wounds came breath that gave me
    life;
They murder'd me that made these fatal marks.
The cause was love, whence grew this mortal hate;
The hate: Lorenzo and young Balthazar;
The love: my son to Bellimperia.                100
But night, the coverer of accursed crimes,
With pitchy silence hush'd these traitors' harms,
And lent them leave, for they had sorted leisure
To take advantage in my garden-plot
Upon my son, my dear Horatio:
There merciless they butcher'd up my boy,
In black, dark night, to pale, dim, cruel death.
He shrieks: I heard (and yet, methinks, I hear)
His dismal outcry echo in the air.
With soonest speed I hasted to the noise,        110
Where hanging on a tree I found my son,

103 sorted] chosen

Through girt with wounds, and slaughter'd as you
   see.
And grieved I, think you, at this spectacle?
Speak, Portaguise, whose loss resembles mine:
If thou canst weep upon thy Balthazar,
'Tis like I wail'd for my Horatio.
And you, my lord, whose reconciled son
March'd in a net, and thought himself unseen,
And rated me for brainsick lunacy,
With "God amend that mad Hieronimo!"—  120
How can you brook our play's catastrophe?
And here behold this bloody handkercher,
Which at Horatio's death I weeping dipp'd
Within the river of his bleeding wounds:
It as propitious, see, I have reserved,
And never hath it left my bloody heart,
Soliciting remembrance of my vow
With these, O, these accursed murderers:
Which now perform'd, my heart is satisfied.
And to this end the Bashaw I became  130
That might revenge me on Lorenzo's life,
Who therefore was appointed to the part,
And was to represent the knight of Rhodes,
That I might kill him more conveniently.
So, Viceroy, was this Balthazar, thy son,
(That Soliman which Bellimperia,
In person of Perseda, murdered)
Solely appointed to that tragic part
That she might slay him that offended her.
Poor Bellimperia miss'd her part in this:  140
For though the story saith she should have died,
Yet I of kindness, and of care to her,
Did otherwise determine of her end;
But love of him whom they did hate too much
Did urge her resolution to be such.

112 Through girt] struck through, pierced  114
Portaguise] Portuguese  118 March'd in a net] *A
proverbial phrase to denote a transparent attempt at deceit* (*Boas*).

And, princes, now behold Hieronimo,
Author and actor in this tragedy,
Bearing his latest fortune in his fist;
And will as resolute conclude his part,
As any of the actors gone before.                    150
And, gentles, thus I end my play;
Urge no more words: I have no more to say.
                              [*He runs to hang himself.*

*King.* O hearken, Viceroy! Hold, Hieronimo!
Brother, my nephew and thy son are slain!
*Vic.* We are betray'd; my Balthazar is slain!
Break ope the doors; run, save Hieronimo.
                    [*They break in and hold* Hieronimo.
Hieronimo,
Do but inform the king of these events;
Upon mine honour, thou shalt have no harm.
*Hier.* Viceroy, I will not trust thee with my life,  160
Which I this day have offered to my son.
Accursed wretch,
Why stayest thou him that was resolv'd to die?
*King.* Speak, traitor! damned, bloody murderer,
    speak!
For now I have thee, I will make thee speak.
Why hast thou done this undeserving deed?
*Vic.* Why hast thou murdered my Balthazar?
*Cast.* Why hast thou butchered both my children
    thus?
*Hier.* O, good words!
As dear to me was my Horatio,                        170
As yours, or yours, or yours, my lord, to you.
My guiltless son was by Lorenzo slain,
And by Lorenzo and that Balthazar
Am I at last revenged thoroughly,
Upon whose souls may heavens be yet avenged
With greater far than these afflictions.
*Cast.* But who were thy confederates in this?

169–92] *For these lines the Fifth Addition was substituted in
1602; see p.* 238.

*Vic.* That was thy daughter Bellimperia;
 For by her hand my Balthazar was slain:
 I saw her stab him.
*King.*                         Why speakest thou not?   180
*Hier.* What lesser liberty can kings afford
 Than harmless silence? then afford it me.
 Sufficeth, I may not, nor I will not tell thee.
*King.* Fetch forth the tortures: traitor as thou art,
 I'll make thee tell.
*Hier.* Indeed,
 Thou mayest torment me, as his wretched son
 Hath done in murd'ring my Horatio:
 But never shalt thou force me to reveal
 The thing which I have vow'd inviolate.        190
 And therefore, in despite of all thy threats,
 Pleas'd with their deaths, and eas'd with their
     revenge,
 First take my tongue, and afterwards my heart.
                         [*He bites out his tongue.*
*King.* O monstrous resolution of a wretch!
 See, Viceroy, he hath bitten forth his tongue,
 Rather than to reveal what we requir'd.
*Cast.* Yet can he write.
*King.* And if in this he satisfy us not,
 We will devise th' extremest kind of death
 That ever was invented for a wretch.        200
         [*Then he makes signs for a knife to mend his pen.*
*Cast.* O, he would have a knife to mend his pen.
*Vic.* Here, and advise thee that thou write the troth.
*King.* Look to my brother! save Hieronimo!
         [*He with a knife stabs the Duke and himself.*
 What age hath ever heard such monstrous deeds?
 My brother, and the whole succeeding hope
 That Spain expected after my decease!—

190 the thing] *Boas pertinently asks what Hieronimo has left
to conceal; but perhaps we are to take this pointless secretiveness as
the climax of his insanity, induced by his long enforced silence.*
202 advise thee] take care

Go, bear his body hence, that we may mourn
The loss of our beloved brother's death;
That he may be entomb'd, whate'er befall;
I am the next, the nearest, last of all.                    210
*Vic.* And thou, Don Pedro, do the like for us:
Take up our hapless son, untimely slain;
Set me with him, and he with woeful me,
Upon the main-mast of a ship unmann'd,
And let the wind and tide haul me along
To Scylla's barking and untamed gulf,
Or to the loathsome pool of Acheron,
To weep my want for my sweet Balthazar:
Spain hath no refuge for a Portingal.
*The trumpets sound a dead march; the* King of Spain *mourning after his brother's body, and the* King of Portingal *bearing the body of his son.*


## SCENE V

*Enter* Ghost *and* Revenge.

*Ghost.* Ay, now my hopes have end in their effects,
When blood and sorrow finish my desires:
Horatio murdered in his father's bower;
Vild Serberine by Pedringano slain;
False Pedringano hang'd by quaint device;
Fair Isabella by herself misdone;
Prince Balthazar by Bellimperia stabb'd;
The Duke of Castile and his wicked son
Both done to death by old Hieronimo;
My Bellimperia fall'n, as Dido fell,                       10
And good Hieronimo slain by himself:
Ay, these were spectacles to please my soul!
Now will I beg at lovely Proserpine
That, by the virtue of her princely doom,
I may consort my friends in pleasing sort,

4 vild] vile        5 quaint device] ingenious trick        6
misdone] killed     15 consort] consort with

And on my foes work just and sharp revenge.
I'll lead my friend Horatio through those fields
Where never-dying wars are still inur'd;
I'll lead fair Isabella to that train
Where pity weeps, but never feeleth pain;      20
I'll lead my Bellimperia to those joys
That vestal virgins and fair queens possess;
I'll lead Hieronimo where Orpheus plays,
Adding sweet pleasure to eternal days.
But say, Revenge—for thou must help, or none—
Against the rest how shall my hate be shown?
*Rev.* This hand shall hale them down to deepest hell,
Where none but Furies, bugs and tortures dwell.
*Ghost.* Then, sweet Revenge, do this at my request:
Let me be judge, and doom them to unrest.      30
Let loose poor Tityus from the vulture's gripe,
And let Don Cyprian supply his room;
Place Don Lorenzo on Ixion's wheel,
And let the lover's endless pains surcease
(Juno forgets old wrath, and grants him ease);
Hang Balthazar about Chimæra's neck,
And let him there bewail his bloody love,
Repining at our joys that are above;
Let Serberine go roll the fatal stone,
And take from Sisyphus his endless moan;       40
False Pedringano, for his treachery,
Let him be dragg'd through boiling Acheron,
And there live, dying still in endless flames,
Blaspheming gods and all their holy names.
*Rev.* Then haste we down to meet thy friends and foes:
To place thy friends in ease, the rest in woes;
For here though death hath end their misery,
I'll there begin their endless tragedy.     [*Exeunt.*

18 inur'd] carried on      28 bugs] bugbears

SCENES ADDED TO

# THE SPANISH TRAGEDY

IN THE EDITION OF

1602

[The additional passages first printed in the edition of 1602 are here reprinted, with the preceding and following lines of the original text added in square brackets where it is necessary to make clear the position of the additions.]

# ANONYMOUS ADDITIONS TO

## *The Spanish Tragedy*

### First Addition, between II. v. 45 and 46.

[For outrage fits our cursed wretchedness.]
Ay me, Hieronimo, sweet husband, speak!
*Hier.* He supp'd with us tonight, frolic and merry,
And said he would go visit Balthazar
At the Duke's palace: there the Prince doth lodge.
He had no custom to stay out so late:
He may be in his chamber; some go see.
Roderigo, ho!

#### *Enter* Pedro *and* Jaques.

*Isab.* Ay me, he raves! sweet Hieronimo!
*Hier.* True, all Spain takes note of it.
Besides, he is so generally beloved;               10
His Majesty the other day did grace him
With waiting on his cup: these be favours
Which do assure me he cannot be short-lived.
*Isab.* Sweet Hieronimo!
*Hier.* I wonder how this fellow got his clothes:
Sirrah, sirrah, I'll know the truth of all:
Jaques, run to the Duke of Castile's presently,
And bid my son Horatio to come home:
I and his mother have had strange dreams tonight.
Do ye hear me, sir?
*Jaques.*                    Ay, sir.
*Hier.*                                   Well, sir, begone.  20
Pedro, come hither; knowest thou who this is?
*Ped.* Too well, sir.

17 presently] at once

*Hier.* Too well! Who, who is it? Peace, Isabella!
　Nay, blush not, man.
*Ped.*　　　　　　　　　It is my Lord Horatio.
*Hier.* Ha, ha! Saint James, but this doth make me
　laugh,
　That there are more deluded than myself.
*Ped.* Deluded?
*Hier.* Ay; I would have sworn myself within this
　hour
　That this had been my son Horatio,
　His garments are so like.　　　　　　　　　30
　Ha! are they not great persuasions!
*Isab.* O, would to God it were not so!
*Hier.* Were not, Isabella? dost thou dream it is?
　Can thy soft bosom entertain a thought
　That such a black deed of mischief should be
　done
　On one so pure and spotless as our son?
　Away, I am ashamed.
*Isab.*　　　　　　　Dear Hieronimo,
　Cast a more serious eye upon thy grief:
　Weak apprehension gives but weak belief.
*Hier.* It was a man, sure, that was hanged up here; 40
　A youth, as I remember: I cut him down.
　If it should prove my son now after all—
　Say you? say you?—Light! lend me a taper;
　Let me look again.—O God!
　Confusion, mischief, torment, death and hell,
　Drop all your stings at once in my cold bosom,
　That now is stiff with horror; kill me quickly.
　Be gracious to me, thou infective night,
　And drop this deed of murder down on me;
　Gird in my waste of grief with thy large darkness, 50
　And let me not survive to see the light
　May put me in the mind I had a son.
*Isab.* O sweet Horatio! O my dearest son!

48 infective] infectious

*Hier.* How strangely had I lost my way to grief!
   [Sweet, lovely rose, ill pluck'd before thy time,]


*Second Addition, replacing* III. ii. 65 *and part of* 66.

[*Lor.* Why so, Hieronimo, use me.]
*Hier.* Who, you, my Lord?
   I reserve your favour for a greater honour;
   This is a very toy, my Lord, a toy.
*Lor.* All's one, Hieronimo, acquaint me with it.
*Hier.* I'faith, my Lord, 'tis an idle thing; I must
      confess
   I ha' been too slack, too tardy, too remiss unto your
      honour.
*Lor.* How now, Hieronimo?
*Hier.* In troth, my Lord, it is a thing of nothing:
   The murder of a son, or so—
   A thing of nothing, my Lord!                           10
[*Lor.*                          Why, then, farewell.]


*Third Addition, between* III. xi. 1 *and* 2.

[1. By your leave, sir.]
*Hier.* 'Tis neither as you think, nor as you think,
   Nor as you think; you're wide all:
   These slippers are not mine, they were my son
      Horatio's.
   My son! and what's a son? A thing begot
   Within a pair of minutes, thereabout;
   A lump bred up in darkness, and doth serve
   To ballace these light creatures we call women;
   And, at nine moneths' end, creeps forth to light.
   What is there yet in a son
   To make a father dote, rave, or run mad?              10
   Being born, it pouts, cries, and breeds teeth.
   What is there yet in a son? He must be fed,

   II. 3 toy] trifle    III. 7 ballace] ballast    8 moneths]
months (*a common spelling, here required by the metre*)

Be taught to go, and speak.  Ay, or yet?
Why might not a man love a calf as well,
Or melt in passion for a frisking kid,
As for a son?  Methinks a young bacon
Or a fine little smooth horse colt
Should move a man as much as doth a son.
For one of these in very little time
Will grow to some good use, whereas a son,          20
The more he grows in stature and in years,
The more unsquar'd, unbevelled he appears;
Reckons his parents among the rank of fools,
Strikes care upon their heads with his mad riots,
Makes them look old before they meet with age.
This is a son!—And what a loss were this,
Considered truly!—O, but my Horatio
Grew out of reach of these insatiate humours!
He loved his loving parents;
He was my comfort, and his mother's joy,           30
The very arm that did hold up our house!
Our hopes were stored up in him,
None but a damned murderer could hate him.
He had not seen the back of nineteen year
When his strong arm unhors'd
The proud Prince Balthazar, and his great mind,
Too full of honour, took him unto mercy—
That valiant but ignoble Portingal!
Well, heaven is heaven still,
And there is Nemesis, and Furies,                  40
And things called whips,
And they sometimes do meet with murderers:
They do not always 'scape, that's some comfort.
Ay, ay, ay; and then time steals on,
And steals, and steals, till violence leaps forth,
Like thunder wrapp'd in a ball of fire,
And so doth bring confusion to them all.
[Good leave have you: nay, I pray you go,]

22 unsquar'd, unbevelled] uneven and unpolished (*Boas*)

*Fourth Addition, between scenes* xii *and* xiii.

## SCENE XIIA

*Enter* Jaques *and* Pedro.

*Jaq.* I wonder, Pedro, why our master thus
    At midnight sends us with our torches light,
    When man, and bird, and beast, are all at rest,
    Save those that watch for rape and bloody murder.
*Ped.* O Jaques, know thou that our master's mind
    Is much distraught, since his Horatio died,
    And—now his aged years should sleep in rest,
    His heart in quiet—like a desperate man,
    Grows lunatic and childish for his son.
    Sometimes, as he doth at his table sit,        10
    He speaks as if Horatio stood by him;
    Then starting in a rage, falls on the earth,
    Cries out "Horatio, where is my Horatio?"
    So that with extreme grief and cutting sorrow
    There is not left in him one inch of man:
    See, where he comes.

*Enter* Hieronimo.

*Hier.* I pry through every crevice of each wall,
    Look on each tree, and search through every brake,
    Beat at the bushes, stamp our grandam earth,
    Dive in the water, and stare up to heaven:     20
    Yet cannot I behold my son Horatio.—
    How now, who's there? spirits, spirits?
*Ped.* We are your servants that attend you, sir.
*Hier.* What make you with your torches in the dark?
*Ped.* You bid us light them, and attend you here.
*Hier.* No, no, you are deceiv'd—not I, you are deceiv'd.
    Was I so mad to bid you light your torches now?
    Light me your torches at the mid of noon,

Whenas the sun-god rides in all his glory:
Light me your torches then.

*Ped.*                    Then we burn daylight.    30

*Hier.* Let it be burnt; Night is a murderous slut,
That would not have her treasons to be seen,
And yonder pale-faced Hecat there, the moon,
Doth give consent to that is done in darkness;
And all those stars that gaze upon her face,
Are aglots on her sleeve, pins on her train;
And those that should be powerful and divine,
Do sleep in darkness when they most should shine.

*Ped.* Provoke them not, fair sir, with tempting words;
The heavens are gracious, and your miseries    40
And sorrow makes you speak, you know not what.

*Hier.* Villain, thou liest, and thou doest nought
But tell me I am mad: thou liest, I am not mad!
I know thee to be Pedro, and he Jaques.
I'll prove it to thee; and were I mad, how could I?
Where was she that same night, when my Horatio
Was murdered? She should have shone: search
    thou the book.
Had the moon shone, in my boy's face there was
    a kind of grace,
That I know—nay, I do know—had the murderer
    seen him,
His weapon would have fall'n and cut the earth,  50
Had he been framed of naught but blood and death.
Alack, when mischief doth it knows not what,
What shall we say to mischief?

*Enter* Isabella.

*Isab.* Dear Hieronimo, come in a-doors,
O, seek not means so to increase thy sorrow.

*Hier.* Indeed, Isabella, we do nothing here;
I do not cry: ask Pedro, and ask Jaques;

29 Whenas] when          30 burn daylight] waste time
36 aglots] ornamental tags

Not I, indeed; we are very merry, very merry.
*Isab.* How? be merry here, be merry here?
  Is not this the place, and this the very tree,      60
  Where my Horatio died, where he was murdered?
*Hier.* Was—do not say what: let her weep it out.
  This was the tree; I set it of a kernel:
  And when our hot Spain could not let it grow,
  But that the infant and the human sap
  Began to wither, duly twice a morning
  Would I be sprinkling it with fountain water.
  At last it grew and grew, and bore and bore,
  Till at the length
  It grew a gallows, and did bear our son:      70
  It bore thy fruit and mine: O wicked, wicked plant!
             *One knocks within at the door.*
  See who knock there.
*Ped.*                  It is a painter, sir.
*Hier.* Bid him come in, and paint some comfort,
  For surely there's none lives but painted comfort.
  Let him come in!—One knows not what may
    chance:
  Gods will that I should set this tree—but even so
  Masters ungrateful servants rear from nought,
  And then they hate them that did bring them up.

           *Enter the* Painter.

*Paint.* God bless you, sir.
*Hier.*          Wherefore? why, thou scornful villain?
  How, where, or by what means should I be
    bless'd?                        80
*Isab.* What wouldst thou have, good fellow?
*Paint.*                    Justice, madam.
*Hier.* O ambitious beggar!
  Wouldst thou have that that lives not in the world?
  Why, all the undelved mines cannot buy
  An ounce of justice,
  'Tis a jewel so inestimable! I tell thee,
  God hath engrossed all justice in his hands,

And there is none but what comes from him.

*Paint.*                                    O, then I see
That God must right me for my murder'd son.

*Hier.* How, was thy son murdered?                    90

*Paint.* Ay, sir; no man did hold a son so dear.

*Hier.* What, not as thine? that's a lie
As massy as the earth: I had a son,
Whose least unvalued hair did weigh
A thousand of thy sons: and he was murdered.

*Paint.* Alas, sir, I had no more but he.

*Hier.* Nor I, nor I: but this same one of mine
Was worth a legion. But all is one.
Pedro, Jaques, go in a-doors; Isabella, go,
And this good fellow here and I                    100
Will range this hideous orchard up and down,
Like to two lions reaved of their young.
Go in a-doors, I say.                    [*Exeunt.*
              *The* Painter *and he sits down.*
Come, let's talk wisely now. Was thy son murdered?

*Paint.* Ay, sir.

*Hier.* So was mine. How dost take it? art thou not
sometimes mad? Is there no tricks that comes before thine eyes?

*Paint.* O Lord, yes, sir.

*Hier.* Art a painter? Canst paint me a tear, or a wound,
a groan, or a sigh? canst paint me such a tree as
this?                    112

*Paint.* Sir, I am sure you have heard of my painting:
my name's Bazardo.

*Hier.* Bazardo! afore God, an excellent fellow! Look
you, sir, do you see, I'd have you paint me in my
gallery, in your oil-colours matted, and draw me
five years younger than I am—do ye see, sir, let
five years go; let them go like the marshal of
Spain—my wife Isabella standing by me, with a
speaking look to my son Horatio, which should

102 reaved] reft, bereft        117 matted] dull

intend to this or some such like purpose: "God
bless thee, my sweet son," and my hand leaning
upon his head, thus, sir; do you see?—may it be
done?                                                    125

*Paint.* Very well, sir.

*Hier.* Nay, I pray, mark me, sir: then, sir, would I
have you paint me this tree, this very tree. Canst
paint a doleful cry?

*Paint.* Seemingly, sir.                                 130

*Hier.* Nay, it should cry; but all is one. Well, sir, paint
me a youth run through and through with
villains' swords, hanging upon this tree. Canst
thou draw a murderer?

*Paint.* I'll warrant you, sir; I have the pattern of the
most notorious villains that ever lived in all
Spain.

*Hier.* O, let them be worse, worse: stretch thine art,
and let their beards be of Judas his own colour,
and let their eye brows jutty over: in any case
observe that. Then, sir, after some violent noise,
bring me forth in my shirt, and my gown under
mine arm, with my torch in my hand, and my
sword reared up thus:—and with these words:

> *What noise is this? who calls Hieronimo?*     145

May it be done?

*Paint.* Yea, sir.

*Hier.* Well, sir; then bring me forth, bring me through
alley and alley, still with a distracted countenance
going along, and let my hair heave up my night-
cap. Let the clouds scowl, make the moon dark, the
stars extinct, the winds blowing, the bells tolling,
the owls shrieking, the toads croaking, the minutes
jarring, and the clock striking twelve. And then
at last, sir, starting, behold a man hanging, and
tottering, and tottering, as you know the wind will

130 seemingly] in semblance        139 Judas ... colour]
red        140 jutty] jut        150 heave] lift        156 totter-
ing] swaying

wave a man, and I with a trice to cut him down.
And looking upon him by the advantage of my
torch, find it to be my son Horatio. There you may
show a passion, there you may show a passion!
Draw me like old Priam of Troy, crying: "The
house is a-fire, the house is a-fire, as the torch over
my head!" Make me curse, make me rave, make
me cry, make me mad, make me well again, make
me curse hell, invocate heaven, and in the end
leave me in a trance—and so forth.            166

*Paint.* And is this the end?

*Hier.* O no, there is no end: the end is death and
madness! As I am never better than when I am
mad: then methinks I am a brave fellow; then
I do wonders: but reason abuseth me, and there's
the torment, there's the hell. At the last, sir, bring
me to one of the murderers; were he as strong as
Hector, thus would I tear and drag him up and
down.            175

*He beats the* Painter *in, then comes out again, with a book
in his hand.*


*Fifth Addition, replacing* IV. iv. 169 *to* 192.

[*Cast.* Why hast thou butchered both my children
thus?]

*Hier.* But are you sure they are dead?

*Cast.*                              Ay, slave, too sure.

*Hier.* What, and yours too?

*Vic.* Ay, all are dead; not one of them survive.

*Hier.* Nay then, I care not; come, and we shall be
friends;
  Let us lay our heads together:
  See, here's a goodly noose will hold them all.

*Vic.* O damned devil, how secure he is!


7 secure] confident

*Hier.* Secure? why, dost thou wonder at it?
  I tell thee, Viceroy, this day I have seen revenge,
  And in that sight am grown a prouder monarch 10
  Than ever sat under the crown of Spain!
  Had I as many lives as there be stars,
  As many heavens to go to as those lives,
  I'd give them all, ay, and my soul to boot,
  But I would see thee ride in this red pool.
*Cast.* Speak, who were thy confederates in this?
*Vic.* That was thy daughter Bellimperia;
  For by her hand my Balthazar was slain:
  I saw her stab him.
*Hier.* Oh, good words!                20
  As dear to me was my Horatio
  As yours, or yours, or yours, my Lord, to you.
  My guiltless son was by Lorenzo slain,
  And by Lorenzo and that Balthazar
  Am I at last revenged thoroughly,
  Upon whose souls may heavens be yet revenged
  With greater far than these afflictions.
  Methinks, since I grew inward with revenge,
  I cannot look with scorn enough on death.
*King.* What, dost thou mock us, slave? Bring tortures
  forth.                             30
*Hier.* Do, do, do; and meantime I'll torture you.
  You had a son, as I take it, and your son
  Should ha' been married to your daughter:
  Ha, was 't not so?—You had a son, too;
  He was my liege's nephew; he was proud
  And politic. Had he lived, he might have come
  To wear the crown of Spain—I think 'twas so.
  'Twas I that killed him; look you, this same hand,
  'Twas it that stabb'd his heart—do ye see, this hand!
  For one Horatio, if you ever knew him: a youth, 40
  One that they hang'd up in his father's garden;

16–27] *These lines are repeated in slightly different order from act* IV *scene* iv *of the original version;* 16–19= 177–80, 20–27= 169–76.     28 inward] intimate

One that did force your valiant son to yield,
While your more valiant son did take him prisoner.
*Vic.* Be deaf, my senses, I can hear no more.
*King.* Fall, heaven, and cover us with thy sad ruins.
*Cast.* Roll all the world within thy pitchy cloud.
*Hier.* Now do I applaud that I have acted.
            *Nunc iners cadat manus!*
Now to express the rupture of my part,
[First take my tongue, and afterward my heart.]

  48] Now may my hand fall still!    49 rupture] breaking off, end

# ARDEN OF FEVERSHAM

# ANONYMOUS

## *Arden of Feversham*

Acted before 1592; printed in 1592.

[In *The Shakespeare Apocrypha*, ed. C. F. Tucker Brooke, Oxford, 1908.]

# THE
# LAMENTA:
## BLE AND TRVE TRA-
## GEDIE OF M. AR-
### DEN OF FEVERSHAM
### IN KENT.

*Who was most wickedlye murdered , by
the meanes of his disloyall and wanton
wyfe, who for the loue she bare to one
Mosbie, hyred two desperat ruffins Blackwill and Shakbag,
to kill him.*

**Wherin** is shewed the great mal-
lice and discimulation of a wicked woman, the vnsatiable desire of filthie lust
and the shamefull end of all
murderers.

*Imprinted at London for Edward*
White, dwelling at the lyttle North
dore of Paules Church at
the signe of the
Gun. 1592.
*

# DRAMATIS PERSONÆ

*Mr. Arden,* of Feversham.
*Franklin,* his Friend.
*Mosbie.*
*Clarke,* a Painter.
*Adam Fowle,* Landlord of the Flower-de-Luce.
*Bradshaw,* a Goldsmith.
*Michael,* Arden's Servant.
*Greene.*
*Richard Reede,* a Sailor.

*Black Will* }
*Shakebag* } Murderers.
*A Prentice.*
*A Ferryman.*
*Lord Cheiny,* and his Men.
*Mayor of Feversham,* and Watch.

*Alice,* Arden's Wife.
*Susan,* Mosbie's Sister.

# THE TRAGEDY OF
# M. ARDEN OF FEVERSHAM

## ACT I

*Enter* Arden *and* Franklin.

*Franklin.* Arden, cheer up thy spirits, and droop no
　　more:
My gracious Lord, the Duke of Somerset,
Hath freely given to thee and to thy heirs,
By letters patents from his Majesty,
All the lands of the Abbey of Feversham.
Here are the deeds, 　　　　　　*[He hands them.*
Sealed and subscribed with his name and the king's:
Read them, and leave this melancholy mood.
*Arden.* Franklin, thy love prolongs my weary life;
And but for thee how odious were this life, 　　10
That shows me nothing but torments my soul,
And those foul objects that offend mine eyes!
Which makes me wish that for this veil of heaven
The earth hung over my head and cover'd me.
Love-letters pass 'twixt Mosbie and my wife,
And they have privy meetings in the town:
Nay, on his finger did I spy the ring
Which at our marriage-day the priest put on.
Can any grief be half so great as this?
*Franklin.* Comfort thyself, sweet friend; it is not
　　strange 　　　　　　　　　　20
That women will be false and wavering.
*Arden.* Ay, but to dote on such a one as he
Is monstrous, Franklin, and intolerable.
*Franklin.* Why, what is he?
*Arden.* A botcher, and no better at the first;

　　　25 botcher] tailor who does repairs

Who, by base brokage getting some small stock,
Crept into service of a nobleman,
And by his servile flattery and fawning
Is now become the steward of his house,
And bravely jets it in his silken gown.                    30
*Franklin.* No nobleman will countenance such a peasant.
*Arden.* Yes, the Lord Clifford, he that loves not me.
But through his favour let him not grow proud;
For were he by the Lord Protector back'd,
He should not make me to be pointed at.
I am by birth a gentleman of blood,
And that injurious riball, that attempts
To violate my dear wife's chastity
(For dear I hold her love, as dear as heaven)
Shall on the bed which he thinks to defile            40
See his dissevered joints and sinews torn,
Whilst on the planchers pants his weary body,
Smear'd in the channels of his lustful blood.
*Franklin.* Be patient, gentle friend, and learn of me
To ease thy grief and save her chastity:
Entreat her fair; sweet words are fittest engines
To rase the flint walls of a woman's breast.
In any case be not too jealious,
Nor make no question of her love to thee;
But, as securely, presently take horse,               50
And lie with me at London all this term;
For women, when they may, will not,
But, being kept back, straight grow outragious.
*Arden.* Though this abhors from reason, yet I'll try it,
And call her forth and presently take leave.
How! Alice!

26 base brokage] sordid commerce        30 jets it] struts
34 Lord Protector] *The Duke of Somerset, Lord Protector till
1552.*        37 injurious riball] insulting wastrel        42
planchers] floor-boards        46 entreat] treat        48
jealious] jealous. *The spelling of the quartos indicates the pronunciation required by the metre; so, too,* outragious *in line* 53.
50 as securely] as if confident

*Here enters* Alice.

*Alice.* Husband, what mean you to get up so early?
  Summer nights are short, and yet you rise ere day.
  Had I been wake, you had not risen so soon.
*Arden.* Sweet love, thou know'st that we two, Ovid-
      like,                                         60
  Have often chid the morning when it 'gan to peep,
  And often wish'd that dark night's purblind steeds
  Would pull her by the purple mantle back,
  And cast her in the ocean to her love.
  But this night, sweet Alice, thou hast kill'd my heart:
  I heard thee call on Mosbie in thy sleep.
*Alice.* 'Tis like I was asleep when I nam'd him,
  For being awake he comes not in my thoughts.
*Arden.* Ay, but you started up and suddenly,
  Instead of him, caught me about the neck.        70
*Alice.* Instead of him? why, who was there but you?
  And where but one is, how can I mistake?
*Franklin.* Arden, leave to urge her over-far.
*Arden.* Nay, love, there is no credit in a dream;
  Let it suffice I know thou lovest me well.
*Alice.* Now I remember whereupon it came:
  Had we no talk of Mosbie yesternight?
*Franklin.* Mistress Alice, I heard you name him once
  or twice.
*Alice.* And thereof came it, and therefore blame not
  me.
*Arden.* I know it did, and therefore let it pass.    80
  I must to London, sweet Alice, presently.
*Alice.* But tell me, do you mean to stay there long?
*Arden.* No longer there till my affairs be done.
*Franklin.* He will not stay above a month at most.
*Alice.* A month? ay me! Sweet Arden, come again
  Within a day or two, or else I die.
*Arden.* I cannot long be from thee, gentle Alice.
  Whilst Michael fetch our horses from the field,
  Franklin and I will down unto the quay;

For I have certain goods there to unload.    90
Meanwhile prepare our breakfast, gentle Alice;
For yet ere noon we'll take horse and away.
                    [*Exeunt* Arden *and* Franklin.
*Alice*. Ere noon he means to take horse and away!
  Sweet news is this.  O that some airy spirit
  Would in the shape and likeness of a horse
  Gallop with Arden 'cross the Ocean,
  And throw him from his back into the waves!
  Sweet Mosbie is the man that hath my heart:
  And he usurps it, having nought but this,
  That I am tied to him by marriage.    100
  Love is a God, and marriage is but words;
  And therefore Mosbie's title is the best.
  Tush! whether it be or no, he shall be mine,
  In spite of him, of Hymen, and of rites.


*Here enters* Adam *of the Flower-de-luce*.

And here comes Adam of the Flower-de-luce;
  I hope he brings me tidings of my love.—
  How now, Adam, what is the news with you?
  Be not afraid; my husband is now from home.
*Adam*. He whom you wot of, Mosbie, Mistress Alice,
  Is come to town, and sends you word by me    110
  In any case you may not visit him.
*Alice*. Not visit him?
*Adam*. No, nor take no knowledge of his being here.
*Alice*. But tell me, is he angry or displeased?
*Adam*. Should seem so, for he is wondrous sad.
*Alice*. Were he as mad as raving Hercules,
  I'll see him, I; and were thy house of force,
  These hands of mine should rase it to the ground,
  Unless that thou would'st bring me to my love.
*Adam*. Nay, an you be so impatient, I'll be gone.  120
*Alice*. Stay, Adam, stay; thou wert wont to be my
      friend.
  Ask Mosbie how I have incurred his wrath;

Bear him from me these pair of silver dice,
With which we play'd for kisses many a time,
And when I lost, I wan, and so did he;
(Such winning and such losing Jove send me!)
And bid him, if his love do not decline,
To come this morning but along my door,
And as a stranger but salute me there:
This may he do without suspect or fear.         130
*Adam.* I'll tell him what you say, and so farewell.
                            [*Exit* Adam.
*Alice.* Do, and one day I'll make amends for all.—
I know he loves me well, but dares not come,
Because my husband is so jealous,
And these my narrow-prying neighbours blab,
Hinder our meetings when we would confer.
But, if I live, that block shall be removed,
And, Mosbie, thou that comes to me by stealth,
Shalt neither fear the biting speech of men
Nor Arden's looks; as surely shall he die        140
As I abhor him and love only thee.

*Here enters* Michael.

How now, Michael, whither are you going?
*Michael.* To fetch my master's nag.
I hope you'll think on me.
*Alice.* Ay; but, Michael, see you keep your oath,
And be as secret as you are resolute.
*Michael.* I'll see he shall not live above a week.
*Alice.* On that condition, Michael, here is my hand:
None shall have Mosbie's sister but thyself.
*Michael.* I understand the painter here hard by    150
Hath made report that he and Sue is sure.
*Alice.* There's no such matter, Michael; believe it not.
*Michael.* But he hath sent a dagger sticking in a heart,
With a verse or two stolen from a painted cloth,
The which I hear the wench keeps in her chest.

125 wan] won      151 sure] betrothed      154 painted
cloth] picture with moral aphorism

Well, let her keep it! I shall find a fellow
That can both write and read and make rhyme too.
And if I do—well, I say no more:
I'll send from London such a taunting letter
As she shall eat the heart he sent with salt      160
And fling the dagger at the painter's head.
*Alice.* What needs all this? I say that Susan's thine.
*Michael.* Why, then I say that I will kill my master,
  Or anything that you will have me do.
*Alice.* But, Michael, see you do it cunningly.
*Michael.* Why, say I should be took, I'll ne'er confess
  That you know anything; and Susan, being a maid,
  May beg me from the gallows of the sheriff.
*Alice.* Trust not to that, Michael.
*Michael.* You cannot tell me, I have seen it, I.      170
  But, mistress, tell her, whether I live or die,
  I'll make her more worth than twenty painters can;
  For I will rid mine elder brother away,
  And then the farm of Bolton is mine own.
  Who would not venture upon house and land,
  When he may have it for a right-down blow?

*Here enters* Mosbie.

*Alice.* Yonder comes Mosbie. Michael, get thee gone,
  And let not him nor any know thy drifts.
                                    [*Exit* Michael.
  Mosbie, my love!
*Mosbie.* Away, I say, and talk not to me now.   180
*Alice.* A word or two, sweet heart, and then I will.
  'Tis yet but early days, thou needest not fear.
*Mosbie.* Where is your husband?
*Alice.* 'Tis now high water, and he is at the quay.
*Mosbie.* There let him be; henceforward know me not.
*Alice.* Is this the end of all thy solemn oaths?
  Is this the fruit thy reconcilement buds?

168 beg me from the gallows] *A maid might redeem the life
of a man betrothed to her, on condition of marriage.*      182
days] in the day

Have I for this given thee so many favours,
Incurr'd my husband's hate, and, out alas!
Made shipwreck of mine honour for thy sake,  190
And dost thou say "henceforward know me not"?
Remember, when I lock'd thee in my closet,
What were thy words and mine; did we not both
Decree to murder Arden in the night?
The heavens can witness, and the world can tell,
Before I saw that falsehood look of thine,
'Fore I was tangled with thy 'ticing speech,
Arden to me was dearer than my soul,—
And shall be still: base peasant, get thee gone,
And boast not of thy conquest over me,  200
Gotten by witchcraft and mere sorcery!
For what hast thou to countenance my love,
Being descended of a noble house,
And match'd already with a gentleman
Whose servant thou may'st be!—and so farewell.

*Mosbie.* Ungentle and unkind Alice, now I see
That which I ever fear'd, and find too true:
A woman's love is as the lightning-flame,
Which even in bursting forth consumes itself.
To try thy constancy have I been strange;  210
Would I had never tried, but lived in hope!

*Alice.* What needs thou try me whom thou never
found false?

*Mosbie.* Yet pardon me, for love is jealous.

*Alice.* So list the sailor to the mermaid's song,
So looks the traveller to the basilisk:
I am content for to be reconcil'd,
And that, I know, will be mine overthrow.

*Mosbie.* Thine overthrow? first let the world dissolve.

*Alice.* Nay, Mosbie, let me still enjoy thy love,
And happen what will, I am resolute.  220
My saving husband hoards up bags of gold
To make our children rich, and now is he
Gone to unload the goods that shall be thine,
And he and Franklin will to London straight.

*Mosbie.* To London, Alice? if thou'lt be rul'd by me,
   We'll make him sure enough for coming there.
*Alice.* Ah, would we could!
*Mosbie.* I happen'd on a painter yesternight,
   The only cunning man of Christendom;
   For he can temper poison with his oil,          230
   That whoso looks upon the work he draws
   Shall, with the beams that issue from his sight,
   Suck venom to his breast and slay himself.
   Sweet Alice, he shall draw thy counterfeit,
   That Arden may by gazing on it perish.
*Alice.* Ay, but Mosbie, that is dangerous,
   For thou, or I, or any other else,
   Coming into the chamber where it hangs, may die.
*Mosbie.* Ay, but we'll have it covered with a cloth
   And hung up in the study for himself.           240
*Alice.* It may not be, for when the picture's drawn,
   Arden, I know, will come and show it me.
*Mosbie.* Fear not; we'll have that shall serve the turn.
   This is the painter's house; I'll call him forth.
*Alice.* But, Mosbie, I'll have no such picture, I.
*Mosbie.* I pray thee leave it to my discretion.
   How! Clarke!

*Here enters* Clarke.

   Oh, you are an honest man of your word! you
      serv'd me well.
*Clarke.* Why, sir, I'll do it for you at any time,
   Provided, as you have given your word,          250
   I may have Susan Mosbie to my wife.
   For, as sharp-witted poets, whose sweet verse
   Make heavenly gods break off their nectar draughts
   And lay their ears down to the lowly earth,
   Use humble promise to their sacred Muse,
   So we that are the poets' favourites
   Must have a love: ay, Love is the painter's Muse,

   226 for coming] against coming, not to come

That makes him frame a speaking countenance,
A weeping eye that witnesses heart's grief.
Then tell me, Master Mosbie, shall I have her? 260
*Alice.* 'Tis pity but he should; he'll use her well.
*Mosbie.* Clarke, here's my hand: my sister shall be
    thine.
*Clarke.* Then, brother, to requite this courtesy,
You shall command my life, my skill, and all.
*Alice.* Ah, that thou could'st be secret.
*Mosbie.* Fear him not; leave; I have talk'd sufficient.
*Clarke.* You know not me that ask such questions.
Let it suffice I know you love him well,
And fain would have your husband made away:
Wherein, trust me, you show a noble mind, 270
That rather than you'll live with him you hate,
You'll venture life, and die with him you love.
The like will I do for my Susan's sake.
*Alice.* Yet nothing could enforce me to the deed
But Mosbie's love. Might I without control
Enjoy thee still, then Arden should not die:
But seeing I cannot, therefore let him die.
*Mosbie.* Enough, sweet Alice; thy kind words makes
    me melt.
Your trick of poisoned pictures we dislike;
Some other poison would do better far. 280
*Alice.* Ay, such as might be put into his broth,
And yet in taste not to be found at all.
*Clarke.* I know your mind, and here I have it for you.
Put but a dram of this into his drink,
Or any kind of broth that he shall eat,
And he shall die within an hour after.
*Alice.* As I am a gentlewoman, Clarke, next day
Thou and Susan shall be married.
*Mosbie.* And I'll make her dowry more than I'll talk
    of, Clarke.
*Clarke.* Yonder's your husband. Mosbie, I'll be
    gone. 290

275 control] restraint

*Here enters* Arden *and* Franklin.

*Alice.* In good time see where my husband comes.
Master Mosbie, ask him the question yourself.
                                    [*Exit* Clarke.
*Mosbie.* Master Arden, being at London yesternight,
The Abbey lands, whereof you are now possess'd,
Were offer'd me on some occasion
By Greene, one of Sir Antony Ager's men:
I pray you, sir, tell me, are not the lands yours?
Hath any other interest herein?
*Arden.* Mosbie, that question we'll decide anon.
Alice, make ready my breakfast, I must hence.   300
                                    [*Exit* Alice.
As for the lands, Mosbie, they are mine
By letters patents from his Majesty.
But I must have a mandate for my wife;
They say you seek to rob me of her love:
Villain, what makes thou in her company?
She's no companion for so base a groom.
*Mosbie.* Arden, I thought not on her, I came to thee;
But rather than I pocket up this wrong——
*Franklin.* What will you do, sir?
*Mosbie.* Revenge it on the proudest of you both.   310
                [*Then* Arden *draws forth* Mosbie's *sword.*
*Arden.* So, sirrah; you may not wear a sword,
The statute makes against artificers;
I warrant that I do. Now use your bodkin,
Your Spanish needle, and your pressing iron,
For this shall go with me; and mark my words,
You goodman botcher, 'tis to you I speak:
The next time that I take thee near my house,
Instead of legs I'll make thee crawl on stumps.
*Mosbie.* Ah, Master Arden, you have injur'd me:
I do appeal to God and to the world.          320
*Franklin.* Why, canst thou deny thou wert a botcher
    once?

    316, 321 botcher] *See note on line* 25.

*Mosbie.* Measure me what I am, not what I was.

*Arden.* Why, what art thou now but a velvet drudge,
  A cheating steward, and base-minded peasant?

*Mosbie.* Arden, now thou hast belch'd and vomited
  The rancorous venom of thy mis-swoll'n heart,
  Hear me but speak: as I intend to live
  With God and his elected saints in heaven,
  I never meant more to solicit her;
  And that she knows, and all the world shall see.  330
  I loved her once;—sweet Arden, pardon me,
  I could not choose, her beauty fired my heart!
  But time hath quench'd these over-raging coals:
  And, Arden, though I now frequent thy house,
  'Tis for my sister's sake, her waiting-maid,
  And not for hers. Mayest thou enjoy her long:
  Hell-fire and wrathful vengeance light on me,
  If I dishonour her or injure thee.

*Arden.* Mosbie, with these thy protestations
  The deadly hatred of my heart is appeased,   340
  And thou and I'll be friends, if this prove true.
  As for the base terms I gave thee late,
  Forget them, Mosbie: I had cause to speak,
  When all the knights and gentlemen of Kent
  Make common table-talk of her and thee.

*Mosbie.* Who lives that is not touch'd with slanderous
    tongues?

*Franklin.* Then, Mosbie, to eschew the speech of men,
  Upon whose general bruit all honour hangs,
  Forbear his house.

*Arden.* Forbear it! nay, rather frequent it more:  350
  The world shall see that I distrust her not.
  To warn him on the sudden from my house
  Were to confirm the rumour that is grown.

*Mosbie.* By my faith, sir, you say true,
  And therefore will I sojourn here a while,
  Until our enemies have talk'd their fill;

348 bruit] report

And then, I hope, they'll cease, and at last confess
How causeless they have injur'd her and me.
*Arden.* And I will lie at London all this Term
　To let them see how light I weigh their words. 360

*Here enters* Alice.

*Alice.* Husband, sit down; your breakfast will be cold.
*Arden.* Come, Master Mosbie, will you sit with us?
*Mosbie.* I cannot eat, but I'll sit for company.
*Arden.* Sirrah Michael, see our horse be ready.
*Alice.* Husband, why pause ye? why eat you not?
*Arden.* I am not well; there's something in this broth
　That is not wholesome: didst thou make it, Alice?
*Alice.* I did, and that's the cause it likes not you.
　*Then she throws down the broth on the ground.*
　There's nothing that I do can please your taste;
　You were best to say I would have poisoned you. 370
　I cannot speak or cast aside my eye,
　But he imagines I have stepp'd awry.
　Here's he that you cast in my teeth so oft:
　Now will I be convinced or purge myself.
　I charge thee speak to this mistrustful man,
　Thou that would'st see me hang, thou, Mosbie, thou:
　What favour hast thou had more than a kiss
　At coming or departing from the town?
*Mosbie.* You wrong yourself and me to cast these
　　doubts:
　Your loving husband is not jealous.　　　　　380
*Arden.* Why, gentle Mistress Alice, cannot I be ill
　But you'll accuse yourself?
　Franklin, thou hast a box of mithridate;
　I'll take a little to prevent the worst.
*Franklin.* Do so, and let us presently take horse;
　My life for yours, ye shall do well enough.

368 likes] pleases　　374 convinced] convicted　　377–8
**a** kiss | At coming or departing] *This would be required by*
*bare civility, as at line* 412.　　　383 mithridate] antidote
to poison

*Alice.* Give me a spoon, I'll eat of it myself;
   Would it were full of poison to the brim,
   Then should my cares and troubles have an end.
   Was ever silly woman so tormented?    390
*Arden.* Be patient, sweet love; I mistrust not thee.
*Alice.* God will revenge it, Arden, if thou dost;
   For never woman lov'd her husband better
   Than I do thee.
*Arden.* I know it, sweet Alice; cease to complain,
   Lest that in tears I answer thee again.
*Franklin.* Come, leave this dallying, and let us away.
*Alice.* Forbear to wound me with that bitter word;
   Arden shall go to London in my arms.
*Arden.* Loth am I to depart, yet I must go.    400
*Alice.* Wilt thou to London, then, and leave me here?
   Ah, if thou love me, gentle Arden, stay.
   Yet, if thy business be of great import
   Go, if thou wilt, I'll bear it as I may;
   But write from London to me every week,
   Nay, every day, and stay no longer there
   Than thou must needs, lest that I die for sorrow.
*Arden.* I'll write unto thee every other tide,
   And so farewell, sweet Alice, till we meet next.
*Alice.* Farewell, husband, seeing you'll have it so; 410
   And, Master Franklin, seeing you take him hence,
   In hope you'll hasten him home, I'll give you this.
                  *[And then she kisseth him.*
*Franklin.* And if he stay, the fault shall not be mine.
   Mosbie, farewell, and see you keep your oath.
*Mosbie.* I hope he is not jealous of me now.
*Arden.* No, Mosbie, no; hereafter think of me
   As of your dearest friend, and so farewell.
          *[Exeunt* Arden, Franklin, *and* Michael.
*Alice.* I am glad he is gone; he was about to stay,
   But did you mark me then how I brake off?
*Mosbie.* Ay, Alice, and it was cunningly performed. 420

   408 tide] *Communication with London was in part by water,*
*as subsequent events in the play show.*

But what a villain is that painter Clarke!

*Alice.* Was it not a goodly poison that he gave?
Why, he's as well now as he was before.
It should have been some fine confection
That might have given the broth some dainty taste:
This powder was too gross and populous.

*Mosbie.* But had he eaten but three spoonfuls more,
Then had he died and our love continued.

*Alice.* Why, so it shall, Mosbie, albeit he live.

*Mosbie.* It is unpossible, for I have sworn　　　430
Never hereafter to solicit thee,
Or, whilst he lives, once more importune thee.

*Alice.* Thou shalt not need, I will importune thee.
What? shall an oath make thee forsake my love?
As if I have not sworn as much myself
And given my hand unto him in the church!
Tush, Mosbie; oaths are words, and words is wind,
And wind is mutable: then, I conclude,
'Tis childishness to stand upon an oath.

*Mosbie.* Well proved, Mistress Alice; yet by your
leave　　　440
I'll keep mine unbroken whilst he lives.

*Alice.* Ay, do, and spare not, his time is but short;
For if thou beest as resolute as I,
We'll have him murdered as he walks the streets.
In London many alehouse ruffins keep,
Which, as I hear, will murther men for gold.
They shall be soundly fee'd to pay him home.

*Here enters* Greene.

*Mosbie.* Alice, what's he that comes yonder? knowest
thou him?

*Alice.* Mosbie, begone: I hope 'tis one that comes
To put in practice our intended drifts.　　　450

[*Exit* Mosbie.

426 populous] common　　　445 ruffins] ruffians
keep] live　　　450 drifts] designs

*Greene.* Mistress Arden, you are well met.
 I am sorry that your husband is from home,
 Whenas my purposed journey was to him:
 Yet all my labour is not spent in vain,
 For I suppose that you can full discourse
 And flat resolve me of the thing I seek.
*Alice.* What is it, Master Greene? If that I may
 Or can with safety, I will answer you.
*Greene.* I heard your husband hath the grant of late,
 Confirmed by letters patents from the king,    460
 Of all the lands of the Abbey of Feversham,
 Generally intitled, so that all former grants
 Are cut off; whereof I myself had one;
 But now my interest by that is void.
 This is all, Mistress Arden; is it true or no?
*Alice.* True, Master Greene; the lands are his in state,
 And whatsoever leases were before
 Are void for term of Master Arden's life;
 He hath the grant under the Chancery seal.
*Greene.* Pardon me, Mistress Arden, I must speak, 470
 For I am touch'd. Your husband doth me wrong
 To wring me from the little land I have.
 My living is my life, onely that
 Resteth remainder of my portion.
 Desire of wealth is endless in his mind,
 And he is greedy-gaping still for gain;
 Nor cares he though young gentlemen do beg,
 So he may scrape and hoard up in his pouch.
 But, seeing he hath taken my lands, I'll value life
 As careless as he is careful for to get:    480
 And tell him this from me, I'll be revenged,
 And so as he shall wish the Abbey lands
 Had rested still within their former state.
*Alice.* Alas, poor gentleman, I pity you,
 And woe is me that any man should want!
 God knows 'tis not my fault: but wonder not

453 Whenas] when, since    457 resolve] inform

Though he be hard to others, when to me,—
Ah, Master Greene, God knows how I am us'd.
*Greene.* Why, Mistress Arden, can the crabbed churl
Use you unkindly? respects he not your birth, 490
Your honourable friends, nor what you brought?
Why, all Kent knows your parentage and what you
are.
*Alice.* Ah, Master Greene, be it spoken in secret here,
I never live good day with him alone:
When he is at home, then have I froward looks,
Hard words and blows to mend the match withal;
And though I might content as good a man,
Yet doth he keep in every corner trulls;
And, weary with his trugs at home,
Then rides he straight to London; there, for-
sooth,                                      500
He revels it among such filthy ones
As counsels him to make away his wife.
Thus live I daily in continual fear,
In sorrow, so depairing of redress
As every day I wish with hearty prayer
That he or I were taken forth the world.
*Greene.* Now trust me, Mistress Alice, it grieveth me
So fair a creature be so abused.
Why, who would have thought the civil sir so
sullen?
He looks so smoothly. Now, fie upon him, churl!
And if he live a day, he lives too long.      511
But frolic, woman! I shall be the man
Shall set you free from all this discontent;
And if the churl deny my interest
And will not yield my lease into my hand,
I'll pay him home, whatever hap to me.
*Alice.* But speak you as you think?
*Greene.* Ay, God's my witness, I mean plain dealing,
For I had rather die than lose my land.

491 what you brought] your dowry

*Alice.* Then, Master Greene, be counselled by me: 520
　　Endanger not yourself for such a churl,
　　But hire some cutter for to cut him short,
　　And here's ten pound to wager them withal;
　　When he is dead, you shall have twenty more,
　　And the lands whereof my husband is possess'd
　　Shall be intitled as they were before.
*Greene.* Will you keep promise with me?
*Alice.* Or count me false and perjur'd whilst I live.
*Greene.* Then here's my hand, I'll have him so dis-
　　patch'd.
　　I'll up to London straight, I'll thither post,　　530
　　And never rest till I have compass'd it.
　　Till then farewell.
*Alice.* Good fortune follow all your forward thoughts.
　　　　　　　　　　　　　　　　[*Exit* Greene.
　　And whosoever doth attempt the deed,
　　A happy hand I wish, and so farewell.—
　　All this goes well: Mosbie, I long for thee
　　To let thee know all that I have contrived.


　　　　*Here enters* Mosbie *and* Clarke.

*Mosbie.* How, now, Alice, what's the news?
*Alice.* Such as will content thee well, sweetheart.
*Mosbie.* Well, let them pass a while, and tell me,
　　Alice,　　　　　　　　　　　　　　　540
　　How have you dealt and tempered with my sister?
　　What, will she have my neighbour Clarke, or no?
*Alice.* What, Master Mosbie! let him woo himself!
　　Think you that maids look not for fair words?
　　Go to her, Clarke; she's all alone within;
　　Michael my man is clean out of her books.
*Clarke.* I thank you, Mistress Arden, I will in;
　　And if fair Susan and I can make a gree,

　　522 cutter] cut-throat　　　523 wager] pay　　　54**1**
tempered] reasoned, persuaded　　　548 gree] agreement

You shall command me to the uttermost,
As far as either goods or life may stretch.    550

                                [*Exit* Clarke.

*Mosbie.* Now, Alice, let's hear thy news.

*Alice.* They be so good that I must laugh for joy,
Before I can begin to tell my tale.

*Mosbie.* Let's hear them, that I may laugh for company.

*Alice.* This morning, Master Greene, Dick Greene I mean,
From whom my husband had the Abbey land,
Came hither, railing, for to know the truth
Whether my husband had the lands by grant.
I told him all, whereat he storm'd amain
And swore he would cry quittance with the churl,  560
And, if he did deny his interest,
Stab him, whatsoever did befall himself.
Whenas I saw his choler thus to rise,
I whetted on the gentleman with words;
And, to conclude, Mosbie, at last we grew
To composition for my husband's death.
I gave him ten pound for to hire knaves,
By some device to make away the churl;
When he is dead, he should have twenty more
And repossess his former lands again.    570
On this we greed, and he is ridden straight
To London, to bring his death about.

*Mosbie.* But call you this good news?

*Alice.* Ay, sweetheart, be they not?

*Mosbie.* 'Twere cheerful news to hear the churl were dead;
But trust me, Alice, I take it passing ill
You would be so forgetful of our state
To make recount of it to every groom.
What! to acquaint each stranger with our drifts,
Chiefly in case of murther, why, 'tis the way    580

563 Whenas] When          566 composition] bargain
571 greed] agreed

To make it open unto Arden's self
And bring thyself and me to ruin both.
Forewarn'd, forearm'd: who threats his enemy,
Lends him a sword to guard himself withal.
*Alice.* I did it for the best.
*Mosbie.* Well, seeing 'tis done, cheerily let it pass.
You know this Greene; is he not religious,
A man, I guess, of great devotion?
*Alice.* He is.
*Mosbie.* Then, sweet Alice, let it pass: I have a drift 590
Will quiet all, whatever is amiss.

*Here enters* Clarke *and* Susan.

*Alice.* How now, Clarke? have you found me false?
Did I not plead the matter hard for you?
*Clarke.* You did.
*Mosbie.* And what? will't be a match?
*Clarke.* A match, ay faith, sir: ay, the day is mine.
The painter lays his colours to the life,
His pencil draws no shadows in his love.
Susan is mine.
*Alice.* You make her blush.                          600
*Mosbie.* What, sister, is it Clarke must be the man?
*Susan.* It resteth in your grant; some words are past,
And haply we be grown unto a match,
If you be willing that it shall be so.
*Mosbie.* Ah, Master Clarke, it resteth at my grant:
You see my sister's yet at my dispose.
But, so you'll grant me one thing I shall ask,
I am content my sister shall be yours.
*Clarke.* What is it, Master Mosbie?
*Mosbie.* I do remember once in secret talk      610
You told me how you could compound by art
A crucifix impoisoned,
That whoso look upon it should wax blind
And with the scent be stifled, that ere long
He should die poison'd that did view it well.

590 drift] design

I would have you make me such a crucifix,
And then I'll grant my sister shall be yours.

*Clarke.* Though I am loth, because it toucheth life,
Yet, rather or I'll leave sweet Susan's love,
I'll do it, and with all the haste I may.          620
But for whom is it?

*Alice.* Leave that to us. Why, Clarke, is it possible
That you should paint and draw it out yourself,
The colours being baleful and impoisoned,
And no ways prejudice yourself withal?

*Mosbie.* Well questioned, Alice; Clarke, how answer
   you that?

*Clarke.* Very easily: I'll tell you straight
How I do work of these impoisoned drugs.
I fasten on my spectacles so close
As nothing can any way offend my sight;          630
Then, as I put a leaf within my nose,
So put I rhubarb to avoid the smell,
And softly as another work I paint.

*Mosbie.* 'Tis very well; but against when shall I have it?

*Clarke.* Within this ten days.

*Mosbie.* 'Twill serve the turn.
Now, Alice, let's in and see what cheer you keep.
I hope, now Master Arden is from home,
You'll give me leave to play your husband's part.

*Alice.* Mosbie, you know, who's master of my heart,
He well may be the master of the house.          641

                                      [*Exeunt.*

# ACT II

## Scene I

*Here enters* Greene *and* Bradshaw.

*Bradshaw.* See you them that comes yonder, Master
   Greene?

*Greene.* Ay, very well: do you know them?

633 softly] easily

*Here enters* Black Will *and* Shakebag.

*Bradshaw.* The one I know not, but he seems a knave
  Chiefly for bearing the other company;
  For such a slave, so vile a rogue as he,
  Lives not again upon the earth.
  Black Will is his name. I tell you, Master Greene,
  At Boulogne he and I were fellow-soldiers,
  Where he play'd such pranks
  As all the camp fear'd him for his villainy:    10
  I warrant you he bears so bad a mind
  That for a crown he'll murther any man.
*Greene.* The fitter is he for my purpose, marry!
*Will.* How now, fellow Bradshaw? Whither away so
  early?
*Bradshaw.* O Will, times are changed: no fellows now,
  Though we were once together in the field;
  Yet thy friend to do thee any good I can.
*Will.* Why, Bradshaw, was not thou and I fellow-
  soldiers at Boulogne, where I was a corporal, and
  thou but a base mercenary groom? No fellows
  now! because you are a goldsmith and have a
  little plate in your shop! You were glad to call
  me "fellow Will," and with a curtsey to the earth,
  "One snatch, good corporal," when I stole the
  half ox from John the victualer, and domineer'd
  with it amongst good fellows in one night.    26
*Bradshaw.* Ay, Will, those days are past with me.
*Will.* Ay, but they be not past with me, for I keep that
  same honourable mind still. Good neighbour
  Bradshaw, you are too proud to be my fellow;
  but were it not that I see more company coming
  down the hill, I would be fellows with you once
  more, and share crowns with you too. But let
  that pass, and tell me whither you go.    34
*Bradshaw.* To London, Will, about a piece of service,
  Wherein haply thou mayest pleasure me.

      25 domineer'd] revelled

*Will.* What is it?

*Bradshaw.* Of late Lord Cheiny lost some plate,
 Which one did bring and sold it at my shop,
 Saying he served Sir Antony Cooke.   40
 A search was made, the plate was found with me,
 And I am bound to answer at the 'size.
 Now, Lord Cheiny solemnly vows,
 If law will serve him, he'll hang me for his plate.
 Now I am going to London upon hope
 To find the fellow. Now, Will, I know
 Thou art acquainted with such companions.

*Will.* What manner of man was he?

*Bradshaw.* A lean-faced writhen knave,
 Hawk-nos'd and very hollow-eyed,   50
 With mighty furrows in his stormy brows;
 Long hair down his shoulders curled;
 His chin was bare, but on his upper lip
 A mutchado, which he wound about his ear.

*Will.* What apparel had he?

*Bradshaw.* A watchet satin doublet all to-torn,
 The inner side did bear the greater show;
 A pair of threadbare velvet hose, seam-rent,
 A worsted stocking rent above the shoe,
 A livery cloak, but all the lace was off;  60
 'Twas bad, but yet it served to hide the plate.

*Will.* Sirrah Shakebag, canst thou remember since we
 troll'd the bowl at Sittingburgh, where I broke
 the tapster's head of the Lion with a cudgel
 stick?

*Shakebag.* Ay, very well, Will.

*Will.* Why, it was with the money that the plate was
 sold for. Sirrah Bradshaw, what wilt thou give
 him that can tell thee who sold thy plate?

*Bradshaw.* Who, I pray thee, good Will?   70

*Will.* Why, 'twas one Jack Fitten. He's now in

42 'size] assize  47 companions] low fellows  49
writhen] twisted, distorted  54 mutchado] moustache
56 to-torn] torn to pieces  63 troll'd] passed round

Newgate for stealing a horse, and shall be ar-
raign'd the next 'size.

*Bradshaw.* Why, then let Lord Cheiny seek Jack Fitten
forth,
For I'll back and tell him who robbed him of his
plate.
This cheers my heart; Master Greene, I'll leave you,
For I must to the Isle of Sheppy with speed.

*Greene.* Before you go, let me entreat you
To carry this letter to Mistress Arden of Feversham
And humbly recommend me to herself.             80

*Bradshaw.* That will I, Master Greene, and so farewell.
Here, Will, there's a crown for thy good news.

> [*Exit* Bradshaw.

*Will.* Farewell, Bradshaw; I'll drink no water for thy
sake whilst this lasts.—Now, gentleman, shall we
have your company to London?

*Greene.* Nay, stay, sirs:
A little more I needs must use your help,
And in a matter of great consequence,
Wherein if you'll be secret and profound,
I'll give you twenty angels for your pains.       90

*Will.* How? twenty angels? give my fellow George
Shakebag and me twenty angels? And if thou'lt
have thy own father slain, that thou may'st
inherit his land, we'll kill him.

*Shakebag.* Ay, thy mother, thy sister, thy brother, or
all thy kin.

*Greene.* Well, this is it: Arden of Feversham
Hath highly wrong'd me about the Abbey land,
That no revenge but death will serve the turn.
Will you two kill him? here's the angels down,   100
And I will lay the platform of his death.

*Will.* Plat me no platforms; give me the money, and
I'll stab him as he stands pissing against a wall,
but I'll kill him.

101, 102 platform] plan

*Shakebag.* Where is he?

*Greene.* He is now at London, in Aldersgate Street.

*Shakebag.* He's dead as if he had been condemned by an Act of Parliament, if once Black Will and I swear his death.

*Greene.* Here is ten pound, and when he is dead,   110 Ye shall have twenty more.

*Will.* My fingers itches to be at the peasant. Ah, that I might be set a-work thus through the year, and that murther would grow to an occupation, that a man might follow without danger of law:— zounds, I warrant I should be warden of the company! Come, let us be going, and we'll bait at Rochester, where I'll give thee a gallon of sack to handsel the match withal.

[*Exeunt.*

## SCENE II

*Here enters* Michael.

*Michael.* I have gotten such a letter as will touch the painter: and thus it is:

*Here enters* Arden *and* Franklin *and hears* Michael *read this letter.*

*My duty remember'd, Mistress Susan, hoping in God you be in good health, as I Michael was at the making hereof. This is to certify you that as the turtle true, when she hath lost her mate, sitteth alone, so I, mourning for your absence, do walk up and down Paul's till one day I fell asleep and lost my master's pantofles. Ah, Mistress Susan, abolish that paltry painter, cut him off by the shins with a frowning look of your crabbed countenance, and think upon Michael, who, drunk with the dregs of your favour, will cleave as fast to your love*

117 bait] stop for food        119 handsel] inaugurate auspiciously        8 pantofles] slippers

*as a plaster of pitch to a gall'd horse-back. Thus hoping*
*you will let my passions penetrate, or rather impetrate*
*mercy of your meek hands, I end*                          15
                *Yours, Michael, or else not Michael.*

*Arden.* Why, you paltry knave,
  Stand you here loitering, knowing my affairs,
  What haste my business craves to send to Kent?
*Franklin.* Faith, friend Michael, this is very ill,    20
  Knowing your master hath no more but you,
  And do ye slack his business for your own?
*Arden.* Where is the letter, sirrah? let me see it.

          *Then he gives him the letter.*

See, Master Franklin, here's proper stuff:
Susan my maid, the painter, and my man,
A crew of harlots, all in love, forsooth;
Sirrah, let me hear no more of this.
Now for thy life once write to her a word!

          *Here enters* Greene, Will, *and* Shakebag.

Wilt thou be married to so base a trull?
'Tis Mosbie's sister: come I once at home,    30
I'll rouse her from remaining in my house.
Now, Master Franklin, let us go walk in Paul's;
Come, but a turn or two, and then away. [*Exeunt.*
*Greene.* The first is Arden, and that's his man,
  The other is Franklin, Arden's dearest friend.
*Will.* Zounds, I'll kill them all three.
*Greene.* Nay, sirs, touch not his man in any case;
  But stand close, and take you fittest standing,
  And at his coming forth speed him:
  To the Nag's Head, there is this coward's haunt. 40
  But now I'll leave you till the deed be done.
                          [*Exit* Greene.

14 impetrate] obtain by request      32 Paul's] *Old St.*
*Paul's was favoured by London merchants and others as a rendezvous*
*and promenade.*

                    K

*Shakebag.* If he be not paid his own, ne'er trust
    Shakebag.

*Will.* Sirrah Shakebag, at his coming forth I'll run
    him through, and then to the Blackfriars, and
    there take water and away.

*Shakebag.* Why, that's the best; but see thou miss him
    not.

*Will.* How can I miss him, when I think on the forty
    angels I must have more?                         50

*Here enters a* Prentice.

*Prentice.* 'Tis very late; I were best shut up my stall,
    For here will be old filching, when the press
    Comes forth of Paul's.

*Then lets he down his window, and it breaks* Black
    Will's *head.*

*Will.* Zounds, draw, Shakebag, draw, I am almost
    kill'd.

*Prentice.* We'll tame you, I warrant.

*Will.* Zounds, I am tame enough already.

*Here enters* Arden, Franklin, *and* Michael.

*Arden.* What troublesome fray or mutiny is this?

*Franklin.* 'Tis nothing but some brabbling paltry fray,
    Devised to pick men's pockets in the throng.    60

*Arden.* Is't nothing else? come, Franklin, let us away.
                                            [*Exeunt.*

*Will.* What 'mends shall I have for my broken head?

*Prentice.* Marry, this 'mends, that if you get you not
    away all the sooner, you shall be well beaten and
    sent to the Counter.              [*Exit* Prentice.

*Will.* Well, I'll be gone, but look to your signs, for I'll
    pull them down all. Shakebag, my broken head
    grieves me not so much as by this means Arden
    hath escaped.

52 old] great      59 brabbling] noisy

*Here enters* Greene.

    I had a glimpse of him and his companion.    70
*Greene.* Why, sirs, Arden's as well as I; I met him and
    Franklin going merrily to the ordinary. What,
    dare you not do it?
*Will.* Yes, sir, we dare do it; but, were my consent to
    give again, we would not do it under ten pound
    more. I value every drop of my blood at a French
    crown. I have had ten pound to steal a dog, and
    we have no more here to kill a man; but that a
    bargain is a bargain, and so forth, you should do
    it yourself.    80
*Greene.* I pray thee, how came thy head broke?
*Will.* Why, thou see'st it is broke, dost thou not?
*Shakebag.* Standing against a stall, watching Arden's
    coming, a boy let down his shop-window, and
    broke his head; whereupon arose a brawl, and
    in the tumult Arden escap'd us and pass'd by
    unthought on. But forbearance is no acquit-
    tance; another time we'll do it, I warrant thee.
*Greene.* I pray thee, Will, make clean thy bloody brow,
    And let us bethink us on some other place    90
    Where Arden may be met with handsomely.
    Remember how devoutly thou hast sworn
    To kill the villain; think upon thine oath.
*Will.* Tush, I have broken five hundred oaths!
    But would'st thou charm me to effect this deed,
    Tell me of gold, my resolution's fee;
    Say thou seest Mosbie kneeling at my knees,
    Off'ring me service for my high attempt,
    And sweet Alice Arden, with a lap of crowns,
    Comes with a lowly curtsey to the earth,    100
    Saying "Take this but for thy quarterage,
    Such yearly tribute will I answer thee."
    Why, this would steel soft-mettled cowardice,

72 ordinary] eating-house    101 quarterage] quarterly
payment    102 answer] guarantee

With which Black Will was never tainted with.
I tell thee, Greene, the forlorn traveller,
Whose lips are glued with summer's parching heat,
Ne'er long'd so much to see a running brook
As I to finish Arden's tragedy.
Seest thou this gore that cleaveth to my face?
From hence ne'er will I wash this bloody stain, 110
Till Arden's heart be panting in my hand.

*Greene.* Why, that's well said; but what saith Shake-
     bag?

*Shakebag.* I cannot paint my valour out with words:
     But, give me place and opportunity,
     Such mercy as the starven lioness,
     When she is dry suck'd of her eager young,
     Shows to the prey that next encounters her,
     On Arden so much pity would I take.

*Greene.* So should it fare with men of firm resolve.
     And now, sirs, seeing this accident             120
     Of meeting him in Paul's hath no success,
     Let us bethink us on some other place
     Whose earth may swallow up this Arden's blood.


*Here enters* Michael.

See, yonder comes his man: and wot you what?
The foolish knave's in love with Mosbie's sister,
And for her sake, whose love he cannot get
Unless Mosbie solicit his suit,
The villain hath sworn the slaughter of his master.
We'll question him, for he may stead us much.—
How now, Michael, whither are you going?   130

*Michael.* My master hath new supp'd,
     And I am going to prepare his chamber.

*Greene.* Where supp'd Master Arden?

*Michael.* At the Nag's Head, at the eighteen-pence

---

129 stead] help   134–5 the eighteen-pence | ordinary]
room in an eating-house where the meal cost eighteen
pence.

ordinary.  How now, Master Shakebag? what,
Black Will!  God's dear lady, how chance your
face is so bloody?

*Will.*  Go to, sirrah, there is a chance in it; this sauci-
ness in you will make you be knock'd.

*Michael.*  Nay, an you be offended, I'll be gone.   140

*Greene.*  Stay, Michael, you may not 'scape us so.
Michael, I know you love your master well.

*Michael.*  Why, so I do; but wherefore urge you that?

*Greene.*  Because I think you love your mistress better.

*Michael.*  So think not I; but say, i'faith, what if I
should?

*Shakebag.*  Come to the purpose, Michael; we hear
You have a pretty love in Feversham.

*Michael.*  Why, have I two or three, what's that to
thee!

*Will.*  You deal too mildly with the peasant.  Thus it is:
'Tis known to us that you love Mosbie's sister;  150
We know besides that you have ta'en your oath
To further Mosbie to your mistress' bed,
And kill your master for his sister's sake.
Now, sir, a poorer coward than yourself
Was never fostered in the coast of Kent:
How comes it then that such a knave as you
Dare swear a matter of such consequence?

*Greene.*  Ah, Will——

*Will.*  Tush, give me leave, there's no more but this:
Sith thou hast sworn, we dare discover all;   160
And hadst thou or should'st thou utter it,
We have devised a complot under hand,
Whatever shall betide to any of us,
To send thee roundly to the devil of hell.
And therefore thus: I am the very man,
Mark'd in my birth-hour by the destinies,
To give an end to Arden's life on earth;
Thou but a member but to whet the knife

162 complot] plot

Whose edge must search the closet of his breast:
Thy office is but to appoint the place,                170
And train thy master to his tragedy;
Mine to perform it when occasion serves.
Then be not nice, but here devise with us
How and what way we may conclude his death.

*Shakebag.* So shalt thou purchase Mosbie for thy
    friend,
And by his friendship gain his sister's love.

*Greene.* So shall thy mistress be thy favourer,
And thou disburd'ned of the oath thou made.

*Michael.* Well, gentlemen, I cannot but confess,
Sith you have urged me so apparently,                180
That I have vowed my master Arden's death;
And he whose kindly love and liberal hand
Doth challenge nought but good deserts of me,
I will deliver over to your hands.
This night come to his house at Aldersgate:
The doors I'll leave unlock'd against you come.
No sooner shall ye enter through the latch,
Over the threshold to the inner court,
But on your left hand shall you see the stairs
That leads directly to my master's chamber:      190
There take him and dispose him as ye please.
Now it were good we parted company;
What I have promised, I will perform.

*Will.* Should you deceive us, 'twould go wrong with
    you.

*Michael.* I will accomplish all I have reveal'd.

*Will.* Come, let's go drink: choler makes me as dry
    as a dog.

*Exeunt* Will, Greene, *and* Shakebag.   *Manet* Michael.

*Michael.* Thus feeds the lamb securely on the down,
Whilst through the thicket of an arbour brake
The hunger-bitten wolf o'erpries his haunt
And takes advantage to eat him up.                 200

171 train] lead, guide        197 securely] carelessly

Ah, harmless Arden, how, how hast thou mis-
    done,
That thus thy gentle life is levell'd at?
The many good turns that thou hast done to me.
Now must I quittance with betraying thee.
I that should take the weapon in my hand
And buckler thee from ill-intending foes,
Do lead thee with a wicked fraudful smile,
As unsuspected, to the slaughter-house.
So have I sworn to Mosbie and my mistress,
So have I promised to the slaughtermen;    210
And should I not deal currently with them,
Their lawless rage would take revenge on me.
Tush, I will spurn at mercy for this once:
Let pity lodge where feeble women lie,
I am resolved, and Arden needs must die.
                        [*Exit* Michael.

# ACT III

## SCENE I

*Enter* Arden *and* Franklin.

*Arden.* No, Franklin, no: if fear or stormy threats,
  If love of me or care of womanhood,
  If fear of God or common speech of men,
  Who mangle credit with their wounding words,
  And couch dishonour as dishonour buds,
  Might join repentance in her wanton thoughts,
  No question then but she would turn the leaf
  And sorrow for her dissolution;

202 levell'd] aimed    206 buckler] shield    211
currently] faithfully    5 couch dishonour as dishonour
buds] nourish the unripe buds of dishonour, as fast as they
appear, till they sprout and grow (*Tucker Brooke*)    6
join] enjoin    8 dissolution] dissolute conduct, dis-
soluteness

But she is rooted in her wickedness,
Perverse and stubborn, not to be reclaim'd;      10
Good counsel is to her as rain to weeds,
And reprehension makes her vice to grow
As Hydra's head that flourish'd by decay.
Her faults, methink, are painted in my face,
For every searching eye to overread;
And Mosbie's name, a scandal unto mine,
Is deeply trenched in my blushing brow.
Ah, Franklin, Franklin, when I think on this,
My heart's grief rends my other powers
Worse than the conflict at the hour of death.      20
*Franklin.* Gentle Arden, leave this sad lament:
She will amend, and so your griefs will cease;
Or else she'll die, and so your sorrows end.
If neither of these two do haply fall,
Yet let your comfort be that others bear
Your woes, twice doubled all, with patience.
*Arden.* My house is irksome; there I cannot rest.
*Franklin.* Then stay with me in London, go not
home.
*Arden.* Then that base Mosbie doth usurp my room
And makes his triumph of my being thence.      30
At home or not at home, where'er I be,
Here, here it lies, ah Franklin, here it lies
That will not out till wretched Arden dies.

### *Here enters* Michael.

*Franklin.* Forget your griefs a while; here comes your
man.
*Arden.* What a-clock is't, sirrah?
*Michael.* Almost ten.
*Arden.* See, see, how runs away the weary time!
Come, Master Franklin, shall we go to bed?
       [*Exeunt* Arden *and* Michael. *Manet* Franklin.

13 flourish'd] *Dyce's conjecture, adopted by Tucker Brooke.*
*The quartos have* perisht.      29 room] place

*Franklin.* I pray you, go before: I'll follow you.
　—Ah, what a hell is fretful jealousy!　　　　40
What pity-moving words, what deep-fetch'd sighs,
What grievous groans and overlading woes
Accompanies this gentle gentleman!
Now will he shake his care-oppressed head,
Then fix his sad eyes on the sullen earth,
Ashamed to gaze upon the open world;
Now will he cast his eyes up towards the heavens,
Looking that ways for redress of wrong:
Sometimes he seeketh to beguile his grief
And tells a story with his careful tongue;　　　50
Then comes his wife's dishonour in his thoughts
And in the middle cutteth off his tale,
Pouring fresh sorrow on his weary limbs.
So woe-begone, so inly charged with woe,
Was never any lived and bare it so.

*Here enters* Michael.

*Michael.* My master would desire you come to bed.
*Franklin.* Is he himself already in his bed?
　　　　　　[*Exit* Franklin. *Manet* Michael.
*Michael.* He is, and fain would have the light away.
　—Conflicting thoughts, encamped in my breast,
Awake me with the echo of their strokes,　　　60
And I, a judge to censure either side,
Can give to neither wished victory.
My master's kindness pleads to me for life
With just demand, and I must grant it him:
My mistress she hath forced me with an oath,
For Susan's sake, the which I may not break,
For that is nearer than a master's love:
That grim-faced fellow, pitiless Black Will,
And Shakebag, stern in bloody stratagem,
　—Two rougher ruffins never lived in Kent,—　70
Have sworn my death, if I infringe my vow,

70 ruffins] ruffians

A dreadful thing to be consider'd of.
Methinks I see them with their bolster'd hair
Staring and grinning in thy gentle face,
And in their ruthless hands their daggers drawn,
Insulting o'er thee with a peck of oaths,
Whilst thou submissive, pleading for relief,
Art mangled by their ireful instruments.
Methinks I hear them ask where Michael is,
And pitiless Black Will cries: "Stab the slave!    80
The peasant will detect the tragedy!"
The wrinkles in his foul death-threat'ning face
Gapes open wide, like graves to swallow men.
My death to him is but a merriment,
And he will murther me to make him sport.
He comes, he comes! ah, Master Franklin, help!
Call on the neighbours, or we are but dead!

*Here enters* Franklin *and* Arden.

*Franklin.* What dismal outcry calls me from my rest?
*Arden.* What hath occasion'd such a fearful cry?
    Speak, Michael: hath any injur'd thee?    90
*Michael.* Nothing, sir; but as I fell asleep,
    Upon the threshold leaning to the stairs,
    I had a fearful dream that troubled me,
    And in my slumber thought I was beset
    With murtherer thieves that came to rifle me.
    My trembling joints witness my inward fear:
    I crave your pardons for disturbing you.
*Arden.* So great a cry for nothing I ne'er heard.
    What? are the doors fast lock'd and all things safe?
*Michael.* I cannot tell; I think I lock'd the doors.    100
*Arden.* I like not this, but I'll go see myself.—
    Ne'er trust me but the doors were all unlock'd:
    This negligence not half contenteth me.
    Get you to bed, and if you love my favour,

73 bolster'd] *perhaps for* bolter'd, *i.e.* matted    81
detect] reveal    92 leaning to] leaning against

Let me have no more such pranks as these.
Come, Master Franklin, let us go to bed.
*Franklin.* Ay, by my faith; the air is very cold.
Michael, farewell; I pray thee dream no more.

[*Exeunt.*

## SCENE II

*Here enters* Will, Greene, *and* Shakebag.

*Shakebag.* Black night hath hid the pleasures of the day,
And sheeting darkness overhangs the earth,
And with the black fold of her cloudy robe
Obscures us from the eyesight of the world,
In which sweet silence such as we triumph.
The lazy minutes linger on their time,
Loth to give due audit to the hour,
Till in the watch our purpose be complete
And Arden sent to everlasting night.
Greene, get you gone, and linger hereabout,    10
And at some hour hence come to us again,
Where we will give you instance of his death.
*Greene.* Speed to my wish, whose will so e'er says no;
And so I'll leave you for an hour or two.

[*Exit* Greene.

*Will.* I tell thee, Shakebag, would this thing were done:
I am so heavy that I can scarce go;
This drowsiness in me bodes little good.
*Shakebag.* How now, Will? become a precisian?
Nay, then let's go sleep, when bugs and fears
Shall kill our courages with their fancy's work.    20
*Will.* Why, Shakebag, thou mistakes me much,
And wrongs me too in telling me of fear.
Were't not a serious thing we go about,
It should be slipp'd till I had fought with thee,
To let thee know I am no coward, I.
I tell thee, Shakebag, thou abusest me.

18 precisian] puritan        19 bugs] bugbears        24
slipp'd] deferred

*Shakebag.* Why, thy speech bewrayed an inly kind of
    fear,
  And savour'd of a weak relenting spirit.
  Go forward now in that we have begun,
  And afterwards attempt me when thou darest.   30
*Will.* And if I do not, heaven cut me off!
  But let that pass, and show me to this house,
  Where thou shalt see I'll do as much as Shakebag.
*Shakebag.* This is the door; but soft, methinks 'tis shut.
  The villain Michael hath deceived us.
*Will.* Soft, let me see, Shakebag; 'tis shut indeed.
  Knock with thy sword, perhaps the slave will hear.
*Shakebag.* It will not be; the white-liver'd peasant
  Is gone to bed, and laughs us both to scorn.
*Will.* And he shall buy his merriment as dear   40
  As ever coistrel bought so little sport:
  Ne'er let this sword assist me when I need,
  But rust and canker after I have sworn,
  If I, the next time that I meet the hind,
  Lop not away his leg, his arm, or both.
*Shakebag.* And let me never draw a sword again,
  Nor prosper in the twilight, cockshut light,
  When I would fleece the wealthy passenger,
  But lie and languish in a loathsome den,
  Hated and spit at by the goers-by,   50
  And in that death may die unpitied,
  If I, the next time that I meet the slave,
  Cut not the nose from off the coward's face
  And trample on it for this villainy.
*Will.* Come, let's go seek out Greene; I know he'll
    swear.
*Shakebag.* He were a villain, an he would not swear.
  'Twould make a peasant swear among his boys,
  That ne'er durst say before but "yea" and "no,"
  To be thus flouted of a coisterel.

41, 59 coistrel, coisterel] base fellow; *the spelling of the
quartos indicates the pronunciation required by the metre.*   47
cockshut light] twilight (O.E.D.)

*Will.* Shakebag, let's seek out Greene, and in the
    morning                             60
At the alehouse butting Arden's house
Watch the out-coming of that prick-ear'd cur,
And then let me alone to handle him.    [*Exeunt.*

## SCENE III

*Here enters* Arden, Franklin, *and* Michael.

*Arden.* Sirrah, get you back to Billingsgate
And learn what time the tide will serve our turn;
Come to us in Paul's.  First go make the bed,
And afterwards go hearken for the flood.
                                [*Exit* Michael.
Come, Master Franklin, you shall go with me.
This night I dream'd that, being in a park,
A toil was pitch'd to overthrow the deer,
And I upon a little rising hill
Stood whistly watching for the herd's approach.
Even there, methought, a gentle slumber took me,  10
And summon'd all my parts to sweet repose;
But in the pleasure of this golden rest
An ill-thew'd foster had removed the toil,
And rounded me with that beguiling home
Which late, methought, was pitch'd to cast the deer.
With that he blew an evil-sounding horn,
And at the noise another herdman came,
With falchion drawn, and bent it at my breast,
Crying aloud, "Thou art the game we seek!"
With this I wak'd and trembled every joint,    20
Like one oscured in a little bush,
That sees a lion foraging about,
And, when the dreadful forest-king is gone,

61 butting] abutting, adjoining       63 let me alone]
trust me       3 Paul's] *See note on* II. ii. 32.      7 toil]
snare     9 whistly] silently      13 ill-thew'd] evil-
natured   foster] forester   21 oscured] obscured, hidden

He pries about with timorous suspect
Throughout the thorny casements of the brake,
And will not think his person dangerless,
But quakes and shivers, though the cause be gone:
So, trust me, Franklin, when I did awake,
I stood in doubt whether I waked or no:
Such great impression took this fond surprise.    30
God grant this vision bedeem me any good.

*Franklin.* This fantasy doth rise from Michael's fear,
Who being awaked with the noise he made,
His troubled senses yet could take no rest;
And this, I warrant you, procured your dream.

*Arden.* It may be so, God frame it to the best:
But oftentimes my dreams presage too true.

*Franklin.* To such as note their nightly fantasies,
Some one in twenty may incur belief;
But use it not, 'tis but a mockery.    40

*Arden.* Come, Master Franklin; we'll now walk in
    Paul's
And dine together at the ordinary,
And by my man's direction draw to the quay,
And with the tide go down to Feversham.
Say, Master Franklin, shall it not be so?

*Franklin.* At your good pleasure, sir; I'll bear you
    company.    [*Exeunt.*


## SCENE IV

*Here enters* Michael *at one door.*
*Here enters* Greene, Will, *and* Shakebag *at another door.*

*Will.* Draw, Shakebag, for here's that villain Michael.

*Greene.* First, Will, let's hear what he can say.

*Will.* Speak, milksop slave, and never after speak.

*Michael.* For God's sake, sirs, let me excuse myself:
For here I swear, by heaven and earth and all,
I did perform the utmost of my task,

31 bedeem] bode        32 fantasy] fancy

And left the doors unbolted and unlock'd.
But see the chance: Franklin and my master
Were very late conferring in the porch,
And Franklin left his napkin where he sat          10
With certain gold knit in it, as he said.
Being in bed, he did bethink himself,
And coming down he found the doors unshut:
He lock'd the gates, and brought away the keys,
For which offence my master rated me.
But now I am going to see what flood it is,
For with the tide my master will away;
Where you may front him well on Rainham Down,
A place well-fitting such a stratagem.

*Will.* Your excuse hath somewhat mollified my
    choler.          20
Why now, Greene, 'tis better now nor e'er it was.

*Greene.* But, Michael, is this true?

*Michael.* As true as I report it to be true.

*Shakebag.* Then, Michael, this shall be your penance,
To feast us all at the Salutation,
Where we will plot our purpose thoroughly.

*Greene.* And, Michael, you shall bear no news of this
    tide,
Because they two may be in Rainham Down
Before your master.

*Michael.* Why, I'll agree to anything you'll have me, 30
So you will except of my company.          [*Exeunt.*

## Scene V

*Here enters* Mosbie.

*Mosbie.* Disturbed thoughts drives me from company
And dries my marrow with their watchfulness;
Continual trouble of my moody brain
Feebles my body by excess of drink,

  18 front] confront, encounter          28 Because] so that
31 except] accept

And nips me as the bitter north-east wind
Doth check the tender blossoms in the spring.
Well fares the man, howe'er his cates do taste,
That tables not with foul suspicion;
And he but pines amongst his delicates,
Whose troubled mind is stuff'd with discontent.  10
My golden time was when I had no gold;
Though then I wanted, yet I slept secure;
My daily toil begat me night's repose,
My night's repose made daylight fresh to me.
But since I climb'd the top bough of the tree
And sought to build my nest among the clouds,
Each gentle stary gale doth shake my bed,
And makes me dread my downfall to the earth.
But whither doth contemplation carry me?
The way I seek to find, where pleasure dwells,  20
Is hedged behind me that I cannot back,
But needs must on, although to danger's gate.
Then, Arden, perish thou by that decree;
For Greene doth ear the land and weed thee up
To make my harvest nothing but pure corn.
And for his pains I'll hive him up a while,
And after smother him to have his wax:
Such bees as Greene must never live to sting.
Then is there Michael and the painter too,
Chief actors to Arden's overthrow;  30
Who when they shall see me sit in Arden's seat,
They will insult upon me for my meed,
Or fright me by detecting of his end.
I'll none of that, for I can cast a bone
To make these curs pluck out each other's throat,
And then am I sole ruler of mine own.
Yet Mistress Arden lives; but she's myself,
And holy Church rites makes us two but one.
But what for that?  I may not trust you, Alice:

7 cates] food    17 stary] stirring (*Bullen*)    24 ear]
plough    32 insult upon] treat with scornful abuse
meed] reward    33 detecting] revealing

You have supplanted Arden for my sake,                    40
And will extirpen me to plant another.
'Tis fearful sleeping in a serpent's bed,
And I will cleanly rid my hands of her.


*Here enters* Alice.

But here she comes, and I must flatter her.—
How now, Alice? what, sad and passionate?
Make me partaker of thy pensiveness:
Fire divided burns with lesser force.
*Alice.* But I will dam that fire in my breast
Till by the force thereof my part consume.
Ah, Mosbie!                                                50
*Mosbie.* Such deep pathaires, like to a cannon's burst
Discharg'd against a ruinated wall,
Breaks my relenting heart in thousand pieces.
Ungentle Alice, thy sorrow is my sore;
Thou know'st it well, and 'tis thy policy
To forge distressful looks to wound a breast
Where lies a heart that dies when thou art sad.
It is not love that loves to anger love.
*Alice.* It is not love that loves to murther love.
*Mosbie.* How mean you that?                               60
*Alice.* Thou knowest how dearly Arden loved me.
*Mosbie.* And then?
*Alice.* And then—conceal the rest, for 'tis too bad,
Lest that my words be carried with the wind,
And publish'd in the world to both our shames.
I pray thee, Mosbie, let our springtime wither;
Our harvest else will yield but loathsome weeds.
Forget, I pray thee, what hath pass'd betwixt us,
For now I blush and tremble at the thoughts!
*Mosbie.* What? are you chang'd?                           70
*Alice.* Ay, to my former happy life again,
From title of an odious strumpet's name

41 extirpen] root up        51 pathaires] passionate outbursts (?)

To honest Arden's wife, not Arden's honest wife.
Ha, Mosbie! 'tis thou has rifled me of that
And made me slanderous to all my kin;
Even in my forehead is thy name engraven,
A mean artificer, that low-born name.
I was bewitched: woe worth the hapless hour
And all the causes that enchanted me!

*Mosbie.* Nay, if you ban, let me breathe curses forth, 80
And if you stand so nicely at your fame,
Let me repent the credit I have lost.
I have neglected matters of import
That would have stated me above thy state,
Forslow'd advantages, and spurn'd at time:
Ay, Fortune's right hand Mosbie hath forsook
To take a wanton giglot by the left.
I left the marriage of an honest maid,
Whose dowry would have weighed down all thy
    wealth,
Whose beauty and demeanour far exceeded thee: 90
This certain good I lost for changing bad,
And wrapp'd my credit in thy company.
I was bewitch'd,—that is no theme of thine,—
And thou unhallowed has enchanted me.
But I will break thy spells and exorcisms,
And put another sight upon these eyes
That showed my heart a raven for a dove.
Thou art not fair, I view'd thee not till now;
Thou art not kind, till now I knew thee not;
And now the rain hath beaten off thy gilt,    100
Thy worthless copper shows thee counterfeit.
It grieves me not to see how foul thou art,
But mads me that ever I thought thee fair.
Go, get thee gone, a copesmate for thy hinds;
I am too good to be thy favourite.

*Alice.* Ay, now I see, and too soon find it true,

80 ban] curse        85 Forslow'd advantages] wasted
opportunities        87 giglot] worthless woman        104
copesmate] paramour

Which often hath been told me by my friends,
That Mosbie loves me not but for my wealth,
Which too incredulous I ne'er believed.
Nay, hear me speak, Mosbie, a word or two;    110
I'll bite my tongue if it speak bitterly.
Look on me, Mosbie, or I'll kill myself:
Nothing shall hide me from thy stormy look.
If thou cry war, there is no peace for me;
I will do penance for offending thee,
And burn this prayer-book, where I here use
The holy word that had converted me.
See, Mosbie, I will tear away the leaves,
And all the leaves, and in this golden cover
Shall thy sweet phrases and thy letters dwell;    120
And thereupon will I chiefly meditate,
And hold no other sect but such devotion.
Wilt thou not look? is all thy love overwhelm'd?
Wilt thou not hear? what malice stops thine ears?
Why speaks thou not? what silence ties thy tongue?
Thou hast been sighted as the eagle is,
And heard as quickly as the fearful hare,
And spoke as smoothly as an orator,
When I have bid thee hear or see or speak,
And art thou sensible in none of these?    130
Weigh all thy good turns with this little fault,
And I deserve not Mosbie's muddy looks.
A fence of trouble is not thicken'd still:
Be clear again, I'll ne'er more trouble thee.
*Mosbie.* O no, I am a base artificer:
My wings are feather'd for a lowly flight.
Mosbie? fie! no, not for a thousand pound.
Make love to you? why, 'tis unpardonable;
We beggars must not breathe where gentles are.
*Alice.* Sweet Mosbie is as gentle as a king,    140
And I too blind to judge him otherwise.
Flowers do sometimes spring in fallow lands,
Weeds in gardens, roses grow on thorns;
So, whatso'er my Mosbie's father was,

Himself is valued gentle by his worth.

*Mosbie.* Ah, how you women can insinuate,
  And clear a trespass with your sweet-set tongue!
  I will forget this quarrel, gentle Alice,
  Provided I'll be tempted so no more.

*Here enters* Bradshaw.

*Alice.* Then with thy lips seal up this new-made
  match.                                        150
*Mosbie.* Soft, Alice, for here comes somebody.
*Alice.* How now, Bradshaw, what's the news with you?
*Bradshaw.* I have little news, but here's a letter
  That Master Greene importuned me to give you.
*Alice.* Go in, Bradshaw; call for a cup of beer;
  'Tis almost supper-time, thou shalt stay with us.
                                      [*Exit* Bradshaw.

*Then she reads the letter.*

*We have miss'd of our purpose at London, but shall per-*
*form it by the way. We thank our neighbour Bradshaw.*
                          *Yours, Richard Greene.*

How likes my love the tenor of this letter?   160
*Mosbie.* Well, were his date complete and expired.
*Alice.* Ah, would it were! Then comes my happy hour:
  Till then my bliss is mix'd with bitter gall.
  Come, let us in to shun suspicion.
*Mosbie.* Ay, to the gates of death to follow thee.
                                      [*Exeunt.*

# Scene VI

*Here enters* Greene, Will, *and* Shakebag.

*Shakebag.* Come, Will, see thy tools be in a readiness!
  Is not thy powder dank, or will thy flint strike fire?
*Will.* Then ask me if my nose be on my face,
  Or whether my tongue be frozen in my mouth.

147 clear a trespass] excuse an offence

Zounds, here's a coil!
You were best swear me on the intergatories
How many pistols I have took in hand,
Or whether I love the smell of gunpowder,
Or dare abide the noise the dag will make,
Or will not wink at flashing of the fire.                    10
I pray thee, Shakebag, let this answer thee,
That I have took more purses in this down
Than e'er thou handled'st pistols in thy life.

*Shakebag.* Ay, haply thou has pick'd more in a throng:
But, should I brag what booties I have took,
I think the overplus that's more than thine
Would mount to a greater sum of money
Than either thou or all thy kin are worth.
Zounds, I hate them as I hate a toad
That carry a muscado in their tongue,                    20
And scarce a hurting weapon in their hand.

*Will.* O Greene, intolerable!
It is not for mine honour to bear this.
Why, Shakebag, I did serve the king at Boulogne,
And thou canst brag of nothing that thou hast done.

*Shakebag.* Why, so can Jack of Feversham,
That sounded for a fillip of the nose,
When he that gave it him holloed in his ear,
And he supposed a cannon-bullet hit him.

*Then they fight.*

*Greene.* I pray you, sirs, list to Aesop's talk:                    30
Whilst two stout dogs were striving for a bone,
There comes a cur and stole it from them both;
So, while you stand striving on these terms of man-
    hood,
Arden escapes us, and deceives us all.

6 intergatories] interrogatories, *i.e.* on oath.        9, 40
dag] pistol                20 muscado] '*Apparently some weapon*'
(O.E.D.)*; or perhaps a* mosquito*?*                27 sounded]
swooned

*Shakebag.* Why, he begun.

*Will.*                              And thou shalt find I'll end;
  I do but slip it until better time:
  But, if I do forget——

  *Then he kneels down and holds up his hands to heaven.*

*Greene.* Well, take your fittest standings, and once more
  Lime your twigs to catch this wary bird.
  I'll leave you, and at your dag's discharge            40
  Make towards, like the longing water-dog
  That coucheth till the fowling-piece be off,
  Then seizeth on the prey with eager mood.
  Ah, might I see him stretching forth his limbs,
  As I have seen them beat their wings ere now!

*Shakebag.* Why, that thou shalt see, if he come this
    way.

*Greene.* Yes, that he doth, Shakebag, I warrant thee:
  But brawl not when I am gone in any case.
  But, sirs, be sure to speed him when he comes,
  And in that hope I'll leave you for an hour.         50
                                      [*Exit* Greene.


  *Here enters* Arden, Franklin, *and* Michael.

*Michael.* 'Twere best that I went back to Rochester:
  The horse halts downright; it were not good
  He travelled in such pain to Feversham;
  Removing of a shoe may haply help it.

*Arden.* Well, get you back to Rochester; but, sirrah, see
  Ye overtake us ere we come to Rainham Down,
  For it will be very late ere we get home.

*Michael.* [*aside*] Ay, God he knows, and so doth
    Will and Shakebag,
  That thou shalt never go further than that down;
  And therefore have I prick'd the horse on purpose, 60
  Because I would not view the massacre.
                                      [*Exit* Michael.

36 slip] defer            42 coucheth] lies down, crouches

*Arden.* Come, Master Franklin, onwards with your
    tale.
*Franklin.* I assure you, sir, you task me much:
    A heavy blood is gathered at my heart,
    And on the sudden is my wind so short
    As hindereth the passage of my speech;
    So fierce a qualm yet ne'er assailed me.
*Arden.* Come, Master Franklin, let us go on softly:
    The annoyance of the dust or else some meat
    You ate at dinner cannot brook with you.    70
    I have been often so, and soon amended.
*Franklin.* Do you remember where my tale did leave?
*Arden.* Ay, where the gentleman did check his wife.
*Franklin.* She being reprehended for the fact,
    Witness produced that took her with the deed,
    Her glove brought in which there she left behind,
    And many other assured arguments,
    Her husband ask'd her whether it were not so.
*Arden.* Her answer then? I wonder how she look'd,
    Having forsworn it with such vehement oaths,    80
    And at the instant so approved upon her.
*Franklin.* First did she cast her eyes down to the
    earth,
    Watching the drops that fell amain from thence;
    Then softly draws she forth her handkercher,
    And modestly she wipes her tear-stain'd face;
    Them hemm'd she out, to clear her voice, should
    seem,
    And with a majesty address'd herself
    To encounter all their accusations.—
    Pardon me, Master Arden, I can no more;
    This fighting at my heart makes short my wind. 90
*Arden.* Come, we are almost now at Rainham Down:
    Your pretty tale beguiles the weary way;
    I would you were in state to tell it out.
*Shakebag.* Stand close, Will, I hear them coming.

73 check] reprove    74 fact] deed    81 approved
upon] proved against

*Here enters* Lord Cheiny *with his men.*

*Will.* Stand to it, Shakebag, and be resolute.

*L. Cheiny.* Is it so near night as it seems,
Or will this black-faced evening have a shower?—
What, Master Arden? you are well met,
I have long'd this fortnight's day to speak with you:
You are a stranger, man, in the Isle of Sheppy. 100

*Arden.* Your honour's always! bound to do you service.

*L. Cheiny.* Come you from London, and ne'er a man
with you?

*Arden.* My man's coming after, but here's
My honest friend that came along with me.

*L. Cheiny.* My Lord Protector's man I take you to be.

*Franklin.* Ay, my good lord, and highly bound to you.

*L. Cheiny.* You and your friend come home and sup
with me.

*Arden.* I beseech your honour pardon me;
I have made a promise to a gentleman,
My honest friend, to meet him at my house;    110
The occasion is great, or else would I wait on you.

*L. Cheiny.* Will you come to-morrow and dine with me,
And bring your honest friend along with you?
I have divers matters to talk with you about.

*Arden.* To-morrow we'll wait upon your honour.

*L. Cheiny.* One of you stay my horse at the top of the
hill.—
What! Black Will? for whose purse wait you?
Thou wilt be hanged in Kent, when all is done.

*Will.* Not hanged, God save your honour;
I am your beadsman, bound to pray for you.    120

*L. Cheiny.* I think thou ne'er saidest prayer in all thy
life.—
One of you give him a crown:—
And, sirrah, leave this kind of life;
If thou beest tainted for a penny-matter,

105 Lord Protector] *See note on* 1. i. 34.    120 beads-
man] one paid to pray for others    124 tainted
attainted, accused

And come in question, surely thou wilt truss.—
Come, Master Arden, let us be going;
Your way and mine lies four miles together.
           [*Exeunt. Manet* Black Will *and* Shakebag.
*Will.* The devil break all your necks at four miles' end!
   Zounds, I could kill myself for very anger!
   His lordship chops me in,                            130
   Even when my dag was levell'd at his heart.
   I would his crown were molten down his throat.
*Shakebag.* Arden, thou hast wondrous holy luck.
   Did ever man escape as thou hast done?
   Well, I'll discharge my pistol at the sky,
   For by this bullet Arden might not die.

### *Here enters* Greene.

*Greene.* What, is he down? is he dispatch'd?
*Shakebag.* Ay, in health towards Feversham, to shame
      us all.
*Greene.* The devil he is! why, sirs, how escap'd he?
*Shakebag.* When we were ready to shoot,             140
   Comes my Lord Cheiny to prevent his death.
*Greene.* The Lord of Heaven hath preserved him.
*Will.* Preserved a fig! The Lord Cheiny hath pre-
      served him,
   And bids him to a feast to his house at Shorlow.
   But by the way once more I'll meet with him,
   And, if all the Cheinys in the world say no,
   I'll have a bullet in his breast to-morrow.
   Therefore come, Greene, and let us to Feversham.
*Greene.* Ay, and excuse ourselves to Mistress Arden:
   O, how she'll chafe when she hears of this!     150
*Shakebag.* Why, I'll warrant you she'll think we dare
      not do it.
*Will.* Why, then let us go, and tell her all the matter,
   And plot the news to cut him off to-morrow.
                                          [*Exeunt.*

125 truss] hang          130 chops . . . in] interrupts

# ACT IV

## SCENE I

*Here enters* Arden *and his wife,* Franklin, *and* Michael.

*Arden.* See how the hours, the gardant of heaven's gate,
Have by their toil removed the darksome clouds,
That Sol may well discern the trampled pace
Wherein he wont to guide his golden car;
The season fits; come, Franklin, let's away.

*Alice.* I thought you did pretend some special hunt,
That made you thus cut short the time of rest.

*Arden.* It was no chase that made me rise so early,
But, as I told thee yesternight, to go
To the Isle of Sheppy, there to dine with my Lord
Cheiny;                                                              10
For so his honour late commanded me.

*Alice.* Ay, such kind husbands seldom want excuses;
Home is a wild cat to a wandering wit.
The time hath been,—would God it were not past,—
That honour's title nor a lord's command
Could once have drawn you from these arms of mine.
But my deserts or your desires decay,
Or both; yet if true love may seem desert,
I merit still to have thy company.

*Franklin.* Why, I pray you, sir, let her go along with
us;                                                                  20
I am sure his honour will welcome her
And us the more for bringing her along.

*Arden.* Content; sirrah, saddle your mistress' nag.

*Alice.* No, begg'd favour merits little thanks;
If I should go, our house would run away,
Or else be stol'n; therefore I'll stay behind.

*Arden.* Nay, see how mistaking you are! I pray thee, go.

*Alice.* No, no, not now.

1 gardant] guardian        3 pace] path

*Arden.* Then let me leave thee satisfied in this,
   That time nor place nor persons alter me,    30
   But that I hold thee dearer than my life.
*Alice.* That will be seen by your quick return.
*Arden.* And that shall be ere night, and if I live.
   Farewell, sweet Alice, we mind to sup with thee.
                       *[Exit Alice.*
*Franklin.* Come, Michael, are our horses ready?
*Michael.* Ay, your horses are ready, but I am not ready,
   for I have lost my purse, with six and thirty
   shillings in it, with taking up of my master's nag.
*Franklin.* Why, I pray you, let us go before,
   Whilest he stays behind to seek his purse.    40
*Arden.* Go to, sirrah, see you follow us to the Isle of
   Sheppy
   To my Lord Cheiny's, where we mean to dine.
       *[Exeunt* Arden *and* Franklin. *Manet* Michael.
*Michael.* So, fair weather after you, for before you lies
   Black Will and Shakebag in the broom close, too
   close for you: they'll be your ferrymen to long
   home.

*Here enters the* Painter.

But who is this? the painter, my co-rival, that
   would needs win Mistress Susan.
*Clarke.* How now, Michael? how doth my mistress
   and all at home?    50
*Michael.* Who? Susan Mosbie? she is your mistress,
   too?
*Clarke.* Ay, how doth she and all the rest?
*Michael.* All's well but Susan; she is sick.
*Clarke.* Sick? Of what disease?
*Michael.* Of a great fe'er.
*Clarke.* A fear of what?
*Michael.* A great fever.

  44 broom close] field of broom     56 fe'er] *Apparently*
*Michael mumbles the word* fever, *but the point is obscure.*

*Clarke.* A fever? God forbid!

*Michael.* Yes, faith, and of a lurden, too, as big as
yourself.                                                                61

*Clarke.* O, Michael, the spleen prickles you. Go to,
you carry an eye over Mistress Susan.

*Michael.* Ay, faith, to keep her from the painter.

*Clarke.* Why more from a painter than from a serving
creature like yourself?

*Michael.* Because you painters make but a painting
table of a pretty wench, and spoil her beauty with
blotting.

*Clarke.* What mean you by that?                                          70

*Michael.* Why, that you painters paint lambs in the
lining of wenches' petticoats, and we serving-men
put horns to them to make them become sheep.

*Clarke.* Such another word will cost you a cuff or a
knock.

*Michael.* What, with a dagger made of a pencil? Faith,
'tis too weak, and therefore thou too weak to win
Susan.

*Clarke.* Would Susan's love lay upon this stroke.

> *Then he breaks* Michael's *head.*

> *Here enters* Mosbie, Greene, *and* Alice.

*Alice.* I'll lay my life, this is for Susan's love.               80
Stay'd you behind your master to this end?
Have you no other time to brabble in
But now when serious matters are in hand?—
Say, Clarke, hast thou done the thing thou promised?

*Clarke.* Ay, here it is; the very touch is death.

*Alice.* Then this, I hope, if all the rest do fail,
Will catch Master Arden,
And make him wise in death that lived a fool.
Why should he thrust his sickle in our corn,

60 lurden] wastrel ( *fever-lurden = disease of idleness* )
63 carry an eye over] keep an eye on        82 brabble]
quarrel noisily

Or what hath he to do with thee, my love,      90
Or govern me that am to rule myself?
Forsooth, for credit sake, I must leave thee!
Nay, he must leave to live that we may love,
May live, may love; for what is life but love?
And love shall last as long as life remains,
And life shall end before my love depart.
*Mosbie.* Why, what's love without true constancy?
Like to a pillar built of many stones,
Yet neither with good mortar well compact
Nor cement to fasten it in the joints,      100
But that it shakes with every blast of wind,
And, being touch'd, straight falls unto the earth,
And buries all his haughty pride in dust.
No, let our love be rocks of adamant,
Which time nor place nor tempest can asunder.
*Greene.* Mosbie, leave protestations now,
And let us bethink us what we have to do.
Black Will and Shakebag I have placed
In the broom close watching Arden's coming;
Let's to them and see what they have done.      110
                                   [*Exeunt.*

## Scene II

*Here enters* Arden *and* Franklin.

*Arden.* Oh, ferryman, where art thou?

*Here enters the* Ferryman.

*Ferryman.* Here, here, go before to the boat, and I will
    follow you.
*Arden.* We have great haste; I pray thee come away.
*Ferryman.* Fie, what a mist is here!
*Arden.* This mist, my friend, is mystical,

105 asunder] sunder, separate      109 broom close] *See
note on* IV. i. 44.

Like to a good companion's smoky brain,
That was half drown'd with new ale overnight.

*Ferryman.* 'Twere pity but his skull were opened to
make more chimney room.                    10

*Franklin.* Friend, what's thy opinion of this mist?

*Ferryman.* I think 'tis like to a curst wife in a little
house, that never leaves her husband till she have
driven him out at doors with a wet pair of eyes;
then looks he as if his house were a-fire, or some
of his friends dead.

*Arden.* Speaks thou this of thine own experience?

*Ferryman.* Perhaps, ay; perhaps, no: For my wife is as
other women are, that is to say, governed by the
moon.                                      20

*Franklin.* By the moon? how, I pray thee?

*Ferryman.* Nay, thereby lies a bargain, and you shall
not have it fresh and fasting.

*Arden.* Yes, I pray thee, good ferryman.

*Ferryman.* Then for this once; let it be midsummer
moon, but yet my wife has another moon.

*Franklin.* Another moon?

*Ferryman.* Ay, and it hath influences and eclipses.

*Arden.* Why, then, by this reckoning you sometimes
play the man in the moon?                  30

*Ferryman.* Ay, but you had not best to meddle with
that moon, lest I scratch you by the face with my
bramble-bush.

*Arden.* I am almost stifled with this fog; come, let's
away.

*Franklin.* And, sirrah, as we go, let us have some more
of your bold yeomanry.

*Ferryman.* Nay, by my troth, sir, but flat knavery.

                                    [*Exeunt.*

23 fresh and fasting] before breakfast, *sc.* soon

## SCENE III

*Here enters* Will *at one door, and* Shakebag *at another.*

*Shakebag.* Oh, Will, where art thou?

*Will.* Here, Shakebag, almost in hell's mouth, where
   I cannot see my way for smoke.

*Shakebag.* I pray thee speak still that we may meet by
   the sound, for I shall fall into some ditch or other,
   unless my feet see better than my eyes.

*Will.* Didst thou ever see better weather to run away
   with another man's wife, or play with a wench at
   pot finger?

*Shakebag.* No; this were a fine world for chandlers, if
   this weather would last; for then a man should
   never dine nor sup without candle-light. But,
   sirrah Will, what horses are those that pass'd? 13

*Will.* Why, didst thou hear any?

*Shakebag.* Ay, that I did.

*Will.* My life for thine, 'twas Arden, and his companion, and then all our labour's lost.

*Shakebag.* Nay, say not so, for if it be they, they may
   haply lose their way as we have done, and then
   we may chance meet with them.          20

*Will.* Come, let us go on like a couple of blind pil-
   grims.

*Then* Shakebag *falls into a ditch.*

*Shakebag.* Help, Will help, I am almost drown'd.

*Here enters the* Ferryman.

*Ferryman.* Who's that that calls for help?

*Will.* 'Twas none here, 'twas thou thyself.

*Ferryman.* I came to help him that call'd for help.
   Why, how now? who is this that's in the ditch?
   You are well enough served to go without a guide
   such weather as this.

*Will.* Sirrah, what companies hath pass'd your ferry
    this morning?                         31
*Ferryman.* None but a couple of gentlemen, that went
    to dine at my Lord Cheiny's.
*Will.* Shakebag, did not I tell thee as much?
*Ferryman.* Why, sir, will you have any letters carried
    to them?
*Will.* No, sir; get you gone.
*Ferryman.* Did you ever see such a mist as this?
*Will.* No, nor such a fool as will rather be hough'd
    than get his way.                       40
*Ferryman.* Why, sir, this is no Hough-Monday; you
    are deceiv'd.—What's his name, I pray you, sir?
*Shakebag.* His name is Black Will.
*Ferryman.* I hope to see him one day hang'd upon a
    hill.                            [*Exit* Ferryman.
*Shakebag.* See how the sun hath clear'd the foggy mist,
    Now we have miss'd the mark of our intent.

*Here enters* Greene, Mosbie, *and* Alice.

*Mosbie.* Black Will and Shakebag, what make you
    here?
    What, is the deed done? is Arden dead?
*Will.* What could a blinded man perform in arms? 50
    Saw you not how till now the sky was dark,
    That neither horse nor man could be discerned?
    Yet did we hear their horses as they pass'd.
*Greene.* Have they escap'd you, then, and pass'd the
    ferry?
*Shakebag.* Ay, for a while; but here we two will stay,
    And at their coming back meet with them once
    more.
    Zounds, I was ne'er so toil'd in all my life
    In following so slight a task as this.

39 hough'd] ham-strung    40 get] go    41 Hough-
Monday] Hick-Monday, *second Monday after Easter, a popular
festival.*

*Mosbie.* How cam'st thou so bewray'd?

*Will.* With making false footing in the dark;   60
  He needs would follow them without a guide.

*Alice.* Here's to pay for a fire and good cheer:
  Get you to Feversham to the Flower-de-luce,
  And rest yourselves until some other time.

*Greene.* Let me alone; it most concerns my state.

*Will.* Ay, Mistress Arden, this will serve the turn,
  In case we fall into a second fog.

          [*Exeunt* Greene, Will, *and* Shakebag.

*Mosbie.* These knaves will never do it, let us give it
  over.

*Alice.* First tell me how you like my new device:
  Soon, when my husband is returning back,   70
  You and I both marching arm in arm,
  Like loving friends, we'll meet him on the way,
  And boldly beard and brave him to his teeth.
  When words grow hot and blows begin to rise,
  I'll call those cutters forth your tenement,
  Who, in a manner to take up the fray,
  Shall wound my husband Hornsby to the death.

*Mosbie.* A fine device! why, this deserves a kiss.

                  [*Exeunt.*


## SCENE IV

### *Here enters* Dick Reede *and a* Sailor.

*Sailor.* Faith, Dick Reede, it is to little end:
  His conscience is too liberal, and he too niggardly
  To part from any thing may do thee good.

*Reede.* He is coming from Shorlow as I understand;
  Here I'll intercept him, for at his house
  He never will vouchsafe to speak with me.
  If prayers and fair entreaties will not serve,
  Or make no battery in his flinty breast,

59 bewray'd] befouled         75 cutters] cut-throats
forth] forth from

*Here enters* Franklin, Arden, *and* Michael.

I'll curse the carle, and see what that will do.
See where he comes to further my intent!—    10
Master Arden, I am now bound to the sea;
My coming to you was about the plot
Of ground which wrongfully you detain from me.
Although the rent of it be very small,
Yet it will help my wife and children,
Which here I leave in Feversham, God knows,
Needy and bare: for Christ's sake, let them have it!

*Arden.* Franklin, hearest thou this fellow speak?
That which he craves I dearly bought of him,
Although the rent of it was ever mine.—    20
Sirrah, you that ask these questions,
If with thy clamorous impeaching tongue
Thou rail on me, as I have heard thou dost,
I'll lay thee up so close a twelve-month's day,
As thou shalt neither see the sun nor moon.
Look to it, for, as surely as I live,
I'll banish pity if thou use me thus.

*Reede.* What, wilt thou do me wrong and threat me too?
Nay, then, I'll tempt thee, Arden, do thy worst.
God, I beseech thee, show some miracle    30
On thee or thine, in plaguing thee for this.
That plot of ground which thou detains from me,
I speak it in an agony of spirit,
Be ruinous and fatal unto thee!
Either there be butcher'd by thy dearest friends,
Or else be brought for men to wonder at,
Or thou or thine miscarry in that place,
Or there run mad and end thy cursed days!

*Franklin.* Fie, bitter knave, bridle thine envious tongue;
For curses are like arrows shot upright,    40
Which falling down light on the shooter's head.

*Reede.* Light where they will! Were I upon the sea,

9 carle] churl, villain            24 lay thee up] send
thee to prison

As oft I have in many a bitter storm,
And saw a dreadful southern flaw at hand,
The pilot quaking at the doubtful storm,
And all the sailors praying on their knees,
Even in that fearful time would I fall down,
And ask of God, whate'er betide of me,
Vengeance on Arden or some misevent
To show the world what wrong the carle hath
    done.                                          50
This charge I'll leave with my distressful wife,
My children shall be taught such prayers as these;
And thus I go, but leave my curse with thee.

                            [*Exeunt* Reede *and* Sailor.

*Arden.* It is the railingest knave in Christendom,
And oftentimes the villain will be mad;
It greatly matters not what he says,
But I assure you I ne'er did him wrong.
*Franklin.* I think so, Master Arden.
*Arden.* Now that our horses are gone home before,
My wife may haply meet me on the way.          60
For God knows she is grown passing kind of late,
And greatly changed from the old humour
Of her wonted frowardness,
And seeks by fair means to redeem old faults.
*Franklin.* Happy the change that alters for the best!
But see in any case you make no speech
Of the cheer we had at my Lord Cheiny's,
Although most bounteous and liberal,
For that will make her think herself more wrong'd,
In that we did not carry her along;            70
For sure she grieved that she was left behind.
*Arden.* Come, Franklin, let us strain to mend our pace,
And take her unawares playing the cook;

            *Here enters* Alice *and* Mosbie.

For I believe she'll strive to mend our cheer.
*Franklin.* Why, there's no better creatures in the world,
Than women are when they are in good humours.

*Arden.* Who is that? Mosbie? what, so familiar?
  Injurious strumpet, and thou ribald knave,
  Untwine those arms.
*Alice.* Ay, with a sugar'd kiss let them untwine.     80
*Arden.* Ah, Mosbie! perjur'd beast! bear this and all!
*Mosbie.* And yet no horned beast; the horns are thine.
*Franklin.* O monstrous! Nay, then 'tis time to draw.
*Alice.* Help, help! they murther my husband.

*Here enters* Will *and* Shakebag.

*Shakebag.* Zounds, who injures Master Mosbie?—Help,
  Will! I am hurt.
*Mosbie.* I may thank you, Mistress Arden, for this
  wound.
                    [*Exeunt* Mosbie, Will, *and* Shakebag.
*Alice.* Ah, Arden, what folly blinded thee?
  Ah, jealous harebrain man, what hast thou done!
  When we, to welcome thy intended sport,
  Came lovingly to meet thee on thy way,     90
  Thou drew'st thy sword, enraged with jealousy,
  And hurt thy friend whose thoughts were free from
    harm:
  All for a worthless kiss and joining arms,
  Both done but merrily to try thy patience.
  And me unhappy that devised the jest,
  Which, though begun in sport, yet ends in blood!
*Franklin.* Marry, God defend me from such a jest!
*Alice.* Could'st thou not see us friendly smile on thee,
  When we join'd arms, and when I kiss'd his cheek?
  Hast thou not lately found me over-kind?     100
  Didst thou not hear me cry, they murther thee?
  Call'd I not help to set my husband free?
  No, ears and all were witch'd; ah me accurs'd
  To link in liking with a frantic man!
  Henceforth I'll be thy slave, no more thy wife,
  For with that name I never shall content thee.
  If I be merry, thou straightways thinks me light;
  If sad, thou sayest the sullens trouble me;

If well attired, thou thinks I will be gadding;
If homely, I seem sluttish in thine eye:   110
Thus am I still, and shall be while I die,
Poor wench, abused by thy misgovernment!

*Arden.* But is it for truth that neither thou nor he
Intendedst malice in your misdemeanour?

*Alice.* The heavens can witness of our harmless
thoughts.

*Arden.* Then pardon me, sweet Alice, and forgive this
fault!
Forget but this and never see the like.
Impose me penance, and I will perform it,
For in thy discontent I find a death,—
A death tormenting more than death itself.   120

*Alice.* Nay, hadst thou loved me as thou dost pretend,
Thou would'st have mark'd the speeches of thy
friend,
Who going wounded from the place, he said
His skin was pierc'd only through my device;
And if sad sorrow taint thee for this fault,
Thou would'st have followed him, and seen him
dress'd,
And cried him mercy whom thou hast misdone:
Ne'er shall my heart be eased till this be done.

*Arden.* Content thee, sweet Alice, thou shalt have thy
will,
Whate'er it be. For that I injur'd thee,   130
And wrong'd my friend, shame scourgeth my
offence;
Come thou thyself, and go along with me,
And be a mediator 'twixt us two.

*Franklin.* Why, Master Arden! know you what you do?
Will you follow him that hath dishonour'd you?

*Alice.* Why, canst thou prove I have been disloyal?

*Franklin.* Why, Mosbie taunts your husband with the
horn.

*Alice.* Ay, after he had reviled him

127 misdone] harmed

By the injurious name of perjur'd beast:
He knew no wrong could spite an jealious man 140
More than the hateful naming of the horn.
*Franklin.* Suppose 'tis true; yet is it dangerous
To follow him whom he hath lately hurt.
*Alice.* A fault confessed is more than half amends;
But men of such ill spirit as yourself
Work crosses and debates 'twixt man and wife.
*Arden.* I pray thee, gentle Franklin, hold thy peace:
I know my wife counsels me for the best.
I'll seek out Mosbie where his wound is dress'd,
And salve this hapless quarrel if I may. 150

[*Exeunt* Arden *and* Alice.

*Franklin.* He whom the devil drives must go perforce.
Poor gentleman, how soon he is bewitch'd!
And yet, because his wife is the instrument,
His friends must not be lavish in their speech.

[*Exit* Franklin.

# ACT V

## SCENE I

*Here enters* Will, Shakebag, *and* Greene.

*Will.* Sirrah Greene, when was I so long in killing a
man?
*Greene.* I think we shall never do it; let us give it over.
*Shakebag.* Nay, Zounds! we'll kill him, though we be
hang'd at his door for our labour.
*Will.* Thou knowest, Greene, that I have lived in
London this twelve years, where I have made
some go upon wooden legs for taking the wall on
me; divers with silver noses for saying "There
goes Black Will!" I have crack'd as many blades
as thou hast done nuts. 11
*Greene.* O monstrous lie!

8–9 taking the wall on me] jostling me off the pavement

*Will.* Faith, in a manner I have. The bawdy-houses
have paid me tribute; there durst not a whore set
up, unless she have agreed with me first for
opening her shop-windows. For a cross word of
a tapster I have pierced one barrel after another
with my dagger, and held him by the ears till
all his beer hath run out. In Thames Street a
brewer's cart was like to have run over me: I
made no more ado, but went to the clerk and cut
all the notches off his tallies and beat them about
his head. I and my company have taken the
constable from his watch, and carried him about
the fields on a coltstaff. I have broken a sergeant's
head with his own mace, and bail'd whom I list
with my sword and buckler. All the tenpenny
alehouses would stand every morning with a
quart pot in their hand, saying, "Will it please
your worship drink?" He that had not done so,
had been sure to have had his sign pull'd down
and his lattice borne away the next night. To
conclude, what have I not done? yet cannot do
this; doubtless, he is preserved by miracle.  34

*Here enters* Alice *and* Michael.

*Greene.* Hence, Will! here comes Mistress Arden.
*Alice.* Ah, gentle Michael, art thou sure they're friends?
*Michael.* Why, I saw them when they both shook
hands.
When Mosbie bled, he even wept for sorrow,
And rail'd on Franklin that was cause of all.
No sooner came the surgeon in at doors,          40
But my master took to his purse and gave him
money,

22 notches off his tallies] *Without them he would be unable to
reckon his accounts or recover his debts* (*Tucker Brooke*).       25
coltstaff] cowl-staff, *a stout stick used for carrying a 'cowl' or
heavy tub, being passed through its handles.*

And, to conclude, sent me to bring you word
That Mosbie, Franklin, Bradshaw, Adam Fowle,
With divers of his neighbours and his friends,
Will come and sup with you at our house this
  night.
*Alice.* Ah, gentle Michael, run thou back again,
And, when my husband walks into the fair,
Bid Mosbie steal from him and come to me;
And this night shall thou and Susan be made sure.
*Michael.* I'll go tell him.                              50
*Alice.* And as thou goest, tell John cook of our guests,
And bid him lay it on, spare for no cost.

                [*Exit* Michael.

*Will.* Nay, an there be such cheer, we will bid our-
  selves.—
Mistress Arden, Dick Greene and I do mean to sup
  with you.
*Alice.* And welcome shall you be. Ah, gentlemen,
How miss'd you of your purpose yesternight?
*Greene.* 'Twas 'long of Shakebag, that unlucky villain.
*Shakebag.* Thou dost me wrong; I did as much as any.
*Will.* Nay then, Mistress Alice, I'll tell you how it was:
When he should have lock'd with both his hilts, 60
He in a bravery flourish'd over his head;
With that comes Franklin at him lustily,
And hurts the slave; with that he slinks away.
Now his way had been to have come hand and feet,
  one and two round, at his costard; he like a fool
  bears his sword-point half a yard out of danger.
  I lie here for my life; if the devil come, an he have
  no more strength than fence, he shall never beat
  me from this ward, I'll stand to it; a buckler in
  a skilful hand is as good as a castle; nay, 'tis better
  than a sconce, for I have tried it.                     71
Mosbie, perceiving this, began to faint:
With that comes Arden with his arming sword,

61 bravery] bravado        65 costard] head        71
sconce] small fort    73 arming] with which he is armed

And thrust him through the shoulder in a trice.
*Alice.* Ay, but I wonder why you both stood still.
*Will.* Faith, I was so amazed, I could not strike.
*Alice.* Ah, sirs, had he yesternight been slain,
  For every drop of his detested blood
  I would have cramm'd in angels in thy fist,
  And kiss'd thee, too, and hugg'd thee in my arms. 80
*Will.* Patient yourself, we cannot help it now.
  Greene and we two will dog him through the fair,
  And stab him in the crowd, and steal away.

*Here enters* Mosbie.

*Alice.* It is unpossible; but here comes he
  That will, I hope, invent some surer means.
  Sweet Mosbie, hide thy arm, it kills my heart.
*Mosbie.* Ay, Mistress Arden, this is your favour.
*Alice.* Ah, say not so; for when I saw thee hurt,
  I could have took the weapon thou let'st fall,
  And run at Arden; for I have sworn      90
  That these mine eyes, offended with his sight,
  Shall never close till Arden's be shut up.
  This night I rose and walk'd about the chamber,
  And twice or thrice I thought to have murther'd
    him.
*Mosbie.* What, in the night? then had we been undone.
*Alice.* Why, how long shall he live?
*Mosbie.* Faith, Alice, no longer than this night.—
  Black Will and Shakebag, will you two perform
  The complot that I have laid?
*Will.* Ay, or else think me a villain.      100
*Greene.* And rather than you shall want, I'll help
  myself.
*Mosbie.* You, Master Greene, shall single Franklin
  forth,
  And hold him with a long tale of strange news,
  That he may not come home till supper-time.

    81 Patient] calm        99 complot] plot

I'll fetch Master Arden home, and we like friends
Will play a game or two at tables here.
*Alice.* But what of all this? how shall he be slain?
*Mosbie.* Why, Black Will and Shakebag lock'd within
　　the counting-house
Shall, at a certain watchword given, rush forth.
*Will.* What shall the watchword be?　　　　　110
*Mosbie.* *Now I take you*; that shall be the word:
But come not forth before in any case.
*Will.* I warrant you. But who shall lock me in?
*Alice.* That will I do; thou'st keep the key thyself.
*Mosbie.* Come, Master Greene, go you along with me.
See all things ready, Alice, against we come.
*Alice.* Take no care for that; send you him home.
　　　　　　　　　　[*Exeunt* Mosbie *and* Greene.
And if he e'er go forth again, blame me.
Come, Black Will, that in mine eyes art fair;
Next unto Mosbie do I honour thee;　　　　120
Instead of fair words and large promises
My hands shall play you golden harmony:
How like you this? say, will you do it, sirs?
*Will.* Ay, and that bravely, too. Mark my device:
Place Mosbie, being a stranger, in a chair,
And let your husband sit upon a stool,
That I may come behind him cunningly,
And with a towel pull him to the ground,
Then stab him till his flesh be as a sieve;
That done, bear him behind the Abbey,　　　130
That those that find him murthered may suppose
Some slave or other kill'd him for his gold.
*Alice.* A fine device! you shall have twenty pound,
And, when he is dead, you shall have forty more,
And, lest you might be suspected staying here,
Michael shall saddle you two lusty geldings;
Ride whither you will, to Scotland, or to Wales,
I'll see you shall not lack, where'er you be.

　　106, 164, *etc.* tables] backgammon　　　114 thou'st]
thou shalt

*Will.* Such words would make one kill a thousand
    men!
  Give me the key; which is the counting-house? 140
*Alice.* Here would I stay and still encourage you;
  But that I know how resolute you are.
*Shakebag.* Tush, you are too faint-hearted; we must
    do it.
*Alice.* But Mosbie will be there, whose very looks
  Will add unwonted courage to my thought,
  And make me the first that shall adventure on
    him.
*Will.* Tush, get you gone; 'tis we must do the deed.
  When this door opens next, look for his death.
                  [Will *and* Shakebag *retire.*
*Alice.* Ah, would he now were here that it might open!
  I shall no more be closed in Arden's arms,    150
  That like the snakes of black Tisiphone
  Sting me with their embracings! Mosbie's arms
  Shall compass me, and, were I made a star,
  I would have none other spheres but those.
  There is no nectar but in Mosbie's lips!
  Had chaste Diana kiss'd him, she like me
  Would grow love-sick, and from her wat'ry bower
  Fling down Endymion, and snatch him up:
  Then blame not me that slay a silly man
  Not half so lovely as Endymion.        160

*Here enters* Michael.

*Michael.* Mistress, my master is coming hard by.
*Alice.* Who comes with him?
*Michael.* Nobody but Mosbie.
*Alice.* That's well, Michael. Fetch in the tables, and
    when thou hast done, stand before the counting-
    house door.

148 s.d. *retire*] *sc.* to *the inner stage, where they remain unseen
by the other characters till line* 235.

*Michael.* Why so?

*Alice.* Black Will is lock'd within to do the deed.

*Michael.* What? shall he die to-night?

*Alice.* Ay, Michael.                                            170

*Michael.* But shall not Susan know it?

*Alice.* Yes, for she'll be as secret as ourselves.

*Michael.* That's brave. I'll go fetch the tables.

*Alice.* But, Michael, hark to me a word or two:
　　When my husband is come in, lock the street-door;
　　He shall be murther'd, or the guests come in.

　　　　　　　　　　　　　　　　[*Exit* Michael.


　　　　　*Here enters* Arden *and* Mosbie.

Husband, what mean you to bring Mosbie home?
Although I wish'd you to be reconciled,
'Twas more for fear of you than love of him.
Black Will and Greene are his companions,        180
And they are cutters, and may cut you short:
Therefore I thought it good to make you friends.
But wherefore do you bring him hither now?
You have given me my supper with his sight.

*Mosbie.* Master Arden, methinks your wife would have
　　me gone.

*Arden.* No, good master Mosbie; women will be
　　prating.
　　Alice, bid him welcome; he and I are friends.

*Alice.* You may enforce me to it, if you will;
　　But I had rather die than bid him welcome.
　　His company hath purchas'd me ill friends,        190
　　And therefore will I ne'er frequent it more.

*Mosbie.* —Oh, how cunningly she can dissemble!

*Arden.* Now he is here, you will not serve me so.

*Alice.* I pray you be not angry or displeased;
　　I'll bid him welcome, seeing you'll have it so.


176 or] before        179 of you] for you, on your behalf
181 cutters] cut-throats        184 given me my supper]
taken away my appetite

You are welcome, Master Mosbie; will you sit
down?

*Mosbie.* I know I am welcome to your loving husband;

But for yourself, you speak not from your heart.

*Alice.* And if I do not, sir, think I have cause.

*Mosbie.* Pardon me, Master Arden; I'll away.   200

*Arden.* No, good Master Mosbie.

*Alice.* We shall have guests enough, though you go
hence.

*Mosbie.* I pray you, Master Arden, let me go.

*Arden.* I pray thee, Mosbie, let her prate her fill.

*Alice.* The doors are open, sir, you may be gone.

*Michael.* —Nay, that's a lie, for I have lock'd the doors.

*Arden.* Sirrah, fetch me a cup of wine, I'll make them
friends.

And, gentle Mistress Alice, seeing you are so stout,

You shall begin! frown not, I'll have it so.

*Alice.* I pray you meddle with that you have to
do.   210

*Arden.* Why, Alice! how can I do too much for him

Whose life I have endangered without cause?

*Alice.* 'Tis true; and, seeing 'twas partly through my
means,

I am content to drink to him for this once.

Here, Master Mosbie! and I pray you, henceforth

Be you as strange to me as I to you.

Your company hath purchased me ill friends,

And I for you, God knows, have undeserved

Been ill spoken of in every place;

Therefore henceforth frequent my house no more.

*Mosbie.* I'll see your husband in despite of you.   221

Yet, Arden, I protest to thee by heaven,

Thou ne'er shalt see me more after this night,

I'll go to Rome rather than be forsworn.

*Arden.* Tush, I'll have no such vows made in my house.

208 stout] obstinate      218 undeserved] undeservedly

*Alice.* Yes, I pray you, husband, let him swear;
  And, on that condition, Mosbie, pledge me here.
*Mosbie.* Ay, as willingly as I mean to live.
*Arden.* Come, Alice, is our supper ready yet?
*Alice.* It will by then you have play'd a game at tables.
*Arden.* Come, Master Mosbie, what shall we play for?
*Mosbie.* Three games for a French crown, sir, and
  please you.                                      233
*Arden.* Content.

*Then they play at the tables.*

*Will.* —Can he not take him yet? what a spite is that?
*Alice.* —Not yet, Will; take heed he see thee not.
*Will.* —I fear he will spy me as I am coming.
*Michael.* —To prevent that, creep betwixt my legs.
*Mosbie.* One ace, or else I lose the game.
*Arden.* Marry, sir, there's two for failing.        240
*Mosbie.* Ah, Master Arden, *now I can take you.*

*Then* Will *pulls him down with a towel.*

*Arden.* Mosbie! Michael! Alice! what will you do?
*Will.* Nothing but take you up, sir, nothing else.
*Mosbie.* There's for the pressing iron you told me of.
                                          [*Stabs him.*
*Shakebag.* And there's for the ten pound in my sleeve.
                                          [*Stabs him.*
*Alice.* What! groans thou? nay, then give me the
  weapon!
  Take this for hindering Mosbie's love and mine.
                                          [*She stabs him.*
*Michael.* O, mistress!
*Will.* Ah, that villain will betray us all.
*Mosbie.* Tush, fear him not; he will be secret.      250
*Michael.* Why, dost thou think I will betray myself?
*Shakebag.* In Southwark dwells a bonny northern lass,
  The widow Chambly; I'll to her house now,

235 *sq.*] Will *speaks from the inner stage.*

And if she will not give me harborough,
I'll make booty of the quean even to her smock.
*Will.* Shift for yourselves; we two will leave you now.
*Alice.* First lay the body in the counting-house.

*Then they lay the body in the Counting-house.*

*Will.* We have our gold; Mistress Alice, adieu;
Mosbie, farewell, and Michael, farewell too. [*Exeunt.*

*Enter* Susan.

*Susan.* Mistress, the guests are at the doors.          260
Hearken, they knock: what, shall I let them in?
*Alice.* Mosbie, go thou and bear them company.
                                      [*Exit* Mosbie.
And, Susan, fetch water and wash away this blood.
*Susan.* The blood cleaveth to the ground and will not
out.
*Alice.* But with my nails I'll scrape away the blood;—
The more I strive, the more the blood appears!
*Susan.* What's the reason, Mistress, can you tell?
*Alice.* Because I blush not at my husband's death.

*Here enters* Mosbie.

*Mosbie.* Now now? what's the matter? is all well?
*Alice.* Ay, well, if Arden were alive again.          270
In vain we strive, for here his blood remains.
*Mosbie.* Why, strew rushes on it, can you not?
This wench doth nothing: fall unto the work.
*Alice.* 'Twas thou that made me murther him.
*Mosbie.* What of that?
*Alice.* Nay, nothing, Mosbie, so it be not known.
*Mosbie.* Keep thou it close, and 'tis unpossible.
*Alice.* Ah, but I cannot! was he not slain by me?
My husband's death torments me at the heart.
*Mosbie.* It shall not long torment thee, gentle Alice;
I am thy husband, think no more of him.          281

254 harborough] harbour

*Here enters* Adam Fowle *and* Bradshaw.

*Bradshaw.* How now, Mistress Arden? what ail you
    weep?
*Mosbie.* Because her husband is abroad so late.
    A couple of ruffins threaten'd him yesternight,
    And she, poor soul, is afraid he should be hurt.
*Adam.* Is't nothing else? tush, he'll be here anon.

*Here enters* Greene.

*Greene.* Now, Mistress Arden, lack you any guests?
*Alice.* Ah, Master Greene, did you see my husband
    lately?
*Greene.* I saw him walking behind the Abbey even
    now.

*Here enters* Franklin.

*Alice.* I do not like this being out so late.—    290
    Master Franklin, where did you leave my busband?
*Franklin.* Believe me I saw him not since morning.
    Fear you not, he'll come anon; meantime
    You may do well to bid his guests sit down.
*Alice.* Ay, so they shall; Master Bradshaw, sit you
    there;
    I pray you, be content, I'll have my will.
    Master Mosbie, sit you in my husband's seat.
*Michael.* —Susan, shall thou and I wait on them?
    Or, an thou say'st the word, let us sit down too.
*Susan.* —Peace, we have other matters now in hand.
    I fear me, Michael, all will be bewrayed.    301
*Michael.* —Tush, so it be known that I shall marry
    thee in the morning, I care not though I be hang'd
    ere night.  But to prevent the worst, I'll buy some
    ratsbane.
*Susan.* —Why, Michael, wilt thou poison thyself?
*Michael.* —No, but my mistress, for I fear she'll tell.
*Susan.* —Tush, Michael; fear not her, she's wise
    enough.

*Mosbie.* Sirrah Michael, give's a cup of beer.—
Mistress Arden, here's to your husband.          310
*Alice.* My husband!
*Franklin.* What ails you, woman, to cry so suddenly?
*Alice.* Ah, neighbours, a sudden qualm came over my
    heart;
My husband's being forth torments my mind.
I know something's amiss, he is not well;
Or else I should have heard of him ere now.
*Mosbie.* —She will undo us through her foolishness.
*Greene.* Fear not, Mistress Arden, he's well enough.
*Alice.* Tell not me; I know he is not well:
He was not wont for to stay thus late.          320
Good Master Franklin, go and seek him forth,
And if you find him, send him home to me,
And tell him what a fear he hath put me in.
*Franklin.* —I like not this; I pray God all be well.
I'll seek him out, and find him if I can.
                    [*Exeunt* Franklin, Mosbie, *and* Greene.
*Alice.* —Michael, how shall I do to rid the rest
    away?
*Michael.* —Leave that to my charge, let me alone.
'Tis very late, Master Bradshaw,
And there are many false knaves abroad,
And you have many narrow lanes to pass.          330
*Bradshaw.* Faith, friend Michael, and thou sayest
    true.
Therefore I pray thee light's forth and lend's a
    link.
                    [*Exeunt* Bradshaw, Adam, *and* Michael.
*Alice.* Michael, bring them to the doors, but do not
    stay;
You know I do not love to be alone.
—Go, Susan, and bid thy brother come:
But wherefore should he come?  Here is nought but
    fear;
Stay, Susan, stay, and help to counsel me.
*Susan.* Alas, I counsel! fear frights away my wits.

*Then they open the counting-house door, and look upon*
Arden.

*Alice.* See, Susan, where thy quondam master lies,
Sweet Arden, smear'd in blood and filthy gore. 340
*Susan.* My brother, you, and I shall rue this deed.
*Alice.* Come, Susan, help to lift his body forth,
And let our salt tears be his obsequies.

*Here enters* Mosbie *and* Greene.

*Mosbie.* Now now, Alice, whither will you bear him?
*Alice.* Sweet Mosbie, art thou come? Then weep that
will:
I have my wish in that I joy thy sight.
*Greene.* Well, it hoves us to be circumspect.
*Mosbie.* Ay, for Franklin thinks that we have murther'd
him.
*Alice.* Ay, but he cannot prove it for his life.
We'll spend this night in dalliance and in sport. 350

*Here enters* Michael.

*Michael.* O mistress, the Mayor and all the watch
Are coming towards our house with glaives and bills.
*Alice.* Make the door fast; let them not come in.
*Mosbie.* Tell me, sweet Alice, how shall I escape?
*Alice.* Out at the back-door, over the pile of wood,
And for one night lie at the Flower-de-luce.
*Mosbie.* That is the next way to betray myself.
*Greene.* Alas, Mistress Arden, the watch will take me
here,
And cause suspicion, where else would be none.
*Alice.* Why, take that way that Mosbie doth;    360
But first convey the body to the fields.

*Then they bear the body into the fields.*

*Mosbie.* Until to-morrow, sweet Alice, now farewell:
And see you confess nothing in any case.

346 joy] enjoy    347 hoves] behoves    357 next]
uickest

*Greene.* Be resolute, Mistress Alice, betray us not,
But cleave to us as we will stick to you.

      [*Exeunt* Mosbie *and* Greene.

*Alice.* Now, let the judge and juries do their worst:
My house is clear, and now I fear them not.

*Susan.* As we went, it snowed all the way,
Which makes me fear our footsteps will be spied.

*Alice.* Peace, fool, the snow will cover them again. 370

*Susan.* But it had done before we came back again.

*Alice.* Hark, hark, they knock! go, Michael, let them
in.

  *Here enters the* Mayor *and the* Watch.

How now, Master Mayor, have you brought my
husband home?

*Mayor.* I saw him come into your house an hour ago.

*Alice.* You are deceived; it was a Londoner.

*Mayor.* Mistress Arden, know you not one that is
called Black Will?

*Alice.* I know none such: what mean these questions?

*Mayor.* I have the Council's warrant to apprehend
him.

*Alice.* —I am glad it is no worse.

Why, Master Mayor, think you I harbour any such?

*Mayor.* We are inform'd that here he is;     381
And therefore pardon us, for we must search.

*Alice.* Ay, search, and spare you not, through every
room:

Were my husband at home, you would not offer this.

   *Here enters* Franklin.

Master Franklin, what mean you come so sad?

*Franklin.* Arden, thy husband and my friend, is slain.

*Alice.* Ah, by whom? Master Franklin, can you tell?

*Franklin.* I know not; but behind the Abbey
There he lies murther'd in most piteous case.

*Mayor.* But, Master Franklin, are you sure 'tis he? 390

*Franklin.* I am too sure; would God I were deceived.

*Alice.* Find out the murtherers, let them be known.

*Franklin.* Ay, so they shall: come you along with us.

*Alice.* Wherefore?

*Franklin.* Know you this hand-towel and this knife?

*Susan.* —Ah, Michael, through this thy negligence
Thou hast betrayed and undone us all.

*Michael.* —I was so afraid I knew not what I did:
I thought I had thrown them both into the well.

*Alice.* It is the pig's blood we had to supper.            400
But wherefore stay you? find out the murtherers.

*Mayor.* I fear me you'll prove one of them yourself.

*Alice.* I one of them? what mean such questions?

*Franklin.* I fear me he was murther'd in this house
And carried to the fields; for from that place
Backwards and forwards may you see
The print of many feet within the snow.
And look about this chamber where we are,
And you shall find part of his guiltless blood;
For in his slipshoe did I find some rushes,            410
Which argueth he was murther'd in this room.

*Mayor.* Look in the place where he was wont to sit.
See, see! his blood! it is too manifest.

*Alice.* It is a cup of wine that Michael shed.

*Michael.* Ay, truly.

*Franklin.* It is his blood, which, strumpet, thou hast
shed.
But if I live, thou and thy complices
Which have conspired and wrought his death shall
rue it.

*Alice.* Ah, Master Franklin, God and heaven can tell
I loved him more than all the world beside.            420
But bring me to him, let me see his body.

*Franklin.* Bring that villain and Mosbie's sister too;
And one of you go to the Flower-de-luce,
And seek for Mosbie, and apprehend him too.

[*Exeunt.*

410 slipshoe] slipper

## SCENE II

*Here enters* Shakebag *solus.*

*Shakebag.*  The widow Chambly, in her husband's days,
  I kept; and now he's dead, she is grown so stout
  She will not know her old companions.
  I came thither, thinking to have had harbour
  As I was wont,
  And she was ready to thrust me out at doors;
  But whether she would or no, I got me up,
  And as she followed me, I spurn'd her down the
    stairs,
  And broke her neck, and cut her tapster's throat,
  And now I am going to fling them in the Thames.
  I have the gold; what care I though it be known!
  I'll cross the water and take sanctuary.          12
                    [*Exit* Shakebag.

## SCENE III

*Here enters the* Mayor, Mosbie, Alice, Franklin, Michael,
                *and* Susan.

*Mayor.*  See, Mistress Arden, where your husband lies;
  Confess this foul fault and be penitent.
*Alice.*  Arden, sweet husband, what shall I say?
  The more I sound his name, the more he bleeds;
  This blood condemns me, and in gushing forth
  Speaks as it falls, and asks me why I did it.
  Forgive me, Arden: I repent me now,
  And, would my death save thine, thou should'st not
    die.
  Rise up, sweet Arden, and enjoy thy love,
  And frown not on me when we meet in heaven:   10
  In heaven I'll love thee, though on earth I did not.

ii. 2 kept] frequented          stout] proud

*Mayor.* Say, Mosbie, what made thee murther him?
*Franklin.* Study not for an answer; look not down:
His purse and girdle found at thy bed's head
Witness sufficiently thou didst the deed;
It bootless is to swear thou didst it not.
*Mosbie.* I hired Black Will and Shakebag, ruffins
both,
And they and I have done this murth'rous deed.
But wherefore stay we? Come and bear me hence.
*Franklin.* Those ruffins shall not escape; I will up to
London,                                                    20
And get the Council's warrant to apprehend them.
                                              [*Exeunt.*


## SCENE IV

*Here enters* Will.

*Will.* Shakebag, I hear, hath taken sanctuary,
But I am so pursued with hues and cries
For petty robberies that I have done,
That I can come unto no sanctuary.
Therefore must I in some oyster-boat
At last be fain to go on board some hoy,
And so to Flushing. There is no staying here.
At Sittingburgh the watch was like to take me,
And had not I with my buckler cover'd my head,
And run full blank at all adventures,                     10
I am sure I had ne'er gone further than that
place;
For the constable had twenty warrants to apprehend
me,
Besides that, I robbed him and his man once at
Gadshill.
Farewell, England; I'll go to Flushing now.
                                              [*Exit* Will.

iii. 13 Study not for] Do not invent          17, 20, &c.
ruffins] ruffians          10 at all adventures] at random

## SCENE V

*Here enters the* Mayor, Mosbie, Alice, Michael, Susan,
*and* Bradshaw.

*Mayor.* Come, make haste, and bring away the pri-
  soners.

*Bradshaw.* Mistress Arden, you are now going to God,
  And I am by the law condemned to die
  About a letter I brought from Master Greene.
  I pray you, Mistress Arden, speak the truth:
  Was I ever privy to your intent or no.

*Alice.* What should I say? You brought me such a
  letter,
  But I dare swear thou knewest not the contents.
  Leave now to trouble me with worldly things,
  And let me meditate upon my saviour Christ,    10
  Whose blood must save me for the blood I shed.

*Mosbie.* How long shall I live in this hell of grief?
  Convey me from the presence of that strumpet.

*Alice.* Ah, but for thee I had never been a strumpet.
  What cannot oaths and protestations do,
  When men have opportunity to woo?
  I was too young to sound thy villainies,
  But now I find it and repent too late.

*Susan.* Ah, gentle brother, wherefore should I die?
  I knew not of it till the deed was done.    20

*Mosbie.* For thee I mourn more than for myself;
  But let it suffice, I cannot save thee now.

*Michael.* And if your brother and my mistress
  Had not promised me you in marriage,
  I had ne'er given consent to this foul deed.

*Mayor.* Leave to accuse each other now,
  And listen to the sentence I shall give.
  Bear Mosbie and his sister to London straight,
  Where they in Smithfield must be executed;
  Bear Mistress Arden unto Canterbury,    30
  Where her sentence is she must be burnt;

Michael and Bradshaw in Feversham must suffer
　　death.

*Alice.* Let my death make amends for all my sins.

*Mosbie.* Fie upon women! this shall be my song;
　　But bear me hence, for I have lived too long.

*Susan.* Seeing no hope on earth, in heaven is my hope.

*Michael.* Faith, I care not, seeing I die with Susan.

*Bradshaw.* My blood be on his head that gave the
　　sentence.

*Mayor.* To speedy execution with them all!　[*Exeunt.*

## EPILOGUE

### *Here enters* Franklin.

*Franklin.* Thus have you seen the truth of Arden's
　　death.
　　As for the ruffins, Shakebag and Black Will,
　　The one took sanctuary, and, being sent for out,
　　Was murther'd in Southwark as he pass'd
　　To Greenwich, where the Lord Protector lay.
　　Black Will was burn'd in Flushing on a stage;
　　Greene was hanged at Osbridge in Kent;
　　The painter fled, and how he died we know not
　　But this above the rest is to be noted:
　　Arden lay murther'd in that plot of ground　　10
　　Which he by force and violence held from Reede;
　　And in the grass his body's print was seen
　　Two years and more after the deed was done.
　　Gentlemen, we hope you'll pardon this naked
　　　　tragedy,
　　Wherein no filed points are foisted in
　　To make it gracious to the ear or eye;
　　For simple truth is gracious enough,
　　And needs no other points of glozing stuff.

**FINIS**

6 stage] scaffold　　　18 glozing] specious

# A WOMAN KILLED WITH KINDNESS

### BY

## THOMAS HEYWOOD

# THOMAS HEYWOOD (*c.* 1573–1641)

## *A Woman Killed with Kindness*

### Acted in 1603; printed in 1607.

[*Dramatic Works*, ed. R. H. Shepherd (Pearson's Reprints), 6 vols., 1874. *A Woman Killed with Kindness* and *The Fair Maid of the West*, ed. K. L. Bates, were published in the inexpensive Belles-Lettres Series, 1917. See also A. M. Clark, *Thomas Heywood*, Oxford, Blackwell, 1931.]

# A
# WOMAN
## KILDE
# with Kindneſſe.

*Written by Tho: Heywood.*

## LONDON
Printed by William Iaggard dwelling in Barbican, and
are to be ſold in Paules Church-yard.
by Iohn Hodgets. 1607.

# The Prologue

I come but like a harbinger, being sent
To tell you what these preparations mean:
Look for no glorious state; our Muse is bent
Upon a barren subject, a bare scene.
We could afford this twig a timber tree,
Whose strength might boldly on yours favours build;
Our russet, tissue; drone, a honey-bee;
Our barren plot, a large and spacious field;
Our course fare, banquets; our thin water, wine;
Our brook, a sea; our bat's eyes, eagle's sight;      10
Our poet's dull and earthy Muse, divine;
Our ravens, doves; our crow's black feathers, white
 But gentle thoughts, when they may give the foil,
 Save them that yield, and spare where they may
  spoil.

 13 foil] *almost, but not quite, a fall, in wrestling*

# DRAMATIS PERSONÆ.

*Sir Francis Acton*, Brother of *Mistress Frankford*.
*Sir Charles Mountford*.
*Master Frankford*.
*Master Wendoll*, Friend to *Frankford*.
*Master Malby*, Friend to *Sir Francis*.
*Master Cranwell*.
*Shafton*, a False Friend to *Sir Charles*.
*Old Mountford*, Uncle to *Sir Charles*.
*Tidy*, Cousin to *Sir Charles*.
*Sandy*.
*Roder*.
*Nicholas*,
*Jenkin*,
*Roger Brickbat*, } Servants to *Frankford*.
*Jack Slime*,
*Spigot*, a Butler,
Sheriff.
A Sergeant, a Keeper, Officers, Falconers, Huntsmen, a
 Coachman, Carters, Servants, Musicians.

*Mistress Frankford*.
*Susan*, Sister of *Sir Charles*.
*Cicely*, Maid to *Mistress Frankford*.
Women Servants.

# A WOMAN KILLED WITH KINDNESS

## Act the First

### Scene I

*Enter* Master John Frankford, Mistress Frankford, Sir Francis Acton, Sir Charles Mountford, Master Malby, Master Wendoll, *and* Master Cranwell.

*Sir Fran.* Some music there: none lead the bride a dance?

*Sir Char.* Yes, would she dance *The Shaking of the Sheets*;
But that's the dance her husband means to lead her.

*Wen.* That's not the dance that every man must dance,
According to the ballad.

*Sir Fran.*                    Music, ho!
By your leave, sister—by your husband's leave,
I should have said—the hand that but this day
Was given you in the church I'll borrow: sound!
This marriage music hoists me from the ground.

*Frank.* Ay, you may caper, you are light and free: 10
Marriage hath yok'd my heels; pray then pardon me.

*Sir Fran.* I'll have you dance too, brother.

*Sir Char.*                    Master Frankford,
You are a happy man, sir; and much joy
Succeed your marriage mirth! you have a wife
So qualified, and with such ornaments
Both of the mind and body. First, her birth
Is noble, and her education such

2 *The Shaking of the Sheets*] *a ballad tune often mentioned, usually with the same double meaning as here*

As might become the daughter of a prince:
Her own tongue speaks all tongues, and her own
    hand
Can teach all strings to speak in their best grace, 20
From the shrill treble to the hoarsest bass.
To end her many praises in one word,
She's beauty and perfection's eldest daughter,
Only found by yours, though many a heart hath
    sought her.

*Frank.* But that I know your virtues and chaste
    thoughts,
I should be jealous of your praise, Sir Charles.

*Cran.* He speaks no more than you approve.

*Mal.* Nor flatters he that gives to her her due.

*Mis. Frank.* I would your praise could find a fitter
    theme
Than my imperfect beauties to speak on;    30
Such as they be, if they my husband please,
They suffice me now I am married:
His sweet content is like a flatt'ring glass,
To make my face seem fairer to mine eye;
But the least wrinkle from his stormy brow
Will blast the roses in my cheeks that grow.

*Sir Fran.* A perfect wife already, meek and patient;
How strangely the word "husband" fits your mouth,
Not married three hours since! Sister, 'tis good;
You, that begin betimes thus, must needs prove 40
Pliant and duteous in your husband's love.—
Godamercies, brother, wrought her to 't already;
"Sweet husband," and a curtsey, the first day!
Mark this, mark this, you that are bachelors,
And never took the grace of honest man;
Mark this, against you marry, this one phrase:
"In a good time that man both wins and woos,
That takes his wife down in her wedding shoes."

*Frank.* Your sister takes not after you, Sir Francis,
All his wild blood your father spent on you:    50

    48 takes ... down] puts her in her place

He got her in his age, when he grew civil;
All his mad tricks were to his land entail'd,
And you are heir to all; your sister, she
Hath to her dower her mother's modesty.

*Sir. Char.* Lord, sir, in what a happy state live you!
This morning, which to many seems a burthen
Too heavy to bear, is unto you a pleasure.
This lady is no clog, as many are:
She doth become you like a well-made suit,
In which the tailor hath us'd all his art:     60
Not like a thick coat of unseason'd frieze,
Forc'd on your back in summer; she's no chain
To tie your neck, and curb you to the yoke;
But she's a chain of gold to adorn your neck.
You both adorn each other, and your hands,
Methinks, are matches: there's equality
In this fair combination; you are both
Scholars, both young, both being descended nobly.
There's music in this sympathy, it carries
Consort, and expectation of much joy,     70
Which God bestow on you, from this first day
Until your dissolution; that's for aye.

*Sir Fran.* We keep you here too long, good brother
    Frankford.
Into the hall; away! go cheer your guests.
What, bride and bridegroom both withdrawn at
    once?
If you be miss'd, the guests will doubt their welcome,
And charge you with unkindness.

*Frank.*             To prevent it,
I'll leave you here, to see the dance within.

*Mis. Frank.* And so will I.

        [*Exeunt* Frankford *and* Mistress Frankford.

*Sir Fran.*         To part you, it were sin.
Now, gallants, while the town-musicians     80
Finger their frets within; and the mad lads

70 consort] harmony        81 fret [ *finger-board divisions*
*on such instruments as the lute*

**M**

And country-lasses, every mother's child,
With nosegays and bridelaces in their hats,
Dance all their country measures, rounds, and jigs,
What shall we do?  Hark, they are all on the
    hoigh;
They toil like mill-horses, and turn as round,—
Marry, not on the toe.  Ay, and they caper,
Not without cutting; you shall see, to-morrow,
The hall-floor peck'd and dinted like a mill-stone,
Made with their high shoes: though their skill be
    small,                                          90
Yet they tread heavy where their hob-nails fall.
*Sir Char.*  Well, leave them to their sports.  Sir Francis
    Acton,
I'll make a match with you; meet me to-morrow
At Chevy-chase, I'll fly my hawk with yours.
*Sir Fran.*  For what?  For what?
*Sir Char.*                      Why, for a hundred pound.
*Sir Fran.*  Pawn me some gold of that.
*Sir Char.*                      Here are ten angels;
I'll make them good a hundred pound to-morrow
Upon my hawk's wing.
*Sir Fran.*                      'Tis a match, 'tis done.
Another hundred pound upon your dogs,
Dare ye, Sir Charles?
*Sir Char.*             I dare: were I sure to lose,   100
I durst do more than that: here 's my hand,
The first course for a hundred pound.
*Sir Fran.*                         A match.
*Wen.*  Ten angels on Sir Francis Acton's hawk;
As much upon his dogs.
*Cran.*  I am for Sir Charles Mountford; I have seen
His hawk and dog both tried.  What, clap you
    hands?
Or is't no bargain?

83 bridelaces] *laces used for binding the sprigs of rosemary
worn at weddings*      85 on the hoigh] *excited*      96 angels]
*gold coins worth ten shillings*

*Wen.*                 Yes, and stake them down:
Were they five hundred, they were all my own.
*Sir Fran.*  Be stirring early with the lark to-morrow;
I'll rise into my saddle ere the sun              110
Rise from his bed.
*Sir Char.*             If there you miss me, say
I am no gentleman: I'll hold my day.
*Sir Fran.*  It holds on all sides.  Come, to-night let's
dance,
Early to-morrow let's prepare to ride;
We had need be three hours up before the bride.
                                    [*Exeunt.*


## Scene II

*Enter* Nick *and* Jenkin, Jack Slime, *and* Roger Brickbat,
*with* Country Wenches, *and two or three* Musicians.

*Jenk.*  Come, Nick, take you Joan Miniver to trace
withal; Jack Slime, traverse you with Cicely
Milk-pail; I will take Jane Trubkin, and Roger
Brickbat shall have Isbel Motley; and now that
they are busy in the parlour, come, strike up,
we'll have a crash here in the yard.              6
*Nick.*  My humour is not compendious; dancing I
possess not, though I can foot it; yet, since I am
fallen into the hands of Cicely Milk-pail, I assent.
*Slime.*  Truly Nick, though we were never brought up
like serving courtiers, yet we have been brought
up with serving creatures, ay, and God's creatures
too; for we have been brought up to serve sheep,
oxen, horses, and hogs, and such like; and, though
we be but country fellows, it may be in the way of
dancing we can do the horse-trick as well as
serving-men.                                     17
*Brick.*  Ay, and the cross-point too.

  1, 2 trace, traverse] dance    6 crash] bout of revelry
16, 18 horse-trick, cross-point] *steps in dancing*

*Jenk.* O Slime, O Brickbat, do not you know that
comparisons are odious? now we are odious ourselves too, therefore there are no comparisons to
be made betwixt us.                                    22

*Nick.* I am sudden, and not superfluous;
  I am quarrelsome, and not seditious;
  I am peaceable, and not contentious;
  I am brief, and not compendious.

*Slime.* Foot it quickly: if the music overcome not my
melancholy, I shall quarrel; and if they do not suddenly strike up, I shall presently strike thee down.

*Jenk.* No quarrelling, for God's sake: truly, if you do,
I shall set a knave between you.                       31

*Slime.* I come to dance, not to quarrel. Come, what
shall it be? *Rogero?*

*Jenk.* *Rogero!* no, we will dance *The Beginning of the
World.*

*Cicely.* I love no dance so well as *John come kiss me now.*

*Nick.* I, that have ere now deserv'd a cushion, call for
the *Cushion-dance.*

*Brick.* For my part, I like nothing so well as *Tom
Tyler.*                                               40

*Jenk.* No, we'll have *The Hunting of the Fox.*

*Slime.* *The Hay, The Hay;* there's nothing like *The
Hay.*

*Nick.* I have said, I do say, and I will say again——

*Jenk.* Every man agree to have it as Nick says.

*All.* Content.

*Nic.* It hath been, it now is, and it shall be——

*Cicely.* What, Master Nicholas, what?

*Nick.* *Put on your smock a' Monday.*

*Jenk.* So the dance will come cleanly off. Come, for
God's sake agree of something; if you like not
that, put it to the musicians; or let me speak for
all, and we'll have *Sellenger's round.*              53

*All.* That, that, that.

31–52] *The dances mentioned are known from other sources,
and descriptions are quoted by Bates.*

*Nick.* No, I am resolv'd, thus it shall be:
  First take hands, then take you to your heels.
*Jenk.* Why, would you have us run away?
*Nick.* No but I would have you shake your heels.
    Music, strike up!
  *They dance.* Nick *dancing speaks stately and scurvily,*
        *the rest after the country fashion.*
*Jenk.* Hey! lively, my lasses! here's a turn for thee! 60
                                        [*Exeunt.*


# Scene III

*Wind horns.* Enter *Sir Charles Mountford, Sir Francis
Acton, Malby, Cranwell, Wendoll, Falconers,* and
                Huntsman.*

*Sir Char.* So; well cast off: aloft, aloft! well flown!
  Oh, now she takes her at the sowse, and strikes her
  Down to the earth, like a swift thunder-clap.
*Wen.* She hath struck ten angels out of my way.
*Sir Fran.* A hundred pound from me.
*Sir Char.*                                What, falconer!
*Fal.* At hand, sir.
*Sir Char.* Now she hath seiz'd the fowl, and 'gins to
    plume her,
  Rebuke her not; rather stand still and chirk her.
  So, seize her gets, her jesses, and her bells:
  Away!                                                  10
*Sir Fran.* My hawk kill'd too.
*Sir Char.*              Ay, but 'twas at the querre,

  59 *s.d. scurvily*] discourteously      1 cast off] *sc. from
the falconer's fist*      2 at the sowse] pouncing straight down
in one swoop      7 plume] pluck      8 Rebuke . . .
chirk] do not alarm her with rough words, but reassure
her by chirping to her. *The old editions read* Rebeck . . .
check. *The emendations and explanations are Bates's*      9 gets,
and jesses] jesses *are straps fastened to the hawk's legs; if the
terms are not synonymous,* gets *may be the straps by which the bells
were attached* (Bates)      11–12 at the querre . . . at the
mount] on the ground . . . on the wing

Not at the mount, like mine.

*Sir Fran.*                    Judgment, my masters.

*Cran.* Yours miss'd her at the ferre.

*Wen.* Ay, but our merlin first had plum'd the fowl,
And twice renew'd her from the river too;
Her bells, Sir Francis, had not both one weight,
Nor was one semi-tune above the other:
Methinks these Milan bells do sound too full,
And spoil the mounting of your hawk.

*Sir Char.*                         'Tis lost.

*Sir Fran.* I grant it not.  Mine likewise seiz'd a fowl 20
Within her talons; and you saw her paws
Full of the feathers: both her petty singles,
And her long singles gripp'd her more than other;
The terrials of her legs were stain'd with blood:
Not of the fowl only she did discomfit
Some of her feathers, but she brake away.
Come, come, your hawk is but a rifler.

*Sir Char.*                            How!

*Sir Fran.* Ay, and your dogs are trindle-tails and curs.

*Sir Char.* You stir my blood.
You keep not a good hound in all your kennel,    30
Nor one good hawk upon your perch.

*Sir Fran.*                       How, knight!

*Sir Char.* So, knight: you will not swagger, sir?

*Sir Fran.* Why, say I did?

*Sir Char.* Why, sir, I say you would gain as much by
        swagg'ring
As you have got by wagers on your dogs;

13 ferre] highest point    14 merlin] *a species of small hawk*
15 renew'd] drove back    22, 23 petty singles . . . long
singles] *the claws of the fore-part of the hawk's foot, the short
outer ones and the longer central ones*    24 terrials] *perhaps
in error for* terrets, *the rings on the hawk's legs*    24–6] *the
sense is*: my hawk drew blood, she did not merely ruffle her
prey's feathers    27 rifler] *a hawk which grips too soon and
catches only feathers*    28 trindle-tails] with curly tails
(*therefore low-bred*)

You will come short in all things.

*Sir Fran.*                              Not in this:
Now I'll strike home.

*Sir Char.*                   Thou shalt to thy long home,
Or I will want my will.

*Sir Fran.* All they that love Sir Francis, follow me.

*Sir Char.* All that affect Sir Charles, draw on my part. 40

*Cran.* On this side heaves my hand.

*Wen.*                              Here goes my heart.

*They divide themselves.* Sir Charles Mountford, Cran-
well, Falconer, *and* Huntsman, *fight against* Sir Francis
Acton, Wendoll, *his* Falconer, *and* Huntsman; *and*
Sir Charles's *side gets the better, beating the others away,
and killing both of* Sir Francis's *men. Exeunt all except*
Sir Charles.

*Sir Char.* My God! what have I done? what have I
    done?
My rage hath plung'd into a sea of blood,
In which my soul lies drown'd.  Poor innocents,
For whom we are to answer!  Well, 'tis done,
And I remain the victor.  A great conquest,
When I would give this right hand, nay, this head,
To breathe in them new life whom I have slain!
Forgive me, God! 'twas in the heat of blood,
And anger quite removes me from myself:        50
It was not I, but rage, did this vile murther;
Yet I, and not my rage, must answer it.
Sir Francis Acton he is fled the field;
With him all those that did partake his quarrel,
And I am left alone, with sorrow dumb,
And in my height of conquest, overcome.


                    *Enter* Susan.

*Susan.* O God! my brother wounded among the dead!
Unhappy jest, that in such earnest ends;
The rumour of this fear stretch'd to my ears,
And I am come to know if you be wounded.        60

*Sir Char.* Oh, sister, sister, wounded at the heart!

*Susan.* My God forbid!

*Sir Char.* In doing that thing which he forbad,
  I am wounded, sister.

*Susan.*                   I hope not at the heart.

*Sir Char.* Yes, at the heart.

*Susan.*                   O God! a surgeon there!

*Sir Char.* Call me a surgeon, sister, for my soul;
  The sin of murther it hath pierc'd my heart,
  And made a wide wound there: but for these
    scratches,
  They are nothing, nothing.

*Susan.*                   Charles, what have you done?
  Sir Francis hath great friends, and will pursue you 70
  Unto the utmost danger of the law.

*Sir Char.* My conscience is become mine enemy,
  And will pursue me more than Acton can.

*Susan.* Oh, fly, sweet brother.

*Sir Char.*                   Shall I fly from thee?
  Why, Sue, art weary of my company?

*Susan.* Fly from your foe.

*Sir Char.*                   You, sister, are my friend,
  And, flying you, I shall pursue my end.

*Susan.* Your company is as my eye-ball dear;
  Being far from you, no comfort can be near;
  Yet fly to save your life: what would I care    80
  To spend my future age in black despair,
  So you were safe? and yet to live one week
  Without my brother Charles, through every check
  My streaming tears would downwards run so rank,
  Till they could set on either side a bank,
  And in the midst a channel; so my face
  For two salt-water brooks shall still find place.

*Sir Char.* Thou shalt not weep so much, for I will stay
  In spite of danger's teeth; I'll live with thee,
  Or I'll not live at all. I will not sell    90
  My country and my father's patrimony,
  Nor thy sweet sight, for a vain hope of life.

*Enter* Sheriff, *with* Officers.

*Sher.*  Sir Charles, I am made the unwilling instrument
     Of your attach and apprehension:
     I am sorry that the blood of innocent men
     Should be of you exacted.  It was told me
     That you were guarded with a troop of friends,
     And therefore I come arm'd.
*Sir Char.*                             O, Master Sheriff,
     I came into the field with many friends,
     But see, they all have left me: only one          100
     Clings to my sad misfortune, my dear sister.
     I know you for an honest gentleman;
     I yield my weapons, and submit to you;
     Convey me where you please.
*Sher.*                             To prison then,
     To answer for the lives of these dead men.
*Susan.*  O God! O God!
*Sir Char.*                  Sweet sister, every strain
     Of sorrow from your heart augments my pain;
     Your grief abounds, and hits against my breast.
*Sher.*  Sir, will you go?
*Sir Char.*          Even where it likes you best.  [*Exeunt.*


# Act the Second

## Scene I

*Enter* Master Frankford *in a study.*

*Frank.*  How happy am I amongst other men,
     That in my mean estate embrace content!
     I am a gentleman, and by my birth,
     Companion with a king; a king's no more.
     I am possess'd of many fair revenues,
     Sufficient to maintain a gentleman.
     Touching my mind, I am studied in all arts;

94 attach] arrest        108 abounds] overflows          5
revenues] *accented as usual* revénues

The riches of my thoughts, and of my time,
Have been a good proficient; but the chief
Of all the sweet felicities on earth,                    10
I have a fair, a chaste, and loving wife;
Perfection all, all truth, all ornament;
If man on earth may truly happy be,
Of these at once possess'd, sure I am he.

*Enter* Nicholas.

*Nick.* Sir, there's a gentleman attends without
    To speak with you.
*Frank.*                    On horseback?
*Nick.*                                    Ay, on horseback.
*Frank.* Entreat him to alight, I will attend him.
    Know'st thou him, Nick?
*Nick.*            Know him, yes; his name's Wendoll:
    It seems he comes in haste: his horse is booted
    Up to the flank in mire, himself all spotted      20
    And stain'd with splashing.  Sure he rid in fear,
    Or for a wager: horse and man both sweat;
    I ne'er saw two in such a smoking heat.
*Frank.* Entreat him in: about it instantly.

                                [*Exit* Nicholas.

    This Wendoll I have noted, and his carriage
    Hath pleas'd me much; by observation
    I have noted many good deserts in him:
    He's affable, and seen in many things,
    Discourses well, a good companion;
    And though of small means, yet a gentleman      30
    Of a good house, though somewhat press'd by want:
    I have preferr'd him to a second place
    In my opinion, and my best regard.

*Enter* Wendoll, Mistress Frankford, *and* Nicholas.

*Mis. Frank.* O Master Frankford, Master Wendoll here
    Brings you the strangest news that e'er you heard.

    9 a good proficient] helping to progress      28 seen]
versed

*Frank.* What news sweet wife? What news, good Master
   Wendoll?

*Wen.* You knew the match made 'twixt Sir Francis
   Acton
  And Sir Charles Mountford.

*Frank.*           True, with their hounds and hawks.

*Wen.* The matches were both play'd.

*Frank.*               Ha, and which won?

*Wen.* Sir Francis, your wife's brother, had the worst, 40
  And lost the wager.

*Frank.*          Why, the worse his chance;
  Perhaps the fortune of some other day
  Will change his luck.

*Mis. Frank.*        Oh, but you hear not all.
  Sir Francis lost, and yet was loth to yield:
  In brief the two knights grew to difference,
  From words to blows, and so to banding sides;
  Where valorous Sir Charles slew in his spleen
  Two of your brother's men; his falconer,
  And his good huntsman, whom he lov'd so well;
  More men were wounded, no more slain outright. 50

*Frank.* Now, trust me, I am sorry for the knight;
  But is my brother safe?

*Wen.*           All whole and sound,
  His body not being blemish'd with one wound:
  But poor Sir Charles is to the prison led,
  To answer at th' assize for them that's dead.

*Frank.* I thank your pains, sir; had the news been
   better
  Your will was to have brought it, Master Wendoll.
  Sir Charles will find hard friends; his case is heinous,
  And will be most severely censur'd on;
  I am sorry for him.—Sir, a word with you:    60
  I know you, sir, to be a gentleman
  In all things; your possibilities but mean:
  Please you to use my table and my purse,
  They are yours.

        59 censur'd on] judged of

*Wen.*                O Lord, sir, I shall never deserve it.
*Frank.* O sir, disparage not your worth too much,
　　You are full of quality and fair desert;
　　Choose of my men which shall attend on you
　　And he is yours.  I will allow you, sir,
　　Your man, your gelding, and your table, all
　　At my own charge; be my companion.        70
*Wen.* Master Frankford, I have oft been bound to you
　　By many favours; this exceeds them all,
　　That I shall never merit your least favour:
　　But, when your last remembrance I forget,
　　Heaven at my soul exact that weighty debt!
*Frank.* There needs no protestation; for I know you
　　Virtuous, and therefore grateful.  Prithee, Nan,
　　Use him with all thy loving'st courtesy.
*Mis. Frank.* As far as modesty may well extend
　　It is my duty to receive your friend.        80
*Frank.* To dinner: come, sir, from this present day,
　　Welcome to me for ever: come, away.

[*Exeunt* Frankford, Mistress Frankford, *and* Wendoll.

*Nick.* I do not like this fellow by no means:
　　I never see him but my heart still earns:
　　Zounds! I could fight with him, yet know not why:
　　The devil and he are all one in my eye.

　　　　　　　*Enter* Jenkin.

*Jenk.* O Nick, what gentleman is that comes to lie at
　　our house? my master allows him one to wait on
　　him, and I believe it will fall to thy lot.
*Nick.* I love my master, by these hilts I do:        90
　　But rather than I'll ever come to serve him,
　　I'll turn away my master.

　　　　　　　*Enter* Cicely.

*Cicely.* Nich'las, where are you, Nich'las? you must
　　come in, Nich'las, and help the young gentleman
　　off with his boots.

　　　　84 earns] grieves

*Nick.* If I pluck off his boots, I'll eat the spurs,
  And they shall stick fast in my throat like burs.
*Cicely.* Then, Jenkin, come you.
*Jenk.* 'Tis no boot for me to deny it. My master
  hath given me a coat here, but he takes pains
  himself to brush it once or twice a day with a
  holly-wand.                                        101
*Cicely.* Come, come, make haste, that you may wash
  your hands again, and help to serve in dinner.
*Jenk.* You may see, my masters, though it be afternoon
  with you, 'tis but early days with us, for we have
  not din'd yet: stay a little, I'll but go in and help
  to bear up the first course, and come to you again
  presently.                                       [*Exeunt.*

## Scene II

*Enter* Malby *and* Cranwell.

*Mal.* This is the sessions-day; pray can you tell me
  How young Sir Charles hath sped? Is he acquit,
  Or must he try the law's strict penalty?
*Cran.* He's clear'd of all, spite of his enemies,
  Whose earnest labours was to take his life:
  But in this suit of pardon he hath spent
  All the revenues that his father left him;
  And he is now turn'd a plain countryman,
  Reform'd in all things. See, sir, here he comes.

*Enter* Sir Charles *and* Keeper.

*Keep.* Discharge your fees, and you are then at
  freedom.                                           10
*Sir Char.* Here, Master Keeper, take the poor remainder
  Of all the wealth I have: my heavy foes

104 my masters] *the actor turns to address the audience: the*
*play would be acted in the afternoon, and the common dining-hour*
*was about mid-day*          105 early days] *early in the day*

Have made my purse light; but, alas, to me
'Tis wealth enough that you have set me free.

*Mal.* God give you joy of your delivery!
I am glad to see you abroad, Sir Charles.

*Sir Char.* The poorest knight in England, Master
    Malby;
My life hath cost me all my patrimony
My father left his son: well, God forgive them
That are the authors of my penury.    20


*Enter* Shafton.

*Shaf.* Sir Charles! a hand, a hand! at liberty?
Now, by the faith I owe, I am glad to see it.
What want you? wherein may I pleasure you?

*Sir Char.* O me! O most unhappy gentleman!
I am not worthy to have friends stirr'd up,
Whose hands may help me in this plunge of want.
I would I were in heaven, to inherit there
Th' immortal birth-right which my Saviour keeps,
And by no unthrift can be bought and sold;
For here on earth what pleasures should we trust? 30

*Shaf.* To rid you from these contemplations,
Three hundred pounds you shall receive of me:
Nay, five for fail. Come, sir, the sight of gold
Is the most sweet receipt for melancholy,
And will revive your spirits: you shall hold law
With your proud adversaries. Tush, let Frank Acton
Wage with his knighthood like expense with me,
And he will sink, he will. Nay, good Sir Charles,
Applaud your fortune, and your fair escape
From all these perils.

*Sir Char.*          O sir, they have undone me.  40
Two thousand and five hundred pound a year
My father at his death possess'd me of;
All which the envious Acton made me spend.

26 plunge] strait, pinch    33 for fail] as a precaution
against shortage    37 Wage] offer as security

And notwithstanding all this large expense
I had much ado to gain my liberty:
And I have now only a house of pleasure,
With some five hundred pounds, reserved
Both to maintain me and my loving sister.

*Shaft.* [*Aside.*] That must I have, it lies convenient
    for me:
If I can fasten but one finger on him,           50
With my full hand I'll gripe him to the heart.
'Tis not for love I proffer'd him this coin,
But for my gain and pleasure.—Come, Sir Charles,
I know you have need of money; take my offer.

*Sir Char.* Sir, I accept it, and remain indebted
Even to the best of my unable power.
Come, gentlemen, and see it tender'd down.
                             [*Exeunt.*

## Scene III

*Enter* Wendoll *melancholy.*

*Wen.* I am a villain if I apprehend
But such a thought: then, to attempt the deed,—
Slave, thou art damn'd without redemption.
I'll drive away this passion with a song.
A song! ha, ha: a song! as if, fond man,
Thy eyes could swim in laughter, when thy soul
Lies drench'd and drowned in red tears of blood.
I'll pray, and see if God within my heart
Plant better thoughts. Why, prayers are medita-
    tions;
And when I meditate (O God, forgive me!)     10
It is on her divine perfections.
I will forget her; I will arm myself
Not to entertain a thought of love to her:
And, when I come by chance into her presence,

46 house of pleasure] country cottage

I'll hale these balls until my eye-strings crack,
From being pull'd and drawn to look that way.

*Enter over the stage,* Frankford, *his wife, and* Nick.

O God! O God! with what a violence
I am hurried to my own destruction.
There goest thou, the most perfectest man
That ever England bred a gentleman;                20
And shall I wrong his bed? Thou God of thunder!
Stay in thy thoughts of vengeance and of wrath,
Thy great, almighty, and all-judging hand
From speedy execution on a villain—
A villain, and a traitor to his friend.

*Enter* Jenkin.

*Jenk.* Did your worship call?
*Wen.* He doth maintain me, he allows me largely
    Money to spend——
*Jenk.* By my faith, so do not you me; I cannot get a
    cross of you.                                  30
*Wen.* My gelding, and my man——
*Jenk.* That's Sorrell and I.
*Wen.* This kindness grows of no alliance 'twixt us——
*Jenk.* Nor is my service of any great acquaintance.
*Wen.* I never bound him to me by desert:
    Of a mere stranger, a poor gentleman,
    A man by whom in no kind he could gain,
    He hath plac'd me in the height of all his thoughts,
    Made me companion with the best and chiefest
    In Yorkshire. He cannot eat without me,        40
    Nor laugh without me: I am to his body
    As necessary as his digestion,
    And equally do make him whole or sick:
    And shall I wrong this man? Base man, ingrate!
    Hast thou the power straight with thy gory hands
    To rip thy image from his bleeding heart?

        15 hale] constrain        30 cross] coin

To scratch thy name from out the holy book
Of his remembrance; and to wound his name
That holds thy name so dear? or rend his heart
To whom thy heart was knit and join'd together? 50
And yet I must: then, Wendoll, be content;
Thus villains, when they would, cannot repent.

*Jenk.* What a strange humour is my new master in!
  Pray God he be not mad: if he should be so, I
  should never have any mind to serve him in
  Bedlam. It may be he is mad for missing of me.

*Wen.* What, Jenkin, where's your mistress?

*Jenk.* Is your worship married?

*Wen.* Why dost thou ask?

*Jenk.* Because you are my master, and if I have a
  mistress, I would be glad, like a good servant, to
  do my duty to her.                          62

*Wen.* I mean where's Mistress Frankford.

*Jenk.* Marry, sir, her husband is riding out of town,
  and she went very lovingly to bring him on his
  way to horse. Do you see, sir? here she comes,
  and here I go.

*Wen.* Vanish.                          [*Exit* Jenkin.


*Enter* Mistress Frankford.

*Mis. Frank.* You are well met, sir; now, in troth, my
  husband,
  Before he took horse, had a great desire   70
  To speak with you: we sought about the house,
  Hallo'd into the fields, sent every way,
  But could not meet you: therefore he enjoin'd me
  To do unto you his most kind commends.
  Nay, more; he wills you, as you prize his love,
  Or hold in estimation his kind friendship,
  To make bold in his absence, and command
  Even as himself were present in the house:

56 Bedlam] *the famous hospital for lunatics*      65 bring
him on his way] accompany him

For you must keep his table, use his servants,
And be a present Frankford in his absence.     80
*Wen.* I thank him for his love.—
    Give me a name, you whose infectious tongues
    Are tipp'd with gall and poison: as you would
    Think on a man that had your father slain,
    Murder'd your children, made your wives base
        strumpets,
    So call me, call me so: print in my face
    The most stigmatic title of a villain,
    For hatching treason to so true a friend.     [*Aside.*
*Mis Frank.* Sir, you are much beholding to my hus-
        band;
    You are a man most dear in his regard.     90
*Wen.* I am bound unto your husband, and you
        too.—
    I will not speak to wrong a gentleman
    Of that good estimation, my kind friend:
    I will not; zounds! I will not. I may choose,
    And I will choose. Shall I be so misled?
    Or shall I purchase to my father's crest
    The motto of a villain? If I say
    I will not do it, what thing can enforce me?
    What can compel me? What sad destiny
    Hath such command upon my yielding thoughts?
    I will not—Ha! some fury pricks me on,     101
    The swift Fates drag me at their chariot-wheel,
    And hurry me to mischief. Speak I must;
    Injure myself, wrong her, deceive his trust.  [*Aside.*
*Mis. Frank.* Are you not well, sir, that you seem thus
        troubled?
    There is sedition in your countenance.
*Wen.* And in my heart, fair angel, chaste and wise.
    I love you: start not, speak not, answer not.
    I love you: nay, let me speak the rest:
    Bid me to swear, and I will call to record     110
    The host of Heaven.

89 beholding] endebted

*Mis. Frank.*                    The host of Heaven forbid
  Wendoll should hatch such a disloyal thought!
*Wen.* Such is my fate; to this suit I was born,
  To wear rich pleasure's crown, or fortune's scorn.
*Mis. Frank.* My husband loves you.
*Wen.*                              I know it.
*Mis. Frank.*                          He esteems you
  Even as his brain, his eye-ball, or his heart.
*Wen.* I have tried it.
*Mis. Frank.* His purse is your exchequer, and his table
  Doth freely serve you.
*Wen.*                So I have found it.
*Mis. Frank.* O! with what face of brass, what brow of
      steel,
  Can you, unblushing, speak this to the face      120
  Of the espous'd wife of so dear a friend?
  It is my husband that maintains your state;
  Will you dishonour him? I am his wife,
  That in your power hath left his whole affairs;
  It is to me you speak.
*Wen.*                    O speak no more!
  For more than this I know, and have recorded
  Within the red-leav'd table of my heart.
  Fair, and of all belov'd, I was not fearful
  Bluntly to give my life into your hand,          130
  And at one hazard all my earthly means.
  Go, tell your husband; he will turn me off,
  And I am then undone: I care not, I;
  'Twas for your sake. Perchance in rage he'll kill me:
  I care not, 'twas for you. Say I incur
  The general name of villain through the world,
  Of traitor to my friend: I care not, I.
  Beggary, shame, death, scandal, and reproach,
  For you I'll hazard all: why, what care I?
  For you I'll live, and in your love I'll die.     140
*Mis. Frank.* You move me, sir, to passion and to
      pity.

      132 turn me off] dismiss me

The love I bear my husband is as precious
As my soul's health.
*Wen.*                I love your husband too,
And for his love I will engage my life;
Mistake me not, the augmentation
Of my sincere affection borne to you
Doth no whit lessen my regard of him.
I will be secret, lady, close as night;
And not the light of one small glorious star
Shall shine here in my forehead, to bewray      150
That act of night.
*Mis. Frank.*          What shall I say?
My soul is wand'ring and hath lost her way.
Oh, Master Wendoll! Oh!
*Wen.*                Sigh not, sweet saint;
For every sigh you breathe draws from my heart
A drop of blood.
*Mis. Frank.*        I ne'er offended yet:
My fault, I fear, will in my brow be writ.
Women that fall, not quite bereft of grace,
Have their offences noted in their face.
I blush and am asham'd. Oh, Master Wendoll,
Pray God I be not born to curse your tongue,   160
That hath enchanted me! This maze I am in
I fear will prove the labyrinth of sin.


*Enter* Nick.

*Wen.* The path of pleasure, and the gate to bliss,
Which on your lips I knock at with a kiss.
*Nick.* [*Aside.*] I'll kill the rogue.
*Wen.* Your husband is from home, your bed's no blab.
Nay, look not down and blush.
                [*Exeunt* Wendoll *and* Mistress Frankford.
*Nick.*                Zounds, I'll stab!
Ay, Nick, was it thy chance to come just in the nick?
I love my master, and I hate that slave;
I love my mistress, but these tricks I like not.   170

My master shall not pocket up this wrong,
I'll eat my fingers first. What say'st thou, metal?
Does not the rascal Wendoll go on legs
That thou must cut off? Hath he not ham-strings
That thou must hough? Nay, metal, thou shalt stand
To all I say. I'll henceforth turn a spy,
And watch them in their close conveyances.
I never look'd for better of that rascal,
Since he came miching first into our house:
It is that Satan hath corrupted her,                    180
For she was fair and chaste. I'll have an eye
In all their gestures. Thus I think of them,
If they proceed as they have done before:
Wendoll's a knave, my mistress is a——        [*Exit.*

## Act the Third

### Scene I

*Enter* Sir Charles Mountford *and* Susan.

*Sir Char.* Sister, you see we are driven to hard shift
  To keep this poor house we have left unsold;
  I am now enforc'd to follow husbandry,
  And you to milk; and do we not live well?
  Well, I thank God.
*Susan.*                       O brother, here's a change,
  Since old Sir Charles died, in our father's house!
*Sir Char.* All things on earth thus change, some up,
    some down;
  Content's a kingdom, and I wear that crown.

*Enter* Shafton *with a* Sergeant.

*Shaf.* Good morrow, good morrow, Sir Charles: what,
    with your sister,

171 pocket up] put up with      172 metal] *he has drawn*
*his dagger at line* 167      177 close conveyances] secret
plots      179 miching] skulking

Plying your husbandry?—Sergeant, stand off.—  10
You have a pretty house here, and a garden,
And goodly ground about it.  Since it lies
So near a lordship that I lately bought,
I would fain buy it of you.  I will give you——
*Sir Char.*  O, pardon me: this house successively
Hath long'd to me and my progenitors
Three hundred year.  My great-great-grandfather,
He in whom first our gentle style began,
Dwelt here; and in this ground, increas'd this mole-
    hill
Unto that mountain which my father left me.    20
Where he the first of all our house began,
I now the last will end, and keep this house,
This virgin title, never yet deflower'd
By any unthrift of the Mountfords' line.
In brief, I will not sell it for more gold
Than you could hide or pave the ground withal.
*Shaf.*  Ha, ha! a proud mind and a beggar's purse!
Where's my three hundred pounds, beside the use?
I have brought it to an execution
By course of law: what, is my money ready?    30
*Sir Char.*  An execution, sir, and never tell me
You put my bond in suit! you deal extremely.
*Shaf.*  Sell me the land, and I'll acquit you straight.
*Sir Char.*  Alas, alas! 'tis all trouble hath left me
To cherish me and my poor sister's life.
If this were sold, our names should then be quite
Raz'd from the bead-roll of gentility.
You see what hard shift we have made to keep it
Allied still to our own name.  This palm, you see,
Labour hath glow'd within; her silver brow,    40
That never tasted a rough winter's blast

15 successively] by succession    16 long'd] belonged
18 gentle style] title of gentility    28 use] interest    29 exe-
cution] *a legal order for seizure of goods or person in default of
payment*    32 put my bond in suit] entered a suit for the re-
covery of the money due under my bond    37 bead-roll] list

Without a mask or fan, doth with a grace
Defy cold winter, and his storms outface.

*Susan.* Sir, we feed sparing, and we labour hard,
We lie uneasy, to reserve to us
And our succession this small plot of ground.

*Sir Char.* I have so bent my thoughts to husbandry,
That I protest I scarcely can remember
What a new fashion is; how silk or satin
Feels in my hand: why, pride is grown to us          50
A mere, mere stranger. I have quite forgot
The names of all that ever waited on me;
I cannot name ye any of my hounds,
Once from whose echoing mouths I heard all the
    music
That e'er my heart desired. What should I say?
To keep this place I have chang'd myself away.

*Shaf.* Arrest him at my suit.—Actions and actions
Shall keep thee in perpetual bondage fast.
Nay, more, I'll sue thee by a late appeal,
And call thy former life in question.          60
The keeper is my friend, thou shalt have irons,
And usage such as I'll deny to dogs:
Away with him!

*Sir Char.* [*To* Susan.] You are too timorous:
But trouble is my master,
And I will serve him truly. My kind sister,
Thy tears are of no force to mollify
This flinty man. Go to my father's brother,
My kinsmen and allies; entreat them for me,
To ransom me from this injurious man,
That seeks my ruin.

*Shaf.*          Come, irons, irons! away;          70
I'll see thee lodg'd far from the sight of day. [*Exeunt.*

*Susan.* My heart's so harden'd with the frost of grief,
Death cannot pierce it through. Tyrant too fell!
So lead the fiends condemned souls to hell.

42 mask] *used as a* veil *for protection against the weather*
51 mere] complete          69 injurious] wrong-doing

*Enter* Sir Francis Acton *and* Malby.

*Sir Fran.* Again to prison! Malby, hast thou seen
    A poor slave better tortur'd?  Shall we hear
    The music of his voice cry from the grate,
    *Meat for the Lord sake?*  No, no, yet I am not
    Throughly reveng'd.  They say he hath **a** pretty
       wench
    Unto his sister: shall I in mercy sake       80
    To him and to his kindred, bribe the fool
    To shame herself by lewd dishonest lust?
    I'll proffer largely but, the deed being done,
    I'll smile to see her base confusion.
*Mal.* Methinks, Sir Francis, you are full reveng'd
    For greater wrongs than he can proffer you.
    See where the poor sad gentlewoman stands.
*Sir Fran.* Ha, ha! now will I flout her poverty,
    Deride her fortunes, scoff her base estate;
    My very soul the name of Mountford hates.    90
    But stay, my heart! oh, what a look did fly
    To strike my soul through with thy piercing eye!
    I am enchanted, all my spirits are fled,
    And with one glance my envious spleen struck dead.
*Susan.* Acton, that seeks our blood!    [*Runs away.*
*Sir Fran.*               O chaste and fair!
*Mal.* Sir Francis, why, Sir Francis! zounds, **in a**
    trance?
    Sir Francis, what cheer, man?  Come, come, how
    is't?
*Sir Fran.* Was she not fair?  Or else this judging eye
    Cannot distinguish beauty.
*Mal.*               She was fair.
*Sir Fran.* She was an angel in a mortal's shape,   100
    And ne'er descended from old Mountford's line.
    But soft, soft, let me call my wits together.
    A poor, poor wench, to my great adversary

    **77** from the grate] *prisoners who could not pay for food were*
*allowed to beg it of passers-by through a grating*

Sister, whose very souls denounce stern war,
One against other. How now, Frank? turn'd fool
Or madman, whether? But no; master of
My perfect senses and directest wits.
Then why should I be in this violent humour
Of passion and of love; and with a person
So different every way, and so oppos'd          110
In all contractions, and still-warring actions?
Fie, fie; how I dispute against my soul!
Come, come; I'll gain her, or in her fair quest
Purchase my soul free and immortal rest. [*Exeunt.*

## Scene II

*Enter three or four* Serving-Men, *one with a voider and a
wooden knife to take away all, another the salt and bread,
another the table-cloth and napkins, another the carpet:*
Jenkin *with two lights after them.*

*Jenk.* So, march in order, and retire in battle array.
     My master and the guests have supp'd already,
     all's taken away: here, now spread for the serving-
     men in the hall. Butler, it belongs to your office.
*But.* I know it, Jenkin. What do you call the gentle-
     man that supp'd there to-night?
*Jenk.* Who, my master?
*But.* No, no; Master Wendoll, he is a daily guest; I
     mean the gentleman that came but this afternoon.
*Jenk.* His name is Master Cranwell. God's light, hark,
     within there, my master calls to lay more billets
     on the fire. Come, come! Lord, how we that
     are in office here in the house are troubled! One
     spread the carpet in the parlour, and stand ready
     to snuff the lights; the rest be ready to prepare

106 whether] which          107 directest] most logical
II. ii. heading *voider*] basket, *into which crumbs were swept
with the* wooden knife     *carpet*] table-cover (*cf. lines* 118-19)

their stomachs. More light in the hall there.
Come, Nich'las.          [*Exeunt all but* Nick.

*Nick.* I cannot eat, but had I Wendoll's heart
   I would eat that; the rogue grows impudent.
   Oh, I have seen such vild notorious tricks,     20
   Ready to make my eyes dart from my head.
   I'll tell my master, by this air I will!
   Fall what may fall, I'll tell him.  Here he comes.

*Enter* Master Frankford, *brushing the crumbs from his
   clothes with a napkin, as newly risen from supper.*

*Frank.* Nich'las, what make you here? why are not you
   At supper in the hall there, with your fellows?
*Nick.* Master, I stay'd your rising from the board,
   To speak with you.
*Frank.*          Be brief, then, gentle Nich'las;
   My wife and guests attend me in the parlour.
   Why dost thou pause?  Now, Nich'las, you want
      money,
   And, unthrift-like, would eat into your wages     30
   Ere you have earn'd it: here's, sir, half a crown;
   Play the good husband, and away to supper.
*Nick.* By this hand, an honourable gentleman! I will
   not see him wrong'd.—Sir, I have serv'd you
   long; you entertain'd me seven years before your
   beard.  You knew me, sir, before you knew my
   mistress.
*Frank.* What of this, good Nich'las?
*Nick.* I never was a make-bate or a knave;
   I have no fault but one: I am given to quarrel,     40
   But not with women.  I will tell you, master,
   That which will make your heart leap from your
      breast,
   Your hair to startle from your head, your ears to
      tingle.

20 vild] vile          32 Play the good husband] do not
waste it          39 make-bate] breeder of strife          43
startle] start up

*Frank.* What preparation's this to dismal news?

*Nick.* 'Sblood, sir! I love you better than your wife;
I'll make it good.

*Frank.* Thou art a knave, and I have much ado
With wonted patience to contain my rage,
And not to break thy pate. Thou art a knave;
I'll turn you, with your base comparisons,
Out of my doors.                                   50

*Nick.*                    Do, do: there is not room
For Wendoll and me too, both in one house.
Oh master, master, that Wendoll is a villain.

*Frank.* Ay, saucy!

*Nick.* Strike, strike, do, strike; yet hear me: I am no
fool,
I know a villain, when I see him act
Deeds of a villain. Master, master, that base slave
Enjoys my mistress, and dishonours you.

*Frank.* Thou hast kill'd me with a weapon whose
sharpen'd point
Hath prick'd quite through and through my
shiv'ring heart:                                   60
Drops of cold sweat sit dangling on my hairs,
Like morning's dew upon the golden flowers,
And I am plung'd into a strange agony.
What didst thou say? If any word that touch'd
His credit or her reputation,
It is as hard to enter my belief
As Dives into heaven.

*Nick.*                    I can gain nothing;
They are two that never wrong'd me. I knew before
'Twas but a thankless office, and perhaps
As much as is my service, or my life                70
Is worth. All this I know; but this and more,
More by a thousand dangers, could not hire me
To smother such a heinous wrong from you.
I saw, and I have said.

*Frank.* [*Aside.*] 'Tis probable; though blunt, yet he
is honest:

Though I durst pawn my life, and on their faith
Hazard the dear salvation of my soul,
Yet in my trust I may be too secure.
May this be true? O, may it, can it be?
Is it by any wonder possible?                          80
Man, woman, what thing mortal may we trust,
When friends and bosom wives prove so unjust?—
What instance hast thou of this strange report?

*Nick.* Eyes, eyes.

*Frank.*          Thy eyes may be deceiv'd, I tell thee:
For should an angel from the heavens drop down,
And preach this to me that thyself hast told,
He should have much ado to win belief;
In both their loves I am so confident.

*Nick.* Shall I discourse the same by circumstance?

*Frank.* No more! to supper, and command your fellows
To attend us and the strangers. Not a word,    91
I charge thee on thy life: be secret then,
For I know nothing.

*Nick.* I am dumb; and, now that I have eas'd my
    stomach,
I will go fill my stomach.

*Frank.*                    Away; be gone.  [*Exit* Nick.
She is well born, descended nobly;
Virtuous her education, her repute
Is in the general voice of all the country
Honest and fair; her carriage, her demeanour,
In all her actions that concern the love        100
To me her husband, modest, chaste, and godly.
Is all this seeming gold plain copper?
But he, that Judas that hath borne my purse,
And sold me for a sin!—O God! O God!
Shall I put up these wrongs? No. Shall I trust
The bare report of this suspicious groom,
Before the double-gilt, the well-hatch'd ore
Of their two hearts? No, I will lose these thoughts:

78 secure] confident    107 well-hatch'd] *perhaps* deeply
engraved

Distraction I will banish from my brow,
And from my looks exile sad discontent; 110
Their wonted favours in my tongue shall flow;
Till I know all, I'll nothing seem to know.
Lights and a table there! Wife, Master Wendoll,
And gentle Master Cranwell.

*Enter* Mistress Frankford, Master Wendoll, Master
Cranwell, Nick, *and* Jenkin, *with cards, carpet, stools,
and other necessaries.*

*Frank.* O, you are a stranger Master Cranwell, you,
And often baulk my house: faith, you are a churl:
Now we have supp'd, a table, and to cards.

*Jenk.* A pair of cards, Nich'las, and a carpet to cover
the table. Where's Cicely with her counters and
her box? Candles and candlesticks there! Fie,
we have such a household of serving creatures!
unless it be Nick and I, there's not one amongst
them all can say bo to a goose. Well said, Nick. 123

*They spread a carpet, set down lights and cards.*

*Mis. Frank.* Come, Master Frankford, who shall take
my part?

*Frank.* Marry, that will I, sweet wife.

*Wen.* No, by my faith, sir; when you are together I
sit out; it must be Mistress Frankford and I, or
else it is no match.

*Frank.* I do not like that match.

*Nick.*—You have no reason, marry, knowing all. 130

*Frank.* 'Tis no great matter neither. Come, Master
Cranwell, shall you and I take them up?

*Cran.* At your pleasure, sir.

*Frank.* I must look to you, Master Wendoll, for you
will be playing false; nay, so will my wife too.

116 baulk] avoid    118 pair] pack    123 well said]
well done    124 take my part] be my partner. *The
double meanings in the names and terms of the card-games here
discussed would gain little by annotation*

*Nick.*—Ay, I will be sworn she will.

*Mis. Frank.* Let them that are taken playing false, forfeit the set.

*Frank.* Content; it shall go hard but I'll take you.

*Cran.* Gentlemen, what shall our game be?    140

*Wen.* Master Frankford, you play best at noddy.

*Frank.* You shall not find it so; indeed you shall not.

*Mis. Frank.* I can play at nothing so well as double ruff.

*Frank.* If Master Wendoll and my wife be together, there's no playing against them at double hand.

*Nick.* I can tell you, sir, the game that Master Wendoll is best at.

*Wen.* What game is that, Nick?

*Nick.* Marry, sir, knave out of doors.

*Wen.* She and I will take you at lodam.    150

*Mis. Frank.* Husband, shall we play at saint?

*Frank.* My saint's turn'd devil.—No, we'll none of saint:
    You are best at new-cut, wife; you'll play at that.

*Wen.* If you play at new-cut, I am soonest hitter of any here, for a wager.

*Frank.* 'Tis me they play on.—Well, you may draw out.
    For all your cunning, 'twill be to your shame;
    I'll teach you, at your new-cut, a new game.
    Come, come.    160

*Cran.* If you cannot agree upon the game, to post and pair.

*Wen.* We shall be soonest pairs; and my good host,
    When he comes late home, he must kiss the post.

*Frank.* Whoever wins, it shall be thy cost.

*Cran.* Faith, let it be vide-ruff, and let's make honours.

*Frank.* If you make honours, one thing let me crave:
    Honour the king and queen; except the knave.

*Wen.* Well, as you please for that.  Lift who shall deal.

138 set] stake    163 kiss the post] be shut out    168
Lift] cut

*Mis. Frank.* The least in sight: what are you, Master
    Wendoll?                                        171
*Wen.* I am a knave.
*Nick.*—I'll swear it.
*Mis. Frank.* I a queen.
*Frank.*—A quean thou shouldst say.—Well, the cards
    are mine;
    They are the grossest pair that e'er I felt.
*Mis. Frank.* Shuffle, I'll cut: would I had never dealt.
*Frank.* I have lost my dealing.
*Wen.*                                        Sir, the fault's in me:
    This queen I have more than my own, you see.
    Give me the stock.
*Frank.*                                        My mind's not on my game.     180
    Many a deal I have lost, the more's your shame.
    You have serv'd me a bad trick, Master Wendoll.
*Wen.* Sir, you must take your lot. To end this strife,
    I know I have dealt better with your wife.
*Frank.* Thou hast dealt falsely then.
*Mis. Frank.* What's trumps?
*Wen.* Hearts: partner, I rub.
*Frank.*—Thou robb'st me of my soul, of her chaste love;
    In thy false dealing thou hast robb'd my heart.
    —Booty you play; I like a loser stand,          190
    Having no heart, or here or in my hand.
    I will give o'er the set; I am not well.
    Come, who will hold my cards?
*Mis. Frank.* Not well, sweet Master Frankford!
    Alas, what ail you? 'Tis some sudden qualm.
*Wen.* How long have you been so, Master Frankford?
*Fran.* Sir, I was lusty, and I had my health,
    But I grew ill when you began to deal.
    Take hence this table. Gentle Master Cranwell,

170 least in sight] *sc.* lowest deals     175 quean] whore
176 grossest pair] *pun on (a)* thickest pack *and (b)* most
obvious couple     178 lost my dealing] misdealt     187
rub] take all the cards of the suit (*sc. hearts*)     190 Booty
you play] you conspire to cheat me

You are welcome; see your chamber at your
  pleasure.                                        200
I am sorry that this megrim takes me so,
I cannot sit and bear you company.
Jenkin, some lights, and show him to his chamber.
                    [*Exeunt* Cranwell *and* Jenkin.
*Mis. Frank.*  A night-gown for my husband; quickly
  there:
It is some rheum or cold.
*Wen.*  Now, in good faith, this illness you have got
By sitting late, without your gown.
*Frank.*  I know it, Master Wendoll.
Go, go to bed, lest you complain like me.
Wife, prythee, wife into my bed-chamber;      210
The night is raw and cold, and rheumatic:
Leave me my gown and light; I'll walk away my
  fit.
*Wen.*  Sweet sir, good night.
*Frank.*  My self, good night.         [*Exit* Wendoll.
*Mis. Frank.*             Shall I attend you, husband?
*Frank.*  No, gentle wife, thou'lt catch cold in thy head;
Prythee, be gone, sweet; I'll make haste to bed.
*Mis. Frank.*  No sleep will fasten on mine eyes, you
  know,
Until you come.
*Frank.*          Sweet Nan, I prythee go.—
                    [*Exit* Mistress Frankford.
I have bethought me: get me, by degrees,
The keys of all my doors, which I will mould   220
In wax, and take their fair impression,
To have by them new keys. This being com-
  pass'd,
At a set hour a letter shall be brought me,
And, when they think they may securely play,
They are nearest to danger. Nick, I must rely
Upon thy trust and faithful secrecy.

204 night-gown] dressing-gown

*Nick.* Build on my faith.
*Frank.*                    To bed then, not to rest;
  Care lodges in my brain, grief in my breast.
                                              [*Exeunt.*


## Act the Fourth

### Scene I

*Enter* Susan, Old Mountford, Sandy, Roder, *and*
Tidy.

*O. Mount.* You say my nephew is in great distress:
  Who brought it to him, but his own lewd life?
  I cannot spare a cross. I must confess
  He was my brother's son: why, niece, what then?
  This is no world in which to pity men.
*Susan.* I was not born a beggar; though his extremes
  Enforce this language from me, I protest
  No fortune of mine own could lead my tongue
  To this base key. I do beseech you, uncle,
  For the name's sake, for Christianity,                    10
  Nay, for God's sake, to pity his distress:
  He is deni'd the freedom of the prison,
  And in the Hole is laid with men condemn'd;
  Plenty he hath of nothing but of irons,
  And it remains in you to free him thence.
*O. Mount.* Money I cannot spare; men should take
    heed;
  He lost my kindred when he fell to need.    [*Exit.*
*Susan.* Gold is but earth, thou earth enough shalt have,
  When thou hast once took measure of thy grave.
  You know me, Master Sandy, and my suit.        20
*Sandy.* I knew you, lady, when the old man liv'd;

IV. i] *Some editors number this scene* III. iii, *starting* Act IV *with
the next scene and numbering the scenes accordingly*        3 cross]
coin          13 the Hole] *one of the worst parts of the Counter
prison*

**N**

I knew you ere your brother sold his land;
Then you were Mistress Sue, trick'd up in jewels;
Then you sung well, play'd sweetly on the flute;
But now I neither know you nor your suit.    [*Exit.*

*Susan.* You, Master Roder, was my brother's tenant,
Rent-free he plac'd you in that wealthy farm
Of which you are possess'd.

*Roder.*                    True, he did;
And have I not there dwelt still for his sake?
I have some business now; but, without doubt,  30
They that have hurl'd him in will help him out.
                                        [*Exit.*

*Susan.* Cold comfort still: what say you, cousin Tidy?
*Tidy.* I say this comes of roysting, swagg'ring.
Call me not cousin: each man for himself.
Some men are born to mirth, and some to sorrow.
I am no cousin unto them that borrow.    [*Exit.*

*Susan.* O charity! why art thou fled to heaven,
And left all things upon this earth uneven?
Their scoffing answers I will ne'er return;
But to myself his grief in silence mourn.        40

        *Enter* Sir Francis Acton *and* Malby.

*Sir Fran.* She is poor, I'll therefore tempt her with
    this gold.
Go, Malby, in my name deliver it,
And I will stay thy answer.

*Mal.* Fair mistress, as I understand, your grief
Doth grow from want, so I have here in store
A means to furnish you, a bag of gold,
Which to your hands I freely tender you.

*Susan.* I thank you, Heavens! I thank you, gentle sir:
God make me able to requite this favour!

*Mal.* This gold Sir Francis Acton sends by me,  50
And prays you——

*Susan.* Acton! O God! that name I'm born to curse:

        **33** roysting] roistering

Hence, bawd! hence, broker! see, I spurn his gold;
My honour never shall for gain be sold.
*Sir Fran.* Stay, lady, stay.
*Susan.*                    From you I'll posting hie,
Even as the doves from feather'd eagles fly.    [*Exit.*
*Sir Fran.* She hates my name, my face: how should I
  woo?
  I am disgrac'd in every thing I do.
  The more she hates me, and disdains my love,
  The more I am rapt in admiration            60
  Of her divine and chaste perfections.
  Woo her with gifts I cannot, for all gifts
  Sent in my name she spurns; with looks I cannot,
  For she abhors my sight; nor yet with letters,
  For none she will receive.  How then, how then?
  Well, I will fasten such a kindness on her
  As shall o'ercome her hate and conquer it.
  Sir Charles, her brother, lies in execution
  For a great sum of money: and, besides,
  The appeal is sued still for my huntsmen's death, 70
  Which only I have power to reverse:
  In her I'll bury all my hate of him.
  Go seek the keeper, Malby, bring me to him:
  To save his body, I his debts will pay;
  To save his life, I his appeal will stay.    [*Exeunt.*

## Scene II

*Enter* Sir Charles Mountford *in prison, with irons,
  his feet bare, his garments all ragged and torn.*

*Sir Char.* Of all on the earth's face most miserable,
  Breathe in this hellish dungeon thy laments:
  Thus like a slave ragg'd, like a felon gyv'd,
  That hurls thee headlong to this base estate!
  O unkind uncle!  O my friends ingrate!
  Unthankful kinsmen!  Mountfords all too base,

53 broker] procurer    68 execution] *see note on* III. i. 29

To let thy name lie fettered in disgrace!
A thousand deaths here in this grave I die;
Fear, hunger, sorrow, cold, all threat my death,
And join together to deprive my breath.          10
But that which most torments me, my dear sister
Hath left to visit me, and from my friends
Hath brought no hopeful answer: therefore I
Divine they will not help my misery.
If it be so, shame, scandal, and contempt
Attend their covetous thoughts; need make their
    graves!
Usurers they live, and may they die like slaves!

*Enter* Keeper.

*Keep.* Knight, be of comfort, for I bring thee freedom
    From all thy troubles.
*Sir Char.*               Then I am doom'd to die;
    Death is the end of all calamity.              20
*Keep.* Live: your appeal is stay'd; the execution
    Of all your debts discharg'd; your creditors
    Even to the utmost penny satisfied.
    In sign whereof, your shackles I knock off;
    You are not left so much indebted to us
    As for your fees; all is discharg'd, all paid:
    Go freely to your house, or where you please,
    After long miseries, embrace your ease.
*Sir Char.* Thou grumblest out the sweetest music to me
    That ever organ play'd.  Is this a dream       30
    Or do my waking senses apprehend
    The pleasing taste of these applausive news?
    Slave that I was, to wrong such honest friends,
    My loving kinsmen, and my near allies.
    Tongue, I will bite thee for the scandal breath'd
    Against such faithful kinsmen: they are all
    Compos'd of pity and compassion,
    Of melting charity, and of moving ruth.

**26** your fees] *due to the gaoler for his services*

That which I spake before was in my rage;
They are my friends, the mirrors of this age,   40
Bounteous and free.  The noble Mountfords' race,
Ne'er bred a covetous thought, or humour base.


*Enter* Susan.

*Susan.*  I can no longer stay from visiting
    My woful brother: while I could, I kept
    My hapless tidings from his hopeful ear.
*Sir Char.* Sister, how much am I indebted to thee,
    And to thy travail!
*Susan.*                What, at liberty?
*Sir Char.* Thou seest I am, thanks to thy industry:
    Oh, unto which of all my courteous friends
    Am I thus bound?  My uncle Mountford, he   50
    Even of an infant lov'd me: was it he?
    So did my cousin Tidy; was it he?
    So Master Roder, Master Sandy too:
    Which of all these did this high kindness do?
*Susan.*  Charles, can you mock me in your poverty,
    Knowing your friends deride your misery?
    Now, I protest I stand so much amaz'd
    To see your bonds free, and your irons knock'd off,
    That I am rapt into a maze of wonder:
    The rather for I know not by what means   60
    This happiness hath chanc'd.
*Sir Char.*                Why, by my uncle,
    My cousins, and my friends; who else, I pray,
    Would take upon them all my debts to pay?
*Susan.*  O brother, they are men all of flint,
    Pictures of marble, and as void of pity
    As chased bears.  I begg'd, I sued, I kneel'd,
    Laid open all your griefs and miseries,
    Which they derided; more than that, denied us
    A part in their alliance; but, in pride,
    Said that our kindred with our plenty died.   70

    66 chased] engraved (*sc. in stone or metal*)

*Sir Char.* Drudges too much—what did they? oh,
 known evil!
 Rich fly the poor, as good men shun the devil.
 Whence should my freedom come? of whom alive,
 Saving of those, have I deserved so well?
 Guess, sister, call to mind, remember me:
 These I have rais'd, these follow the world's guise;
 Whom rich in honour, they in woe despise.

*Susan.* My wits have lost themselves, let's ask the
 keeper.

*Sir Char.* Gaoler!

*Keep.* At hand, sir.         80

*Sir Char.* Of courtesy resolve me one demand.
 What was he took the burthen of my debts
 From off my back, stay'd my appeal to death,
 Discharg'd my fees, and brought me liberty?

*Keep.* A courteous knight, one call'd Sir Francis Acton.

*Susan.* Acton!

*Sir Char.*     Ha! Acton! O me, more distress'd
 In this than all my troubles! hale me back,
 Double my irons, and my sparing meals
 Put into halves, and lodge me in a dungeon
 More deep, more dark, more cold, more comfort-
  less.           90
 By Acton freed! not all thy manacles
 Could fetter so my heels as this one word
 Hath thrall'd my heart; and it must now lie bound
 In more strict prison than thy stony gaol.
 I am not free, I go but under bail.

*Keep.* My charge is done, sir, now I have my fees,
 As we get little, we will nothing leese.   [*Exit.*

*Sir Char.* By Acton freed, my dangerous opposite!
 Why, to what end? on what occasion? ha!
 Let me forget the name of enemy,    100
 And with indifference balance this high favour:
 Ha!

75 remember] remind  97 leese] lose  98 opposite]
adversary (*cf. line* 115)

*Susan.*—His love to me, upon my soul 'tis so!
　That is the root from whence these strange things
　　grow.
*Sir Char.* Had this proceeded from my father, he
　That by the law of nature is most bound
　In offices of love, it had deserv'd
　My best employment to requite that grace:
　Had it proceeded from my friends or him,
　From them this action had deserv'd my life;　110
　And from a stranger more, because from such
　There is less expectation of good deeds.
　But he, nor father, nor ally, nor friend,
　More than a stranger, both remote in blood,
　And in his heart oppos'd my enemy—
　That this high bounty should proceed from him!
　Oh, there I lose myself! What should I say,
　What think, what do, his bounty to repay?
*Susan.* You wonder, I am sure, whence this strange
　　kindness　　　　　　　　　　　　　　120
　Proceeds in Acton. I will tell you, brother:
　He dotes on me, and oft hath sent me gifts,
　Letters and tokens: I refus'd them all.
*Sir Char.* I have enough; though poor, my heart is set,
　In one rich gift to pay back all my debt.　[*Exeunt.*

## Scene III

*Enter* Frankford, *and* Nick *with keys, and a letter in his
hand.*

*Frank.* This is the night that I must play the trick
　To try two seeming angels. Where's my keys?
*Nick.* They are made according to your mould in wax:
　I bade the smith be secret, gave him money,
　And here they are. The letter, sir.
*Frank.* True, take it, there it is;

　　　　110 From them] on their part

And when thou seest me in my pleasant'st vein,
Ready to sit to supper, bring it me.
*Nick.* I'll do't, make no more question but I'll do't.
                                                    [*Exit.*

*Enter* Mistress Frankford, Cranwell, Wendoll, *and*
                          Jenkin.

*Mis. Frank.* Sirrah, 'tis six o'clock already struck!  10
Go bid them spread the cloth and serve in supper.
*Jenk.* It shall be done, forsooth, mistress. Where is
     Spigot, the butler, to give us out  salt and
     trenchers?                                *Exit.*
*Wen.* We that have been a-hunting all the day
Come with prepared stomachs. Master Frankford,
We wish'd you at our sport.
*Frank.* My heart was with you, and my mind was on
     you.
     Fie, Master Cranwell! you are still thus sad?
     A stool, a stool. Where's Jenkin, and where's Nick?
     'Tis supper-time at least an hour ago.          21
     What's the best news abroad?
*Wen.*                             I know none good.
*Frank.*—But I know too much bad.

*Enter* Butler *and* Jenkin *with a table-cloth, bread,*
                *trenchers, and salt.*

*Cran.* Methinks, sir, you might have that interest
In your wife's brother, to be more remiss
In his hard dealing against poor Sir Charles,
Who, as I hear, lies in York Castle, needy,
And in great want.        [*Exeunt* Butler *and* Jenkin.
*Frank.* Did not more weighty business of my own
     Hold me away, I would have labour'd peace      30
     Betwixt them, with all care; indeed I would, sir.
*Mis. Frank.* I'll write unto my brother earnestly
     In that behalf.

     24–5 interest|In . . . to be more remiss] influence with . . .
to make him less strict

*Wen.*                              A charitable deed,
  And will beget the good opinion
  Of all your friends that love you, Mistress Frankford.
*Frank.* That's you for one; I know you love Sir
      Charles—
  And my wife too—well.
*Wen.*                         He deserves the love
  Of all true gentlemen; be yourselves judge.
*Frank.* But supper, ho! Now as thou lov'st me, Wendoll,
  Which I am sure thou dost, be merry pleasant,  40
  And frolic it to-night. Sweet Master Cranwell,
  Do you the like. Wife, I protest my heart
  Was ne'er more bent on sweet alacrity.
  Where be those lazy knaves to serve in supper?

*Enter* Nick.

*Nick.* Sir, here's a letter.
*Frank.* Whence comes it? and who brought it?
*Nick.* A stripling that below attends your answer,
  And, as he tells me, it is sent from York.
*Frank.* Have him into the cellar; let him taste
  A cup of our March beer: go, make him drink.  50
                              [*Reads the letter.*
*Nick.* I'll make him drunk, if he be a Trojan.
*Frank.* My boots and spurs! where's Jenkin? God
      forgive me,
  How I neglect my business! Wife, look here;
  I have a matter to be tried to-morrow
  By eight o'clock, and my attorney writes me,
  I must be there betimes with evidence,
  Or it will go against me. Where's my boots?

*Enter* Jenkin *with boots and spurs.*

*Mis. Frank.* I hope your business craves no such des-
      patch
  That you must ride to-night.

---

43 alacrity] liveliness          51 Trojan] *slang* for hard
drinker

*Wen.*—I hope it doth.

*Frank.*                    God's me! no such despatch!    60
Jenkin, my boots.  Where's Nick?  Saddle my
    roan,
And the grey dapple for himself.  Content ye,
It much concerns me.  Gentle Master Cranwell,
And Master Wendoll, in my absence use
The very ripest pleasure of my house.

*Wen.*  Lord! Master Frankford, will you ride to-night?
The ways are dangerous.

*Frank.*                    Therefore will I ride
Appointed well; and so shall Nick my man.

*Mis. Frank.*  I'll call you up by five o'clock to-morrow.

*Frank.*  No, by my faith, wife, I'll not trust to that; 70
'Tis not such easy rising in a morning
From one I love so dearly: no, by my faith,
I shall not leave so sweet a bedfellow,
But with much pain.  You have made me a sluggard
Since I first knew you.

*Mis. Frank.*                    Then, if you needs will go
This dangerous evening, Master Wendoll,
Let me entreat you bear him company.

*Wen.*  With all my heart, sweet mistress.  My boots
    there!

*Frank.*  Fie, fie, that for my private business
I should disease my friend, and be a trouble    80
To the whole house!  Nick!

*Nick.*  Anon, sir.

*Frank.*  Bring forth my gelding.—        [*Exit* Nick.
                    As you love me, sir,
Use no more words: a hand, good Master Cranwell.

*Cran.*  Sir, God be your good speed!

*Frank.*  Good night, sweet Nan; nay, nay, a kiss and
    part.
—Dissembling lips, you suit not with my heart. [*Exit.*

*Wen.*  How business, time, and hours, all gracious
    prove,

80 disease] inconvenience

And are the furthers to my new-born love!
I am husband now in Master Frankford's place, 90
And must command the house.  My pleasure is
We will not sup abroad so publicly,
But in your private chamber, Mistress Frankford.
*Mis. Frank.*  O, sir, you are too public in your love,
And Master Frankford's wife——
*Cran.*                            Might I crave favour,
I would entreat you I might see my chamber;
I am on the sudden grown exceeding ill,
And would be spar'd from supper.
*Wen.*                            Light there, ho!
See you want nothing, sir; for, if you do,
You injure that good man, and wrong me too. 100
*Cran.*  I will make bold: good night.        [*Exit.*
*Wen.*                            How all conspire
To make our bosom sweet, and full entire!
Come, Nan, I prythee let us sup within.
*Mis. Frank.*  Oh, what a clog unto the soul is sin!
We pale offenders are still full of fear;
Every suspicious eye brings danger near,
When they whose clear hearts from offence are
    free
Despise report, base scandals do outface,
And stand at mere defiance with disgrace.
*Wen.*  Fie, fie! you talk too like a puritan.        110
*Mis. Frank.*  You have tempted me to mischief, Master
    Wendoll:
I have done I know not what.  Well, you plead
    custom;
That which for want of wit I granted erst,
I now must yield through fear.  Come, come, let's
    in;
Once o'er shoes, we are straight o'er head in sin.
*Wen.*  My jocund soul is joyful above measure;
I'll be profuse in Frankford's richest treasure.
                                        [*Exeunt.*

    102 bosom] *perhaps* privacy        105 still] always

## Scene IV

*Enter* Cicely, Jenkin, *and* Butler *and other* Serving-men.

*Jenk.* My mistress and Master Wendoll, my master,
sup in her chamber to-night. Cicely, you are
preferr'd from being the cook to be chambermaid:
of all the loves betwixt thee and me, tell me what
thou think'st of this!

*Cicely.* Mum; there's an old proverb,—when the cat's
away, the mouse may play.

*Jenk.* Now you talk of a cat, Cicely, I smell a rat.

*Cicely.* Good words, Jenkin, lest you be call'd to
answer them.                                    10

*Jenk.* Why, God make my mistress an honest woman!
are not these good words? Pray God my new
master play not the knave with my old master! is
there any hurt in this? God send no villainy
intended! and, if they do sup together, pray God
they do not lie together! God make my mistress
chaste, and make us all His servants! what harm
is there in all this? Nay, more; here is my hand,
thou shalt never have my heart unless thou say
Amen.                                           20

*Cicely.* Amen, I pray God, I say.

### *Enter* Serving-man.

*Serv.* My mistress sends that you should make less
noise, to lock up the doors, and see the household
all got to bed: you, Jenkin, for this night are made
the porter to see the gates shut in.

*Jenk.* Thus, by little and little, I creep into office.
Come, to kennel, my masters, to kennel; 'tis
eleven o'clock, already.

*Serv.* When you have lock'd the gates in, you must
send up the keys to my mistress.                30

3 preferr'd] promoted

*Cicely.* Quickly, for God's sake, Jenkin, for I must
carry them. I am neither pillow nor bolster, but
I know more than both.

*Jenk.* To bed, good Spigot; to bed, good honest
serving-creatures; and let us sleep as snug as pigs
in pease-straw. [*Exeunt.*

## Scene V

### *Enter* Frankford *and* Nick.

*Frank.* Soft, soft; we have tied our geldings to a tree,
Two flight-shot off, lest by their thundering hoofs
They blab our coming back. Hear'st thou no noise?

*Nick.* Hear! I hear nothing but the owl and you.

*Frank.* So; now my watch's hand points upon twelve,
And it is dead midnight. Where are my keys?

*Nick.* Here, sir.

*Frank.* This is the key that opes my outward gate;
This is the hall-door; this my withdrawing chamber;
But this, that door that's bawd unto my shame, 10
Fountain and spring of all my bleeding thoughts,
Where the most hallowed order and true knot
Of nuptial sanctity hath been profan'd;
It leads to my polluted bed-chamber,
Once my terrestrial heaven, now my earth's hell,
The place where sins in all their ripeness dwell.
But I forget myself: now to my gate.

*Nick.* It must ope with far less noise than Cripple-gate,
or your plot's dash'd.

*Frank.* So, reach me my dark lanthorn to the rest; 20
Tread softly, softly.

*Nick.* I will walk on eggs this pace.

IV. v.] *The mentions of place show that this scene begins outside
the house and progresses without interruption, as the Elizabethan stage
permitted, to the threshold of the bedchamber* 2 flight-shot]
bow-shot 18 Cripple-gate] *one of the great gates of London*

*Frank.* A general silence hath surpris'd the house,
And this is the last door. Astonishment,
Fear, and amazement play against my heart,
Even as a madman beats upon a drum.
Oh, keep my eyes, you Heavens, before I enter,
From any sight that may transfix my soul;
Or, if there be so black a spectacle,
Oh, strike mine eyes stark blind; or, if not so,    30
Lend me such patience to digest my grief
That I may keep this white and virgin hand
From any violent outrage or red murther!
And with that prayer I enter.                [*Exit.*
*Nick.*                     Here's a circumstance.
A man may be made cuckold in the time
That he's about it. An the case were mine,
As 'tis my master's,—'sblood that he makes me
    swear!—
I would have plac'd his action, enter'd there;
I would, I would——


                    *Enter* Frankford.
*Frank.* Oh! oh!                                    40
*Nick.* Master, 'sblood! master! master!
*Frank.* O me unhappy! I have found them lying
Close in each other's arms, and fast asleep.
But that I would not damn two precious souls,
Bought with my Saviour's blood, and send them,
    laden
With all their scarlet sins upon their backs,
Unto a fearful judgment, their two lives
Had met upon my rapier.
*Nick.* 'Sblood, master, have you left them sleeping still?
Let me go wake them.
*Frank.*             Stay, let me pause a while.    50
O God! O God! that it were possible
To undo things done; to call back yesterday!

    34] *modern editors begin a new scene here, but see note on* IV.
**v.** *above*

That Time could turn up his swift sandy glass,
To untell the days, and to redeem these hours!
Or that the sun
Could, rising from the west, draw his coach back-
    ward,
Take from th' account of time so many minutes,
Till he had all these seasons call'd again,
Those minutes, and those actions done in them,
Even from her first offence; that I might take her 60
As spotless as an angel in my arms!
But, oh! I talk of things impossible,
And cast beyond the moon. God give me patience!
For I will in and wake them.                *[Exit.*
*Nick.*                        Here's patience perforce;
He needs must trot afoot that tires his horse.

*Enter* Wendoll, *running over the stage in a night-gown,
he after him with his sword drawn; the maid in her smock
stays his hand, and clasps hold on him. He pauses for
a while.*

*Frank.* I thank thee, maid; thou, like the angel's hand,
Hast stay'd me from a bloody sacrifice.
Go, villain, and my wrongs sit on thy soul
As heavy as this grief doth upon mine!
When thou record'st my many courtesies,          70
And shalt compare them with thy treacherous heart,
Lay them together, weigh them equally,
'Twill be revenge enough. Go, to thy friend
A Judas: pray, pray, lest I live to see
Thee, Judas-like, hang'd on an elder-tree.

*Enter* Mistress Frankford *in her smock, night-gown,
and night attire.*

*Mis. Frank.* Oh, by what word, what title, or what
    name,

65 s.d. *night-gown*] dressing-gown          70 record'st]
rememberest

Shall I entreat your pardon? Pardon! oh!
I am as far from hoping such sweet grace
As Lucifer from heaven. To call you husband—
O me, most wretched! I have lost that name,    80
I am no more your wife.

*Nick.*                         'Sblood, sir, she sounds.

*Frank.* Spare thou thy tears, for I will weep for thee;
And keep thy count'nance, for I'll blush for thee.
Now, I protest, I think 'tis I am tainted,
For I am most asham'd; and 'tis more hard
For me to look upon thy guilty face,
Than on the sun's clear brow. What wouldst thou
    speak?

*Mis. Frank.* I would I had no tongue, no ears, no eyes,
No apprehension, no capacity.
When do you spurn me like a dog? when tread me 90
Under your feet? when drag me by the hair?
Though I deserve a thousand thousand fold
More than you can inflict: yet, once my husband,
For womanhood, to which I am a shame,
Though once an ornament—even for His sake
That hath redeem'd our souls, mark not my face
Nor hack me with your sword: but let me go
Perfect and undeformed to my tomb.
I am not worthy that I should prevail
In the least suit; no, not to speak to you,    100
Nor look on you; nor to be in your presence.
Yet, as an abject, this one suit I crave;
This granted, I am ready for my grave.    [*Kneels.*

*Frank.* My God, with patience arm me! Rise, nay,
    rise,
And I'll debate with thee. Was it for want
Thou play'dst the strumpet? Wast thou not supplied
With every pleasure, fashion, and new toy
Nay, even beyond my calling?

*Mis. Frank.*                         I was.

81 sounds] swoons

*Frank.* Was it then disability in me?

Or in thine eye seem'd he a properer man?    110

*Mis. Frank.* Oh, no.

*Frank.* Did I not lodge thee in my bosom? wear thee
Here in my heart?

*Mis. Frank.*            You did.

*Frank.*                    I did, indeed;
Witness my tears I did.
Go, bring my infants hither.

*Enter* Servant *with two* Children.

            O Nan! O Nan!
If neither fear of shame, regard of honour,
The blemish of my house, nor my dear love
Could have withheld thee from so lewd a fact,
Yet for these infants, these young harmless souls,
On whose white brows thy shame is character'd, 120
And grows in greatness as they wax in years,—
Look but on them, and melt away in tears.
Away with them! lest, as her spotted body
Hath stain'd their names with stripe of bastardy,
So her adulterous breath may blast their spirits
With her infectious thoughts.  Away with them!
                [*Exeunt* Servant *and* Children.

*Mis. Frank.* In this one life I die ten thousand deaths.

*Frank.* Stand up, stand up; I will do nothing rashly;
I will retire a while into my study,
And thou shalt hear thy sentence presently.    130
                            [*Exit.*

*Mis. Frank.* 'Tis welcome, be it death.  O me base
    strumpet,
That, having such a husband, such sweet children,
Must enjoy neither! Oh, to redeem my honour,
I would have this hand cut off, these my breasts
    sear'd,
Be rack'd, strappado'd, put to any torment:

110 properer] handsomer    118 fact] deed        135
strappado'd] tortured

Nay, to whip but this scandal out, I would hazard
The rich and dear redemption of my soul.
He cannot be so base as to forgive me;
Nor I so shameless to accept his pardon.
O women, women, you that have yet kept        140
Your holy matrimonial vow unstain'd,
Make me your instance: when you tread awry,
Your sins, like mine, will on your conscience lie.

*Enter* Cicely, Spigot, *all the serving-men and*
Jenkin, *as newly come out of bed.*

*All.* O mistress, mistress, what have you done, mistress?
*Nick.* 'Sblood, what a caterwauling keep you here!
*Jenk.* O Lord, mistress, how comes this to pass? My
    master is run away in his shirt, and never so much
    as call'd me to bring his clothes after him.
*Mis. Frank.* See what guilt is! here stand I in this
    place,
    Asham'd to look my servants in the face.        150

*Enter* Master Frankford *and* Cranwell; *whom seeing*
*she falls on her knees.*

*Frank.* My words are register'd in Heaven already,
    With patience hear me. I'll not martyr thee,
    Nor mark thee for a strumpet; but with usage
    Of more humility torment thy soul,
    And kill thee even with kindness.
*Cran.*                      Master Frankford——
*Frank.* Good Master Cranwell!—Woman, hear thy
    judgment.
    Go make thee ready in thy best attire;
    Take with thee all thy gowns, all thy apparel;
    Leave nothing that did ever call thee mistress,
    Or by whose sight, being left here in the house,  160
    I may remember such a woman by.
    Choose thee a bed and hangings for a chamber;
    Take with thee every thing that hath thy mark;

And get thee to my manor seven mile off,
Where live; 'tis thine; I freely give it thee.
My tenants by shall furnish thee with wains
To carry all thy stuff, within two hours,—
No longer will I limit thee my sight.
Choose which of all my servants thou likest best,
And they are thine to attend thee.

*Mis. Frank.*                    A mild sentence.    170

*Frank.* But, as thou hop'st for Heaven, as thou believ'st
Thy name's recorded in the book of life,
I charge thee never after this sad day
To see me, or to meet me, or to send
By word or writing, gift, or otherwise,
To move me, by thyself, or by thy friends;
Nor challenge any part in my two children.
So, farewell, Nan! for we will henceforth be
As we had never seen, ne'er more shall see.

*Mis. Frank.* How full my heart is, in my eyes
  appears;                                   180
What wants in words, I will supply in tears.

*Frank.* Come, take your coach, your stuff; all must
  along;
Servants and all, make ready; all be gone.
It was thy hand cut two hearts out of one.
                                      [*Exeunt.*


## Act the Fifth

### Scene I

*Enter* Sir Charles Mountford, *gentleman-like, and*
          Susan, *gentlewoman-like.*

*Susan.* Brother, why have you trick'd me like a bride,
Bought me this gay attire, these ornaments?
Forget you our estate, our poverty?

*Sir Char.* Call me not brother, but imagine me

  168 limit thee] admit thee to          1 trick'd] tricked
out, dressed

Some barbarous outlaw, or uncivil kern;
For if thou shutt'st thy eye, and only hear'st
The words that I shall utter, thou shalt judge me
Some staring ruffian, not thy brother Charles.
O Susan!——

*Susan.* O brother, what doth this strange language
    mean? 10

*Sir Char.* Dost love me, sister? wouldst thou see me live
A bankrupt beggar in the world's disgrace,
And die indebted to my enemies?
Wouldst thou behold me stand like a huge beam
In the world's eye, a bye-word and a scorn?
It lies in thee of these to acquit me free,
And all my debt I may out-strip by thee.

*Susan.* By me! why, I have nothing, nothing left;
I owe even for the clothes upon my back;
I am not worth——

*Sir Char.*          O sister, say not so; 20
It lies in you my downcast state to raise,
To make me stand on even points with the world.
Come, sister, you are rich; indeed you are;
And in your power you have, without delay,
Acton's five hundred pound back to repay.

*Susan.* Till now I had thought you lov'd me. By mine
    honour
(Which I have kept as spotless as the moon),
I ne'er was mistress of that single doit
Which I reserv'd not to supply your wants;
And do you think that I would hoard from you? 30
Now, by my hopes in Heaven, knew I the means
To buy from the slavery of your debts
(Especially from Acton, whom I hate),
I would redeem it with my life or blood.

*Sir Char.* I challenge it; and, kindred set apart,
Thus, ruffian-like, I lay siege to your heart.
What do I owe to Acton?

5 kern] rascal     28 doit] *small coin worth half a farthing*
35 challenge it] claim the fulfilment of it

*Susan.* Why some five hundred pounds; towards
      which, I swear,
   In all the world I have not one denier.
*Sir Char.* It will not prove so. Sister, now resolve me: 40
   What do you think (and speak your conscience)
   Would Acton give, might he enjoy your bed?
*Susan.* He would not shrink to spend a thousand
      pound,
   To give the Mountfords' name so deep a wound.
*Sir Char.* A thousand pound! I but five hundred owe;
   Grant him your bed, he's paid with interest so.
*Susan.* O brother!
*Sir Char.*            O sister! only this one way,
   With that rich jewel you my debts may pay:
   In speaking this my cold heart shakes with shame,
   Nor do I woo you in a brother's name,            50
   But in a stranger's. Shall I die in debt
   To Acton, my grand foe, and you still wear
   The precious jewel that he holds so dear?
*Susan.* My honour I esteem as dear and precious
   As my redemption.
*Sir Char.*               I esteem you, sister,
   As dear, for so dear prizing it.
*Susan.*                        Will Charles
   Have me cut off my hands, and send them Acton?
   Rip up my breast, and with my bleeding heart
   Present him, as a token?
*Sir Char.*                  Neither, sister:
   But hear me in my strange assertion.            60
   Thy honour and my soul are equal in my regard;
   Nor will thy brother Charles survive thy shame.
   His kindness, like a burthen hath surcharged me,
   And under his good deeds I stooping go,
   Not with an upright soul. Had I remain'd
   In prison still, there doubtless I had died:
   Then, unto him that freed me from that prison,
   Still do I owe this life. What mov'd my foe

   39 denier] *another small coin*      40 resolve] tell

To enfranchise me? 'Twas, sister, for your love.
With full five hundred pounds he bought your
love,                                          70
And shall he not enjoy it? Shall the weight
Of all this heavy burthen lean on me,
And will not you bear part? You did partake
The joy of my release, will you not stand
In joint-bond bound to satisfy the debt?
Shall I be only charg'd?

*Susan.*                        But that I know
These arguments come from an honour'd mind,
As in your most extremity of need
Scorning to stand in debt to one you hate,—
Nay, rather would engage your unstain'd honour 80
Than to be held ingrate,—I should condemn you.
I see your resolution, and assent;
So Charles will have me, and I am content.

*Sir Char.* For this I trick'd you up.

*Susan.*                        But here's a knife,
To save mine honour, shall slice out my life.

*Sir Char.* Ay, now thou pleasest me a thousand time
More in that resolution than thy grant.—
Observe her love; to soothe it to my suit,
Her honour she will hazard, though not lose:
To bring me out of debt, her rigorous hand   90
Will pierce her heart. O wonder! that will choose,
Rather than stain her blood, her life to lose.—
Come, you sad sister to a woeful brother,
This is the gate: I'll bear him such a present,
Such an acquittance for the knight to seal,
As will amaze his senses, and surprise
With admiration all his fantasies.

*Enter* Sir Francis Acton *and* Malby.

*Susan.* Before his unchaste thoughts shall seize on me,
'Tis here shall my imprison'd soul set free.

*Sir Fran.* How! Mountford with his sister, hand in
hand!                                          100

What miracle's afoot?

*Mal.*                        It is a sight
Begets in me much admiration.

*Sir Char.* Stand not amaz'd to see me thus attended:
Acton, I owe thee money, and being unable
To bring thee the full sum in ready coin,
Lo! for thy more assurance, here's a pawn:
My sister, my dear sister, whose chaste honour
I prize above a million: here, nay, take her;
She's worth your money, man; do not forsake her.

*Sir Fran.* I would he were in earnest!          110

*Susan.* Impute it not to my immodesty,
My brother being rich in nothing else
But in his interest that he hath in me,
According to his poverty hath brought you
Me, all his store; whom howsoe'er you prize
As forfeit to your hand, he values highly,
And would not sell, but to acquit your debt,
For any emperor's ransom.

*Sir Fran.*                        —Stern heart, relent;
Thy former cruelty at length repent.
Was ever known, in any former age,          120
Such honourable wrested courtesy?
Lands, honours, life, and all the world forego,
Rather than stand engag'd to such a foe.

*Sir Char.* Acton, she is too poor to be thy bride,
And I too much oppos'd to be thy brother.
There, take her to thee: if thou hast the heart
To seize her as a rape, or lustful prey;
To blur our house, that never yet was stain'd;
To murther her that never meant thee harm;
To kill me now, whom once thou sav'dst from
death;          130
Do them at once: on her all these rely,
And perish with her spotted chastity.

*Sir Fran.* You overcome me in your love, Sir Charles;
I cannot be so cruel to a lady

102 admiration] wonder

I love so dearly.  Since you have not spar'd
To engage your reputation to the world,
Your sister's honour, which you prize so dear,
Nay, all the comforts which you hold on earth,
To grow out of my debt, being your foe,
Your honour'd thoughts, lo! thus I recompense:  140
Your metamorphis'd foe receives your gift
In satisfaction of all former wrongs.
This jewel I will wear here in my heart;
And, where before I thought her for her wants
Too base to be my bride, to end all strife,
I seal you my dear brother, her my wife.

*Susan.* You still exceed us: I will yield to fate,
And learn to love, where I till now did hate.

*Sir Char.* With that enchantment you have charm'd
        my soul,
And made me rich even in those very words:  150
I pay no debt, but am indebted more;
Rich in your love, I never can be poor.

*Sir Fran.* All's mine is yours; we are alike in state,
Let's knit in love what was oppos'd in hate.
Come, for our nuptials we will straight provide,
Blest only in our brother and fair bride.    [*Exeunt.*


## Scene II

*Enter* Cranwell, Frankford, *and* Nick.

*Cran.* Why do you search each room about your
        house,
Now that you have despatch'd your wife away?

*Frank.* O sir, to see that nothing may be left
That ever was my wife's.  I lov'd her dearly,
And when I do but think of her unkindness,
My thoughts are all in hell; to avoid which torment,
I would not have a bodkin or a cuff,

144 where] whereas        for her wants] because of her
poverty

A bracelet, necklace, or rebato wire,
Nor any thing that ever was call'd hers,
Left me, by which I might remember her.　　10
Seek round about.
*Nick.* 'Sblood, master! here's her lute flung in a corner.
*Frank.* Her lute! O God! upon this instrument
Her fingers have run quick division,
Sweeter than that which now divides our hearts.
These frets have made me pleasant, that have now
Frets of my heart-strings made. O Master Cranwell,
Oft hath she made this melancholy wood,
Now mute and dumb for her disastrous chance,
Speak sweetly many a note, sound many a strain
To her own ravishing voice, which being well
　　strung,　　21
What pleasant strange airs have they jointly sung!
Post with it after her. Now nothing's left;
Of her and hers I am at once bereft.
*Nick.* I'll ride and overtake her; do my message,
And come back again.　　　　　　　[*Exit.*
*Cran.*　　　　　　　Mean time, sir, if you please,
I'll to Sir Francis Acton, and inform him
Of what hath pass'd betwixt you and his sister.
*Frank.* Do as you please. How ill am I bested,　　29
To be a widower ere my wife be dead!　　[*Exeunt.*


# Scene III

*Enter* Mistress Frankford, *with* Jenkin, *her maid*
Cicely, *her* Coachman, *and three* Carters.

*Mis. Frank.* Bid my coach stay: why should I ride in
　　state,
Being hurl'd so low down by the hand of fate?

8 rebato wire] *frame supporting the upstanding ruff*　　14
run quick division] executed a rapid melodic passage
16 frets] *see note on* I. i. 81

A seat like to my fortunes let me have;
Earth for my chair, and for my bed a grave.

*Jenk.* Comfort, good mistress; you have watered your
coach with tears already: you have but two mile
now to go to your manor. A man cannot say
by my old master Frankford as he may say by
me, that he wants manors, for he hath three or
four; of which this is one that we are going to
now.                                                      11

*Cicely.* Good mistress, be of good cheer; sorrow, you
see, hurts you, but helps you not: we all mourn
to see you so sad.

*Carter.* Mistress, I spy one of my landlord's men
Come riding post: 'tis like he brings some news.

*Mis. Frank.* Comes he from Master Frankford, he is
welcome;
So are his news because they come from him.

*Enter* Nick.

*Nick.* There!

*Mis. Frank.* I know the lute; oft have I sung to thee:
We both are out of tune, both out of time.         21

*Nick.* Would that had been the worst instrument that
e'er you played on. My master commends him
to ye; there's all he can find that was ever yours:
he hath nothing left that ever you could lay claim
to but his own heart, an he could afford you that.
All that I have to deliver you is this: he prays you
to forget him, and so he bids you farewell.

*Mis. Frank.* I thank him; he is kind, and ever was.
All you that have true feeling of my grief,         30
That know my loss, and have relenting hearts,
Gird me about, and help me with your tears
To wash my spotted sins: my lute shall groan;
It cannot weep, but shall lament my moan.

9 manors] *the pun on* manors *and* manners *was an old
favourite*

*Enter* Wendoll, *apart.*

*Wen.* Pursu'd with horror of a guilty soul,
  And with the sharp scourge of repentance lash'd,
  I fly from my own shadow.  O my stars!
  What have my parents in their lives deserv'd,
  That you should lay this penance on their son?
  When I but think of Master Frankford's love,    40
  And lay it to my treason, or compare
  My murthering him for his relieving me,
  It strikes a terror like a lightning's flash
  To scorch my blood up.  Thus I, like the owl,
  Asham'd of day, live in these shadowy woods,
  Afraid of every leaf or murmuring blast,
  Yet longing to receive some perfect knowledge
  How he hath dealt with her.
              *Sees* Mistress Frankford.
                        O my sad fate!
  Here, and so far from home, and thus attended!
  O God! I have divorc'd the truest turtles    50
  That ever liv'd together, and being divided
  In several places, make their several moan;
  She in the fields laments, and he at home.
  So poets write that Orpheus made the trees
  And stones to dance to his melodious harp,
  Meaning the rustic and the barbarous hinds,
  That had no understanding part in them:
  So she from these rude carters tears extracts,
  Making their flinty hearts with grief to rise,
  And draw down rivers from their rocky eyes.—    60
*Mis. Frank.* If you return unto your master, say
  (Though not from me; for I am all unworthy
  To blast his name so with a strumpet's tongue)
  That you have seen me weep, wish myself dead:
  Nay, you may say too, for my vow is pass'd,
  Last night you saw me eat and drink my last.
  This to your master you may say and swear;

                41 lay] compare

For it is writ in Heaven, and decreed here.

*Nick.* I'll say you wept: I'll swear you made me sad.
Why how now, eyes? what now? what's here to do?
I am gone, or I shall straight turn baby too.    71

*Wen.*—I cannot weep, my heart is all on fire:
Curst be the fruits of my unchaste desire!

*Mis. Frank.* Go, break this lute upon my coach's wheel,
As the last music that I e'er shall make;
Not as my husband's gift, but my farewell
To all earth's joy; and so your master tell.

*Nick.* If I can for crying.

*Wen.*                         —Grief, have done,
Or like a madman I shall frantic run.

*Mis. Frank.* You have beheld the woefull'st wretch on
    earth;                                       80
A woman made of tears: would you had words
To express but what you see! My inward grief
No tongue can utter; yet unto your power
You may describe my sorrow, and disclose
To thy sad master my abundant woes.

*Nick.* I'll do your commendations.

*Mis. Frank.*                         Oh no:
I dare not so presume; nor to my children:
I am disclaim'd in both; alas, I am.
Oh, never teach them, when they come to speak,
To name the name of mother: chide their tongue,
If they by chance light on that hated word;    91
Tell them 'tis naught; for, when that word they
    name,
Poor pretty souls! they harp on their own shame.

*Wen.*—To recompense her wrongs, what canst thou
    do?
Thou hast made her husbandless and childless too.

*Mis. Frank.* I have no more to say. Speak not for me;
Yet you may tell your master what you see.

*Nick.* I'll do't.                              [*Exit.*

88 disclaim'd] deprived of a claim

*Wen.*—I'll speak to her, and comfort her in grief.
Oh! but her wound cannot be cur'd with words.
No matter though, I'll do my best good-will      101
To work a cure on her whom I did kill.
*Mis. Frank.* So, now unto my coach, then to my home,
So to my death-bed; for from this sad hour
I never will nor eat, nor drink, nor taste
Of any cates that may preserve my life:
I never will nor smile, nor sleep, nor rest;
But when my tears have wash'd my black soul white,
Sweet Saviour, to Thy hands I yield my sprite.
*Wen.* O Mistress Frankford——
*Mis. Frank.*                    Oh, for God's sake fly!
The devil doth come to tempt me ere I die.      111
My coach! this fiend, that with an angel's face
Courted mine honour, till he sought my wrack,
In my repentant eyes seems ugly black.

> [*Exeunt all, except* Wendoll *and* Jenkin, *the* Carters
> *whistling.*

*Jenk.* What, my young master that fled in his shirt!
How come you by your clothes again? You have
made our house in a sweet pickle, have you not,
think you? What, shall I serve you still, or cleave
to the old house?      119
*Wen.* Hence, slave! away with thy unseason'd mirth!
Unless thou canst shed tears, and sigh, and howl,
Curse thy sad fortunes, and exclaim on fate,
Thou art not for my turn.
*Jenk.* Marry, an you will not, another will: farewell,
and be hang'd! Would you had never come to
have kept this coil within our doors; we shall ha'
you run away like a sprite again.      [*Exit.*
*Wen.* She's gone to death; I live to want and woe;
Her life, her sins, and all upon my head.
And I must now go wander, like a Cain,      130
In foreign countries and remoted climes,

106 cates] cakes, food      126 kept this coil] caused
this trouble

Where the report of my ingratitude
Cannot be heard.  I'll over first to France,
And so to Germany and Italy;
Where when I have recovered, and by travel
Gotten those perfect tongues, and that these rumours
May in their height abate, I will return:
And I divine (however now dejected)
My worth and parts being by some great man
    prais'd,                                            139
At my return I may in court be rais'd.        [*Exit.*


## Scene IV

*Enter* Sir Francis Acton, Sir Charles Mountford,
Cranwell, Malby, *and* Susan.

*Sir Fran.* Brother, and now my wife, I think these
    troubles
Fall on my head by justice of the Heavens,
For being so strict to you in your extremities:
But we are now aton'd.  I would my sister
Could with like happiness o'ercome her griefs,
As we have ours.
*Susan.* You tell us, Master Cranwell, wondrous things,
Touching the patience of that gentleman,
With what strange virtue he demeans his grief.
*Cran.* I told you what I was a witness of;             10
It was my fortune to lodge there that night.
*Sir Fran.* O that same villain Wendoll! 'twas his
    tongue
That did corrupt her; she was of herself
Chaste, and devoted well.  Is this the house?

136 gotten . . . tongues] learned those languages perfectly
V. iv.] *The scene evidently shifts without interruption in the action
from the approaches to the Manor, to its interior, and to the threshold of
the bed-chamber, which is revealed by drawing the curtain of the
inner stage at line 40.  Modern editors mark fresh scenes at lines*
22 *and* 40.        4 atoned] reconciled

*Cran.* Yes, sir, I take it, here your sister lies.

*Sir Fran.* My brother Frankford show'd too mild a
    spirit
  In the revenge of such a loathed crime;
  Less than he did, no man of spirit could do:
  I am so far from blaming his revenge,
  That I commend it. Had it been my case,    20
  Their souls at once had from their breasts been
    freed:
  Death to such deeds of shame is the due meed.

*Enter* Jenkin *and* Cicely.

*Jenk.* O my mistress, my mistress, my poor mistress.

*Cicely.* Alas that ever I was born! what shall I do
  for my poor mistress?

*Sir Char.* Why, what of her?

*Jenk.* O Lord, sir, she no sooner heard that her brother
  and his friends were come to see how she did,
  but she, for very shame of her guilty conscience,
  fell into such a swoon, that we had much ado to
  get life into her.    31

*Susan.* Alas that she should bear so hard a fate!
  Pity it is repentance comes too late.

*Sir Fran.* Is she so weak in body?

*Jenk.* O sir, I can assure you there's no hope of life in
  her, for she will take no sustenance: she hath
  plainly starv'd herself, and now she's as lean as
  a lath. She ever looks for the good hour. Many
  gentlemen and gentlewomen of the country are
  come to comfort her.    40

*Enter* Mistress Frankford, *in her bed.*

*Mal.* How fare you, Mistress Frankford?

*Mis. Frank.* Sick, sick, oh, sick. Give me some air,
  I pray you.

40 s.d.] *see note on* v. iv *above*

Tell me, oh, tell me where is Master Frankford?
Will not he deign to see me ere I die?

*Mal.* Yes, Mistress Frankford: divers gentlemen,
Your loving neighbours, with that just request
Have mov'd, and told him of your weak estate:
Who, though with much ado to get belief,
Examining of the general circumstance,
Seeing your sorrow and your penitence,          50
And hearing therewithal the great desire
You have to see him ere you left the world,
He gave to us his faith to follow us,
And sure he will be here immediately.

*Mis. Frank.* You have half reviv'd me with those
pleasing news;
Raise me a little higher in my bed.
Blush I not, brother Acton? Blush I not, Sir Charles?
Can you not read my fault writ in my cheek?
Is not my crime there, tell me, gentlemen?

*Sir Char.* Alas, good mistress, sickness hath not left you
Blood in your face enough to make you blush.    61

*Mis. Frank.* Then sickness, like a friend, my fault
would hide.
Is my husband come? My soul but tarries
His arrive, and I am fit for Heaven.

*Sir Fran.* I came to chide you, but my words of hate
Are turn'd to pity and compassionate grief.
I came to rate you; but my brawls, you see,
Melt into tears, and I must weep by thee.
Here's Master Frankford now.

### *Enter* Frankford.

*Frank.* Good-morrow, brother; good-morrow, gentle-
men:
God, that hath laid this cross upon our heads,   71
Might (had He pleas'd) have made our cause of
meeting
On a more fair and a more contented ground;
But He that made us, made us to this woe.

*Mis. Frank.* And is he come? Methinks that voice I
 know.

*Frank.* How do you, woman?

*Mis. Frank.* Well, Master Frankford, well; but shall
 be better,

 I hope, within this hour. Will you vouchsafe,

 Out of your grace and your humanity,

 To take a spotted strumpet by the hand?  80

*Frank.* This hand once held my heart in faster bonds

 Than now 'tis gripp'd by me. God pardon them

 That made us first break hold!

*Mis. Frank.*      Amen, amen.

 Out of my zeal to Heaven, whither I am now
  bound,

 I was so impudent to wish you here;

 And once more beg your pardon. O good man,

 And father to my children, pardon me,

 Pardon, oh, pardon me! My fault so heinous is,

 That if you in this world forgive it not,

 Heaven will not clear it in the world to come. 90

 Faintness hath so usurp'd upon my knees

 That kneel I cannot, but on my heart's knees

 My prostrate soul lies thrown down at your feet

 To beg your gracious pardon. Pardon, oh, pardon
  me!

*Frank.* As freely, from the low depth of my soul,

 As my Redeemer hath forgiven His death,

 I pardon thee; I will shed tears for thee,

 Pray with thee; and, in mere pity

 Of thy weak state, I'll wish to die with thee.

*All.* So do we all.

*Nick.*    So will not I;    100

 I'll sigh and sob, but, by my faith, not die.

*Sir Fran.* O Master Frankford, all the near alliance

 I lose by her shall be supplied in thee:

 You are my brother by the nearest way;

 Her kindred hath fallen off, but yours doth
  stay.

*Frank.* Even as I hope for pardon at that day
  When the great Judge of Heaven in scarlet sits,
  So be thou pardon'd. Though thy rash offence
  Divorc'd our bodies, thy repentant tears
  Unite our souls.
*Sir Char.*      Then comfort, Mistress Frankford; 110
  You see your husband hath forgiven your fall;
  Then rouse your spirits, and cheer your fainting
    soul.
*Susan.* How is it with you?
*Sir Fran.*                How do you feel yourself?
*Mis. Frank.* Not of this world.
*Frank.* I see you are not, and I weep to see it.
  My wife, the mother to my pretty babes!
  Both those lost names I do restore thee back,
  And with this kiss I wed thee once again:
  Though thou art wounded in thy honour'd name,
  And with that grief upon thy death-bed liest, 120
  Honest in heart, upon my soul, thou diest.
*Mis. Frank.* Pardon'd on earth, soul, thou in Heaven
    art free.
  Once more thy wife, dies thus embracing thee. [*Dies.*
*Frank.* New married, and new widow'd. Oh! she's
    dead,
  And a cold grave must be her nuptial bed.
*Sir Char.* Sir, be of good comfort; and your heavy
    sorrow
  Part equally amongst us: storms divided
  Abate their force, and with less rage are guided.
*Cran.* Do, Master Frankford; he that hath least part
  Will find enough to drown one troubled heart. 130
*Sir Fran.* Peace with thee, Nan. Brothers, and gentle-
    men,
  All we that can plead interest in her grief,
  Bestow upon her body funeral tears.
  Brother, had you with threats and usage bad
  Punish'd her sin, the grief of her offence
  Had not with such true sorrow touch'd her heart.

*Frank.*  I see it had not: therefore on her grave
  Will I bestow this funeral epitaph,
  Which on her marble tomb shall be engrav'd.
  In golden letters shall these words be fill'd,   140
  *Here lies she whom her husband's kindness kill'd.*

FINIS.

140 fill'd] *perhaps* inlaid

# The Epilogue

An honest crew, disposed to be merry,
Came to a tavern by, and call'd for wine:
The drawer brought it, smiling like a cherry,
And told them it was pleasant, neat, and fine.
Taste it, quoth one. He did so. Fie! quoth he,
This wine was good; now't runs too near the lee.

Another sipp'd, to give the wine his due,
And said unto the rest it drunk too flat;
The third said, it was old; the fourth, too new;
Nay, quoth the fifth, the sharpness likes me not.    10
Thus, gentlemen, you see how in one hour
The wine was new, old, flat, sharp, sweet, and sour.

Unto this wine we do allude our play;
Which some will judge too trivial, some too grave;
You as our guests we entertain this day,
And bid you welcome to the best we have.
Excuse us, then; good wine may be disgrac'd,
When every several mouth hath sundry taste.


4 neat, and fine] pure and clear          10 likes] pleases
13 allude] compare